The Vintage

MENCKEN

D0557301

The Vintage

MENCKEN

★

Gathered by

Alistair Cooke

Vintage Books

A Division of Random House, Inc.

New York

Vintage Books Edition, March 1990

ISBN: 679-72895-3
Library of Congress Cataloging-in-Publication Data: 89-40542

Display typography by Rebecca Aidlin

Manufactured in the United States of America
10 9 8 7 6 5 4 3 2 1

AN INTRODUCTION TO H. L. MENCKEN

BY *Alistair Cooke*

This book was put together in a period which, in spite of the anxious humility forced on us by the atom and hydrogen bombs, has much in common with the 1920's that Mencken came to immortalize and to deflate. Since his day there are slicker types of demagogues in politics and new schools of necromancy in advertising, show business, industry, psychiatry, and public relations, to go no further. Following their antics in these later days as a newspaper reporter, I have often thought that Mencken should be living and writing at this hour. So this volume is meant incidentally to recall to the tamed radicals who cut their intellectual teeth on him what manner of man he was; but mainly to introduce to a generation that never read him a writer who more and more strikes me as the master craftsman of daily journalism in the twentieth century. He has written nothing since his stroke in 1948, and it is surely no secret that he ceased to be a missionary force long before then. To be precise, it was the Roosevelt era that brought him to the mat.

At first glance, the New Deal might appear to offer just the sort of target he loved: a big popular idol, an idealist in the Wilsonian tradition who was yet undismayed by the shifts and audacities necessary to get his own way; moreover, a liberal with the further stigma of having gone back on a patrician upbringing for "the people's" sake. But as a matter of record the New Deal was Mencken's Waterloo, and Roosevelt his Wellington. To jeer at democratic government when it paid off in *filet mignon* and a car in every garage was one thing. To pipe the same tune in the unfunny days of 12,-000,000 unemployed was another. Mencken's thunder issued from an unmaterial mind, but also from a full stomach. In the thirties it impressed only those who feared the hungrier chorus of the breadlines. It was always plain that Mencken had a clear eye for the realities that conceived the Roosevelt period. He saw that the way ahead for America lay between no such simple choices as he had laid down between "the aristocrat"—the "first-rate man" speaking his mind—and the "boo-boisie" that had no mind to speak. But this thesis was his specialty, and in a vulgar time it had made him famous. He naturally came to hate the man and the shift of history that made it an anachronism. The decline of his prestige was very swift, and he was honest enough to recognize it. In the middle 1930's he all but abandoned the preoccupation of his palmy days, his self-chosen trade as "a critic of ideas." He turned to his old hobby of the American language, rewrote once again the original volume, and, to clinch his reputation—if it was ever in doubt—as the classical authority on the English of the United States, put out in the next ten years two magnificent Supplements to the parent work. As he moved into his sixties he amused himself by putting on paper a few recollections of his childhood in Baltimore. These fugitive magazine pieces blossomed into a three-volume autobiography, completed by the end of 1943. After the war he concerned himself almost wholly with his notes on the language, but he roused himself in 1948 to cover the presidential nominating conventions. In the fall of that year he came down with a cerebral thrombosis.

When it seemed, seven years ago, that Mencken was on the point of death, I first thought of collecting the best of his work, putting the stress on the newspaper pieces that had outlived more pretentious stuff and on the memoirs in which emerged the beautiful, well-tempered, and funny style of his later years. My obituary of him, written in dutiful haste on a November night while its subject lay in an oxygen tent, is happily still in galley proof in the home office of the *Manchester Guardian*. And since Mencken was born in 1880, what was intended as a memorial tribute has turned into a seventy-fifth birthday present.

For the newcomers to this prince of journalists, a brief account of his life, from his birth into his prime, may be in order. Henry Louis Mencken was born on September 12, 1880, in Baltimore, Maryland. His family, which he was proud to discover was in the collateral line of one Luder Mencke, a learned lawyer who employed Johann Sebastian Bach as a choirmaster, left Germany in the turbulent exodus of 1848, and his grandfather settled in the German section of Baltimore as a cigar-maker. His son, August, in time started his own tobacco business, which did very well indeed and would have cushioned a more docile son through manhood, matrimony, and middle age. But young Henry, the first born of three sons and a daughter, discovered *Huckleberry Finn* at the age of nine, an event he was later to describe as "the most stupendous of my whole life."

It was enough to turn him for a few absorbed years into a bookworm, until—in his late teens—he abandoned his heavy reading "in favor of life itself." The marvels of the ordinary life around him provoked in him a warm desire "to lay in all the worldly wisdom of a police lieutenant, a bartender, a shyster lawyer, and a midwife." Newspaper work appeared to him to offer this reward in the shortest order, and on the Monday morning after his father died, in January 1899, he put on his best suit and appeared in the city room of the Baltimore *Morning Herald*. There was nothing for him, and on the many nights he came hopefully back he was waved away by the night editor. But he turned up mechanically every night for a month and was at last sent off to see how a rural suburb had survived a blizzard. He found nothing more remarkable than the rumor of a horse-stealing, a five-line report of which, however, appeared in the *Herald* next morning, to the ecstasy of its author (*see* page 26).

From then on, Mencken would be a newspaperman all his life, and it was the title he liked best. Being also a man proud of his roots, he resisted—through the most fabulous fame in American journalistic history— all allurements to move to New York, Chicago, and other metropolises. He stayed in Baltimore and of Baltimore, continuing to live to this day in the modest house his family had taken him to when he was three years old. After six years on the *Herald*, he moved in his twenties to the Baltimore *Sunpapers*, with whom he stayed on and off as an editorial writer, columnist, and reporter down to the time of his stroke. Even when he was editing the *Smart Set* and the *American Mercury*, he remained never more than a few nights a week in New York, and got on the train as soon as possible to repair from what he called "a third-rate Babylon" to the frowzier charms of Baltimore and "the immense protein factory of Chesapeake Bay."

Almost from the start Mencken had a reputation among Baltimore newsmen as a boy wonder, in the sense that he learned everything that can be practically learned about a newspaper in a few years, and that he was extraordinarily industrious and fertile. But he showed in his early youth very few gleams of the invective style that was to make him within a decade or two the terror of the lawmakers, the churches, the businessmen, and the respectable citizenry, first of Baltimore and then of the whole Republic. But the ferment was stewing in him and needed only some strong precipitate to cause him to explode. Nietzsche and Bernard Shaw were the missing sparks. He discovered them in his mid-twenties, matched himself favorably against their Olympian stature, and decided on his life work: to be the native American Voltaire, the enemy of all puritans, the heretic in the Sunday school, the one-man demolition crew of the genteel tradition, the unregenerate neighborhood brat who stretches a string in the alley to trip the bourgeoisie on its pious homeward journey.

The *Sunpapers* soon gave Mencken, aside from his reporting duties, a daily column in which to let off steam. And he at once began to scald all the most respected institutions of the land, peeling off with a daily vengeance the layers of Victorianism that still encrusted American and English life. He did this in a prose that started as a drunken parody of almost any iconoclast he admired. Nietzsche suggested the outlandish metaphors, Macaulay the feigned omniscience, Ambrose Bierce the sheer shockability, and some local journalistic oldsters the flamboyance that was then fashionable in American newspaper writing. Shaw taught him most, and it is possible that the stranger to American writing will at first think of Mencken, as I did, as a windier, inferior Shaw. At his best he offered to the young something of the same tonic: the joy of seeing the enemy soundly hog-tied and handcuffed, the sense of sharing the empyrean with an archangel. Both men are superior popular educators who kick up a terrific dust on the intellectual middle plateau between the philistine and the first-rate scholar.

What makes both of them more memorable than many of their betters is their style.

But the pleasures of Shaw's prose, like the pleasures of most sermons, are a good deal more malicious than they are advertised. And without wanting to prolong a comparison that is invidious, and perhaps scandalously unfair to Shaw's superior intellect and satirical power, I should like to note that Mencken, for one thing, is devoid of malice, for another of puritanism, and so he wholly lacks the shrill spinster note that in the end wearies all but the most dedicated of Shaw's disciples. Shaw is a drum-beater, an evangelist, a hedgehog (in Isaiah Berlin's vivid metaphor) who relates everything he sees and feels to a central vision of what he believes life ought to be. Mencken not only had an innate, foxy suspicion of all hedgehogs; his attempts to focus into a single theory his observations on politics and beliefs are defeated by his insight into the politicians who practice the politics and the human beings who hold the beliefs. And if this is a defeat, it is also the triumph of a first-rate fox over a second-rate hedgehog. What has stood the test of time and the exhaustion of the Mencken cult is not, it seems to me, his orderly essays on religion or his healthy but noisy crusade against the genteel tradition; it is his reflections on "the sex uproar" of the Twenties, his reports of political conventions and evolution trials, an evening with Valentino, the memory of a minor revolution in Cuba, a devastating comment on the Gray-Snyder murder—indeed, much of what book-writers with one foot already in obscurity call "transient" journalism. The one prepared indictment that keeps its clarion freshness through the years is that against the plutocracy. This may be because every time the United States is launched on a new prosperity, the plutocrats take to the bridge again to dictate our values while the country-club guests reappear to set the tone of our seagoing manners. The long peroration to "The National Letters," written in 1920, is a classic diagnosis of a disease that seems to afflict us about once every quarter-century; and a Mencken twenty years younger, writing it in 1950, need hardly have blotted a sentence.

Looking over the whole range of his work today, we can see that if he was overrated in his day as a thinker (though not more so than his victims), he was vastly underrated as a humorist with one deadly sensible eye on the behavior of the human animal. He helped along this misconception by constantly reminding people that he was a critic of ideas, which was true only as the ideas were made flesh. He was, in fact, a humorist by instinct and a superb craftsman by temperament. So that when all his private admirations were aped and exhausted, there emerged the style of H. L. Mencken, purified and mellowed in later years, a style flexible, fancy-free, ribald, and always beautifully lucid: a native product unlike any other style in the language.

This Introduction is beginning to turn into an essay, and I had better keep the reader no longer from the pleasures to come. I wanted to avoid yet another collection of random pieces with little shape or order. The Mencken bed-book has already appeared. It is H. L.'s own huge anthology known as *A Mencken Chrestomathy*. I have followed his sensible instinct here only in reprinting almost nothing of his youthful work and very little of his political musings later than 1933. But I wanted to do something that was beyond the purpose of the *Chrestomathy*, namely to give to the new Mencken reader a running account of his life as he wrote and lived it. This means that I have begun with his own memories of his childhood and early newspaper days, even though they were written as late as the 1940's, in his most mature style. Similarly, I have sandwiched in his account of a newspaper expedition to the Caribbean at the period when the experience came his way. The only part of his writing that is not represented here is his immense contribution to the study of the language. There are many short delightful passages and a flick of mischief on nearly every page, but his linguistic writing is most impressive by the sheer mass and sustained excellence of its scholarship. Its quality can no more be suggested in a few pages than the suspense of *The Emperor Jones* can be conveyed by a few tappings of the tom-tom that is heard throughout the play.

The introductory notes are mostly Mencken's own. Where they are not, I have initialed them. It remains for me only to say how grateful I am to Hamilton Owens and Clement Vitek for letting me raid the files of the *Sunpapers* at indecently short notice; and to the stalwart Blanche and Alfred Knopf for their philosophical tolerance of a working newspaperman who is always on the wing. Finally, I must express my gratitude and affection to the master himself, who blessed this project from the rather helpless sidelines on which he sits these days with so much humor and fortitude.

A. C.

Summer 1955

CONTENTS

CONTENTS

The Vintage

MENCKEN

HLM＊HLM＊HLM＊HLM

In the following pages a ＊ indicates an omission from the text as originally published.

INTRODUCTION TO THE UNIVERSE
[*1883*]
(FROM *Happy Days*, 1940)

AT the instant I first became aware of the cosmos we all infest I was sitting in my mother's lap and blinking at a great burst of lights, some of them red and others green, but most of them only the bright yellow of flaring gas. The time: the evening of Thursday, September 13, 1883, which was the day after my third birthday. The place: a ledge outside the second-story front windows of my father's cigar factory at 368 Baltimore street, Baltimore, Maryland, U.S.A., fenced off from space and disaster by a sign bearing the majestic legend: AUG. MENCKEN & BRO. The occasion: the third and last annual Summer Nights' Carnival of the Order of Orioles, a society that adjourned *sine die,* with a thumping deficit, the very next morning, and has since been forgotten by the whole human race.

At that larval stage of my life, of course, I knew nothing whatever about the Order of Orioles, just as I knew nothing whatever about the United States, though I had been born to their liberties, and was entitled to the protection of their army and navy. All I was aware of, emerging from the unfathomable abyss of nonentity, was the fact that the world I had just burst into seemed to be very brilliant, and that peeping at it over my father's sign was somewhat hard on my still gelatinous bones. So I made signals of distress to my mother and was duly hauled into her lap, where I first dozed and then snored away until the lights went out, and the family buggy wafted me home, still asleep.

★

THE BALTIMORE OF THE EIGHTIES
[1880's]
(FROM *Happy Days*, 1940)

The city into which I was born in 1880 had a reputation all over for what the English, in their real-estate advertising, are fond of calling the amenities. So far as I have been able to discover by a labored search of contemporary travel-books, no literary tourist, however waspish he may have been about Washington, Niagara Falls, the prairies of the West, or even Boston and New York, ever gave Baltimore a bad notice. They all agreed, often with lubricious gloats and gurgles, (*a*) that its indigenous victualry was unsurpassed in the Republic, (*b*) that its native Caucasian females of all ages up to thirty-five were of incomparable pulchritude, and as amiable as they were lovely, and (*c*) that its home-life was spacious, charming, full of creature comforts, and highly conducive to the facile and orderly propagation of the species.

There was some truth in all these articles, but not, I

regret to have to add, too much. Perhaps the one that came closest to meeting scientific tests was the first. Baltimore lay very near the immense protein factory of Chesapeake Bay, and out of the bay it ate divinely. I well recall the time when prime hard crabs of the channel species, blue in color, at least eight inches in length along the shell, and with snow-white meat almost as firm as soap, were hawked in Hollins street of Summer mornings at ten cents a dozen. The supply seemed to be almost unlimited, even in the polluted waters of the Patapsco river, which stretched up fourteen miles from the bay to engulf the slops of the Baltimore canneries and fertilizer factories. Any poor man could go down to the banks of the river, armed with no more than a length of stout cord, a home-made net on a pole, and a chunk of cat's meat, and come home in a couple of hours with enough crabs to feed his family for two days. Soft crabs, of course, were scarcer and harder to snare, and hence higher in price, but not much. More than once, hiding behind my mother's apron, I helped her to buy them at the door for two-and-a-twelfth cents apiece. And there blazes in my memory like a comet the day when she came home from Hollins market complaining with strange and bitter indignation that the fishmongers there—including old Harris, her favorite—had begun to *sell* shad roe. Hitherto, stretching back to the first settlement of Baltimore Town, they had always thrown it in with the fish. Worse, she reported that they had now entered upon an illegal combination to lift the price of the standard shad of twenty inches—enough for the average family, and to spare—from forty cents to half a dollar. When my father came home for lunch and heard this incredible news, he predicted formally that the Republic would never survive the Nineteenth Century.

Terrapin was not common eating in those days, any more than it is in these, but that was mainly because few women liked it, just as few like it today. It was then assumed that their distaste was due to the fact that its consumption involved a considerable lavage with fortified wines, but they still show no honest enthusiasm for it, though Prohibition converted many of them into very adept and eager boozers. It was not, in my infancy, within the reach of the proletariat, but it was certainly not beyond the bourgeoisie. My mother, until well past the turn of the century, used to buy pint jars of the picked meat in Hollins market, with plenty of rich, golden eggs scattered through it, for a dollar a jar. For the same price it was possible to obtain *two* wild ducks of respectable if not royal species—and the open season ran gloriously from the instant the first birds wandered in from Labrador to the time the last stragglers set sail for Brazil. So far as I can remember, my mother never bought any of these ducks, but that was only because the guns, dogs and eagle eye of my uncle Henry, who lived next door, kept us oversupplied all Winter.

Garden-truck was correspondingly cheap, and so was fruit in season. Out of season we seldom saw it at all. Oranges, which cost sixty cents a dozen, came in at Christmas, and not before. We had to wait until May for strawberries, asparagus, fresh peas, carrots, and even radishes. But when the huge, fragrant strawberries of Anne Arundel county (pronounced Ann'ran'l) appeared at last they went for only five cents a box. All Spring the streets swarmed with hucksters selling such things: they called themselves, not hucksters, but Arabs (with the first *a* as in *day*), and announced their wares with loud, raucous, unintelligible cries, much worn down by phonetic decay. In Winter the principal howling was done by colored men selling shucked oysters out of huge cans. In the dark backward and abysm of time their cry must have been simply "Oysters!", but generations of Aframerican larynxes had debased it to "Awneeeeeee!", with the final *e*'s prolonged until the vendor got out of breath. He always wore a blue-and-white checked apron, and that apron was also the uniform of the colored butlers of the Baltimore gentry when engaged upon their morning work—sweeping the sidewalk, scouring the white marble front steps, polishing up the handle of the big front door, and bragging about their white folks to their colleagues to port and starboard.

Oysters were not too much esteemed in the Baltimore of my youth, nor are they in the Baltimore of today. They were eaten, of course, but not often, for serving them raw at the table was beyond the usual domestic technic of the time, and it was difficult to cook them in any fashion that made them consonant with contemporary ideas of elegance. Fried, they were fit only to be devoured at church oyster-suppers, or gobbled in oyster-bays by drunks wandering home from scenes of revelry. The more celebrated oyster-houses of Baltimore—for example, Kelly's in Eutaw street—were patronized largely by such lamentable characters. It was their playful custom to challenge foolish-looking strangers to wash down a dozen raw Chincoteagues with half a tumbler of Maryland rye: the town belief was that this combination was so deleterious as to be equal to the kick of a mule. If the stranger survived, they tried to inveigle him into eating another dozen with sugar sprinkled on them: this dose was supposed to be almost certainly fatal. I grew up believing that the only man in history who had ever actually swallowed it and lived was John L. Sullivan.

There is a saying in Baltimore that crabs may be prepared in fifty ways and that all of them are good. The range of oyster dishes is much narrower, and they are much less attractive. Fried oysters I have just mentioned. Stewed, they are undoubtedly edible, but only in the sorry sense that oatmeal or boiled rice is edible. Certainly no Baltimorean not insane would argue that an oyster stew has any of the noble qualities of the two great crab soups—shore style (with vegetables) and bisque (with cream). Both of these masterpieces were on tap in the old Rennert Hotel when I lunched there daily (years after the term of the present narrative) and both were magnificent. The Rennert also offered an oyster pot-pie that had its points, but the late Jeff Davis, manager of the hotel (and the last public virtuoso of Maryland cookery), once confessed to me that its flavor was really due to a sly use of garlic. Such concoctions as panned and scalloped oysters have never been eaten in my time by connoisseurs, and oyster fritters (always called flitters in Baltimore) are to be had only at free-for-all oyster-roasts and along the wharves. A roasted oyster, if it be hauled off the fire at the exact instant the shell opens, is not to be sniffed at, but getting it down is a troublesome business, for the shell is too hot to be handled without mittens. Despite this inconvenience, there are still oyster-roasts in Baltimore on Winter Sunday afternoons, and since the collapse of Prohibition they have been drawing pretty good houses. When the Elks give one they hire a militia armory, lay in a thousand kegs of beer, engage 200 waiters, and prepare for a mob. But the mob is not attracted by the oysters alone; it comes mainly to eat hot-dogs, barbecued beef and sauerkraut and to wash down these lowly victuals with the beer.

The greatest crab cook of the days I remember was Tom McNulty, originally a whiskey drummer but in the end sheriff of Baltimore, and the most venerated oyster cook was a cop named Fred. Tom's specialty was made by spearing a slice of bacon on a large fork, jamming a soft crab down on it, holding the two over a charcoal brazier until the bacon had melted over the crab, and then slapping both upon a slice of hot toast. This titbit had its points, I assure you, and I never think of it without deploring Tom's too early translation to bliss eternal. Fred devoted himself mainly to oyster flitters. The other cops rolled and snuffled in his masterpieces like cats in catnip, but I never could see much virtue in them. It was always my impression, perhaps in error, that he fried them in curve grease borrowed from the street railways. He was an old-time Model T flat-foot, not much taller than a fire-plug, but as big around the middle as a load of hay. At the end of a busy afternoon he would be spattered from head to foot with blobs of flitter batter and wild grease.

It was the opinion of my father, as I have recorded, that all the Baltimore beers were poisonous, but he nevertheless kept a supply of them in the house for visiting plumbers, tinners, cellar-inspectors, tax-assessors and so on, and for Class D social callers. I find by his bill file that he paid $1.20 for a case of twenty-four bottles. His own favorite malt liquor was Anheuser-Busch, but he also made occasional experiments with the other brands that were then beginning to find a national market: some of them to survive to this day, but the most perished under Prohibition. His same bill file shows that on December 27, 1883, he paid Courtney, Fairall & Company, then the favorite fancy grocers of Baltimore, $4 for a gallon of Monticello whiskey. It retails now for from $3 to $3.50 a *quart*. In those days it was always straight, for the old-time Baltimoreans regarded blends with great suspicion, though many of the widely-advertised brands of Maryland rye were of that character. They drank straight whiskey straight, disdaining both diluents and chases. I don't recall ever seeing my father drink a high-ball; the thing must have existed in his day, for he lived on to 1899, but he probably regarded its use as unmanly and ignoble. Before every meal, including breakfast, he ducked into the cupboard in the dining-room and poured out a substantial hooker of rye, and when he emerged he was always sucking in a great whiff of air to cool off his tonsils. He regarded this appetizer as necessary to his wellbeing. He said that it was the best medicine he had ever found for toning up his stomach.

How the stomachs of Baltimore survived at all in

those days is a pathological mystery. The standard evening meal tended to be light, but the other two were terrific. The repertoire for breakfast, beside all the known varieties of pancake and porridge, included such things as ham and eggs, broiled mackerel, fried smelts, beef hash, pork chops, country sausage, and even—God help us all!—what would now be called Welsh rabbit. My father, save when we were in the country, usually came home for lunch, and on Saturdays, with no school, my brother Charlie and I sat in. Our favorite Winter lunch was typical of the time. Its main dishes were a huge platter of Norfolk spots or other pan-fish, and a Himalaya of corn-cakes. Along with this combination went succotash, buttered beets, baked potatoes, string beans, and other such hearty vegetables. When oranges and bananas were obtainable they followed for dessert—sliced, and with a heavy dressing of grated cocoanut. The calorie content of two or three helpings of such powerful aliments probably ran to 3000. We'd all be somewhat subdued afterward, and my father always stretched out on the dining-room lounge for a nap. In the evening he seldom had much appetite, and would usually complain that cooking was fast going downhill in Baltimore, in accord with the general decay of human society. Worse, he would warn Charlie and me against eating too much, and often he undertook to ration us. We beat this sanitary policing by laying in a sufficiency in the kitchen before sitting down to table. As a reserve against emergencies we kept a supply of ginger snaps, mushroom crackers, all-day suckers, dried apricots and solferino taffy in a cigar-box in our bedroom. In fear that it might spoil, or that mice might sneak up from the cellar to raid it, we devoured this stock at frequent intervals, and it had to be renewed.

The Baltimoreans of those days were complacent beyond the ordinary, and agreed with their envious visitors that life in their town was swell. I can't recall ever hearing anyone complain of the fact that there was a great epidemic of typhoid fever every Summer, and a wave of malaria every Autumn, and more than a scattering of smallpox, especially among the colored folk in the alleys, every Winter. Spring, indeed, was the only season free from serious pestilence, and in Spring the communal laying off of heavy woolen underwear was always followed by an epidemic of colds. Our house in Hollins street, as I first remember it, was heated by Latrobe stoves, the invention of a Baltimore engineer. They had mica windows (always called isinglass) that made a cheery glow, but though it was warm enough within the range of that glow on even the coldest Winter days, their flues had little heat to spare for the rooms upstairs. My brother and I slept in Canton-flannel nightdrawers with feathers above us and underneath, but that didn't help us much on January mornings when all the windows were so heavily frosted that we couldn't see outside. My father put in a steam-heating plant toward the end of the eighties—the first ever seen in Hollins street—, but such things were rare until well into the new century. The favorite central heating device for many years was a hot-air furnace that was even more inefficient than the Latrobe stove. The only heat in our bathroom was supplied from the kitchen, which meant that there was none at all until the hired girl began to function below. Thus my brother and I were never harassed by suggestions of morning baths, at least in Winter. Whenever it was decided that we had reached an intolerable degree of grime, and measures were taken to hound us to the bathroom, we went into the vast old zinc-lined tub together, and beguiled the pains of getting clean by taking toy boats along. Once we also took a couple of goldfish, but the soap killed them almost instantly.

At intervals of not more than a month in Winter a water-pipe froze and burst, and the whole house was cold and clammy until the plumbers got through their slow-moving hocus-pocus. Nothing, in those days, seemed to work. All the house machinery was constantly out of order. The roof sprang a leak at least three times a year, and I recall a day when the cellar was flooded by a broken water-main in Hollins street, and my brother and I had a grand time navigating it in wooden washtubs. No one, up to that time, had ever thought of outfitting windows with fly-screens. Flies overran and devoured us in Summer, immense swarms of mosquitoes were often blown in from the swamps to the southwest, and a miscellany of fantastic moths, gnats, June-bugs, beetles, and other insects, some of them of formidable size and pugnacity, buzzed around the gas-lights at night.

We slept under mosquito canopies, but they were of flimsy netting and there were always holes in them, so that when a mosquito or fly once got in he had us all to himself, and made the most of it. It was not uncommon, in Summer, for a bat to follow the procession. When this happened my brother and I turned out with brooms, baseball bats and other weapons, and pursued the hunt to a kill. The carcass was always nailed to the backyard fence the next morning, with the wings stretched out as far as possible, and boys would come from blocks around to measure and admire it. Whenever an insect of unfamiliar species showed up we tried to capture it, and if we succeeded we kept it alive in a pill-box or baking-powder can. Our favorite among pill-boxes was the one that held Wright's Indian Vegetable Pills (which my father swallowed every time he got into a low state), for it was made of thin sheets of wood veneer, and was thus more durable than the druggists' usual cardboard boxes.

Every public place in Baltimore was so furiously beset by bugs of all sorts that communal gatherings were impossible on hot nights. The very cops on the street corners spent a large part of their time slapping mosquitoes and catching flies. Our pony Frank had a fly-net, but it operated only when he was in motion; in his leisure he was as badly used as the cops. When arc-lights began to light the streets, along about 1885, they attracted so many beetles of gigantic size that their glare was actually obscured. These beetles at once acquired the name of electric-light bugs, and it was believed that the arc carbons produced them by a kind of spontaneous generation, and that their bite was as dangerous as that of a tarantula. But no Baltimorean would ever admit categorically that this Congo-like plague of flying things, taking one day with another, was really serious, or indeed a plague at all. Many a time I have seen my mother leap up from the dinner-table to engage the swarming flies with an improvised punkah, and heard her rejoice and give humble thanks simultaneously that Baltimore was not the sinkhole that Washington was.

These flies gave no concern to my brother Charlie and me; they seemed to be innocuous and even friendly compared to the chiggers, bumble-bees and hornets that occasionally beset us. Indeed, they were a source of pleasant recreation to us, for very often, on hot Summer evenings, we would retire to the kitchen, stretch out flat on our backs on the table, and pop away at them with slingshots as they roosted in dense clumps upon the ceiling. Our favorite projectile was a square of lemon-peel, roasted by the hired girl. Thus prepared, it was tough enough to shoot straight and kill certainly, but when it bounced back it did not hurt us. The hired girl, when she was in an amiable mood, prepared us enough of these missiles for an hour's brisk shooting, and in the morning she had the Red Cross job of sweeping the dead flies off the ceiling. Sometimes there were hundreds of them, lying dead in sticky windrows. When there were horse-flies from the back alley among them, which was not infrequently, they leaked red mammalian blood, which was an extra satisfaction to us. The stables that lined the far side of the alley were vast hatcheries of such flies, some of which reached a gigantic size. When we caught one we pulled off its wings and watched it try idiotically to escape on foot, or removed its legs and listened while it buzzed in a loud and futile manner. The theory taught in those days was that creatures below the warm-blooded level had no feelings whatever, and in fact rather enjoyed being mutilated. Thus it was an innocent and instructive matter to cut a worm into two halves, and watch them wriggle off in opposite directions. Once my brother and I caught a turtle, chopped off its head, and were amazed to see it march away headless. That experience, in truth, was so astonishing as to be alarming, and we never monkeyed with turtles thereafter. But we got a good deal of pleasure, first and last, out of chasing and butchering toads, though we were always careful to avoid taking them in our hands, for the juice of their kidneys was supposed to cause warts.

At the first smell of hot weather there was a tremendous revolution in Hollins street. All the Brussels carpets in the house were jimmied up and replaced by sleazy Chinese matting, all the haircloth furniture was covered with linen covers, and every picture, mirror, gas bracket and Rogers group was draped in fly netting. The carpets were wheelbarrowed out to Steuart's hill by professional carpet beaters of the African race, and there flogged and flayed until the heaviest lick yielded no more dust. Before the mattings could be laid all the floors had to be scrubbed, and every picture and mirror had to be taken down and polished. Also, the lace curtains had to come down, and the ivory-colored Holland shades that hung in Winter had to be changed to blue ones, to filter out the Summer sun. The lace curtains were always laundered before being put away—a formidable operation involving stretching them on huge frameworks set up on trestles in the backyard. All this uproar was repeated in reverse at the ides of September. The mattings came up, the carpets went down, the furniture was stripped of its covers, the pictures, mirrors and gas brackets lost their netting, and the blue Holland shades were displaced by the ivory ones. It always turned out, of course, that the flies of Summer had got through the nettings with ease, and left every picture peppered with their calling cards. The large pier mirror between the two windows of the parlor usually got a double dose, and it took the hired girl half a day to renovate it, climbing up and down a ladder in the clumsy manner of a policeman getting over a fence, and dropping soap, washrags, hairpins and other gear on the floor.

The legend seems to prevail that there were no sewers in Baltimore until after the World War, but that is something of an exaggeration. Our house in Hollins street was connected with a private sewer down the alley in the rear as early as I have any recollection of it, and so were many other houses, especially in the newer parts of the town. But I should add that we also had a powder-room in the backyard for the accommodation of laundresses, whitewashers and other visiting members of the domestic faculty, and that there was a shallow sink under it that inspired my brother and me with considerable dread. Every now and then some child in West Baltimore fell into such a sink, and had to be hauled out, besmeared and howling, by the cops. The one in our yard was pumped out and fumigated every Spring by a gang of colored men who arrived on a wagon that was called an O.E.A.—*i.e.*, odorless excavating apparatus. They discharged this social-minded duty with great fervor and dispatch, and achieved non-odoriferousness, in the innocent Aframerican way, by burning buckets of rosin and tar. The whole neighborhood choked on the black, greasy, pungent smoke for hours afterward. It was thought to be an effective preventive of cholera, smallpox and tuberculosis.

All the sewers of Baltimore, whether private or public, emptied into the Back Basin in those days, just as all those of Manhattan empty into the North and East rivers to this day. But I should add that there was a difference, for the North and East rivers have swift tidal currents, whereas the Back Basin, distant 170 miles from the Chesapeake capes, had only the most lethargic. As a result it began to acquire a powerful aroma every Spring, and by August smelled like a billion polecats. This stench radiated all over downtown Baltimore, though in Hollins street we hardly ever detected it. Perhaps that was due to the fact that West Baltimore had rival perfumes of its own—for example, the emanation from the Wilkins hair factory in the Frederick road, a mile or so from Union Square. When a breeze from the southwest, bouncing its way over the Wilkins factory, reached Hollins street the effect was almost that of poison gas. It happened only seldom, but when it happened it was surely memorable. The householders of the vicinage always swarmed down to the City Hall the next day and raised blue hell, but they never got anything save promises. In fact, it was not until the Wilkinses went into the red and shut down their factory that the abomination abated—and its place was then taken, for an unhappy year or two, by the degenerate cosmic rays projected from a glue factory lying in the same general direction. No one, so far as I know, ever argued that these mephitic blasts were salubrious, but it is a sober fact that town opinion held that the bouquet of the Back Basin was. In proof thereof it was pointed out that the clerks who sweated all Summer in the little coops of offices along the Light street and Pratt street wharves were so remarkably long-lived that many of them appeared to be at least 100 years old, and that the colored stevedores who loaded and unloaded the Bay packets were the strongest, toughest, drunkenest and most thieving in the whole port.

The Baltimore of the eighties was a noisy town, for the impact of iron wagon tires on hard cobblestone was almost like that of a hammer on an anvil. To be sure, there was a dirt road down the middle of every street, kept in repair by the accumulated sweepings of the sidewalks, but this cushioned track was patronized only by hay-wagons from the country and like occasional traffic: milk-men, grocery deliverymen and other such regulars kept to the areas where the cobbles were naked, and so made a fearful clatter. In every way, in fact, city life was much noiser then than it is now. Children at play were not incarcerated in playgrounds and policed by hired ma'ms, but roved the open streets, and most of their games involved singing or yelling. At Christmas-time they began to blow horns at least a week before the great day, and kept it up until all the horns were disabled, and in Summer they began celebrating the Fourth far back in June and were still exploding fire-crackers at the end of July. Nearly every house had a dog in it, and nearly all the dogs barked more or less continuously from 4 a.m. until after midnight. It was still lawful to keep chickens in backyards, and many householders did so. All within ear range of Hollins street appeared to divide them as to sex in the proportion of a hundred crowing roosters to one clucking hen. My grandfather Mencken once laid in a coop of Guineas, unquestionably the noisiest species of *Aves* known to science. But his wife, my step-grandmother, had got in a colored clergyman to steal them before the neighbors arrived with the police.

In retired by-streets grass grew between the cobblestones to almost incredible heights, and it was not uncommon for colored rag-and-bone men to pasture their undernourished horses on it. On the steep hill making eastward from the Washington Monument, in the very heart of Baltimore, some comedian once sowed wheat, and it kept on coming up for years thereafter. Every Spring the Baltimore newspapers would report on the prospects of the crop, and visitors to the city were taken to see it. Most Baltimoreans of that era, in fact, took a fierce, defiant pride in the bucolic aspects of their city. They would boast that it was the only great seaport on earth in which dandelions grew in the streets in Spring. They believed that all such vegetation was healthful, and kept down chills and fever. I myself once had proof that the excess of litter in the streets was not without its value to mankind. I was riding the pony Frank when a wild thought suddenly seized him, and he bucked me out of the saddle in the best manner of a Buffalo Bill bronco. Unfortunately, my left foot was stuck in the stirrup, and so I was dragged behind him as he galloped off. He had gone at least a block before a couple of colored boys stopped him. If the cobblestones of Stricker street had been bare I'd not be with you to-day. As it was, I got no worse damage than a series of harsh scourings running from my neck to my heels. The colored boys took me to Reveille's livery-stable, and stopped the bloodshed with large gobs of spider web. It was the hemostatic of choice in Baltimore when I was young. If, perchance, it spread a little tetanus, then the Baltimoreans blamed the mercies of God.

ADVENTURES OF A Y.M.C.A. LAD [*1894*]
(FROM *Heathen Days*, 1943)

When I reach the shades at last it will no doubt astonish Satan to discover, on thumbing my *dossier,* that I was once a member of the Y.M.C.A. Yet a fact is a fact. What is more remarkable, I was not recruited by a missionary to the heathen, but joined at the suggestion of my father, who enjoyed and deserved the name of an infidel. I was then a little beyond fourteen years old, and a new neighborhood branch of the Y, housed in a nobby pressed-brick building, had just been opened in West Baltimore, only a few blocks from our home in Hollins street. The whole upper floor was given over to a gymnasium, and it was this bait, I gathered, that fetched my father, for I was already a bookworm and beginning to be a bit round-shouldered, and he often exhorted me to throw back my shoulders and stick out my chest.

Apparently he was convinced that exercise on the wooden horse and flying rings would cure my scholarly stoop, and make a kind of grenadier of me. If so, he was in error, for I remain more or less Bible-backed to this day, and am often mistaken for a Talmudist. All that the Y.M.C.A.'s horse and rings really accomplished was to fill me with an ineradicable distaste, not only for Christian endeavor in all its forms, but also for every variety of callisthenics, so that I still begrudge the tri-fling exertion needed to climb in and out of a bathtub, and hate all sports as rabidly as a person who likes sports hates common sense. If I had my way no man guilty of golf would be eligible to any office of trust or profit under the United States, and all female athletes would be shipped to the white-slave corrals of the Argentine.

Indeed, I disliked that gymnasium so earnestly that I never got beyond its baby-class, which was devoted to teaching freshmen how to hang their clothes in the lockers, get into their work-suits, and run around the track. I was in those days a fast runner and could do the 100 yards, with a fair wind, in something better than fourteen seconds, but how anyone could run on a quad-rangular track with sides no more than fifty feet long was quite beyond me. The first time I tried it I slipped and slid at all four corners, and the second time I came down with a thump that somehow contrived to skin both my shins. The man in charge of the establishment —the boys all called him Professor—thereupon put me to the punching-bag, but at my fourth or fifth wallop it struck back, and I was floored again. After that I tried all the other insane apparatus in the place, includ-ing the horizontal bars, but I always got into trouble very quickly, and never made enough progress to hurt myself seriously, which might have been some comfort, at least on the psychological side. There were other boys who fell from the highest trapezes, and had to be sent home in hacks, and yet others who broke their arms or legs and were heroic figures about the building for months afterward, but the best I ever managed was a bloody nose, and that was caused, not by my own enterprise, but by another boy falling on me from somewhere near the roof. If he had landed six inches farther inshore he might have fractured my skull or broken my neck, but all he achieved was to scrape my nose. It hurt a-plenty, I can tell you, and it hurt still worse when the Professor doused it with arnica, and splashed a couple of drops into each of my eyes.

Looking back over the years, I see that that ghastly gymnasium, if I had continued to frequent it, might have given me an inferiority complex, and bred me up a foe of privilege. I was saved, fortunately, by a congenital complacency that has been a godsend to me, more than once, in other and graver situations. Within a few weeks I was classifying all the boys in the place in the inverse order of their diligence and prowess, and that classification, as I have intimated, I adhere to at the present moment. The youngsters who could leap from bar to bar without slipping and were facile on the trapeze I equated with simians of the genus *Hylobates,* and convinced myself that I was surprised when they showed a capacity for articulate speech. As for the weight-lifters, chinners, somersaulters, leapers and other such virtuosi of striated muscle, I dismissed them as *Anthropoidea* far inferior, in all situations calling for taste or judgment, to schoolteachers or mules.

I should add that my low view of these prizemen was unaccompanied by personal venom; on the contrary, I got on with them very well, and even had a kind of liking for some of them—that is, in their private capacities.

Very few, I discovered, were professing Christians, though the Y.M.C.A., in those days even more than now, was a furnace of Protestant divinity. They swore when they stubbed their toes, and the older of them entertained us youngsters in the locker-room with their adventures in amour. The chief free-and-easy trysting-place in West Baltimore, at the time, was a Baptist church specializing in what was called "young people's work." It put on gaudy entertainments, predominantly secular in character, on Sunday nights, and scores of the poor working girls of the section dropped in to help with the singing and lasso beaux. I gathered from the locker-room talk that some of those beaux demanded dreadful prices for their consent to the lassoing. Whether this boasting was true or not I did not know, for I never attended the Sabbath evening orgies myself, but at all events it showed that those who did so were of an antinomian tendency, and far from ideal Y.M.C.A. fodder. When the secretaries came to the gymnasium to drum up customers for prayer-meetings downstairs the Lotharios always sounded razzberries and cleared out.

On one point all hands were agreed, and that was on the point that the Professor was what, in those days, was called a pain in the neck. When he mounted a bench and yelled "Fellows!" my own blood always ran cold, and his subsequent remarks gave me a touch of homicidal mania. Not until many years afterward, when a certain eminent politician* in Washington took to radio crooning, did I ever hear a more offensive voice. There were tones in it like the sound of molasses dripping from a barrel. It was not at all effeminate, but simply saccharine. Had I been older in worldly wisdom it would have suggested to me a suburban curate gargling over the carcass of a usurer who had just left the parish its richest and stupidest widow. As I was, an innocent boy, I could only compare it to the official chirp-

* I.e., F.D.R. A.G.

ing of a Sunday-school superintendent. What the Professor had to say was usually sensible enough, and I don't recall him ever mentioning either Heaven or Hell; it was simply his tone and manner that offended me. He is now dead, I take it, for many years, and I only hope that he has had good luck *post mortem,* but while he lived his harangues to his students gave me a great deal of unnecessary pain, and definitely slanted my mind against the Y.M.C.A. Even when, many years later, I discovered as a newspaper correspondent that the Berlin outpost thereof, under the name of the *christliche Verein junger Männer,* was so enlightened that it served beer in its lamissary, I declined to change my attitude.

But I was driven out of the Y.M.C.A. at last, not by the Professor nor even by his pupils in the odoriferous gymnasium—what a foul smell, indeed, a gymnasium has! how it suggests a mixture of Salvation Army, elephant house, and county jail!—but by a young member who, so far as I observed, never entered the Professor's domain at all. He was a pimply, officious fellow of seventeen or eighteen, and to me, of course, he seemed virtually a grown man. The scene of his operations was the reading-room, whither I often resorted in self-defense when the Professor let go with "Fellows!" and began one of his hortations. It was quiet there, and though most of the literature on tap was pietistic I enjoyed going through it, for my long interest in the sacred sciences had already begun. One evening, while engaged upon a pamphlet detailing devices for catching boys and girls who knocked down part of their Sunday-school money, I became aware of the pimply one, and presently saw him go to a bookcase and select a book. Dropping into a chair, he turned its pages feverishly, and presently he found what he seemed to be looking for, and cleared his throat to attract attention. The four or five of us at the long table all looked up.

"See here, fellows," he began—again that ghastly "fellows!"—"let me have your ears for just a moment. Here is a book"—holding it up—"that is worth all the other books ever written by mortal man. There is nothing like it on earth except the One Book that our Heavenly Father Himself gave us. It is pure gold, pure meat. There is not a wasted word in it. Every syllable is a perfect gem. For example, listen to this—"

What it was he read I don't recall precisely, but I remember that it was some thumping and appalling platitude or other—something on the order of "Honesty is the best policy," "A guilty conscience needs no accuser," or "It is never too late to mend." I guessed at first that he was trying to be ironical, but it quickly appeared that he was quite serious, and before his audience managed to escape he had read forty or fifty such specimens of otiose rubbish, and following nearly every one of them he indulged himself in a little homily, pointing up its loveliness and rubbing in its lesson. The poor ass, it appeared, was actually enchanted, and wanted to spread his joy. It was easy to recognize in him the anti-social animus of a born evangelist, but there was also something else—a kind of voluptuous delight in the shabby and preposterous, a perverted aestheticism like that of a latter-day movie or radio fan, a wild will to roll in and snuffle balderdash as a cat rolls in and snuffles catnip. I was, as I have said, less than fifteen years old, but I had already got an overdose of such blah in the McGuffey Readers and penmanship copybooks of the time, so I withdrew as quickly as possible, unhappily aware that even the Professor was easier to take than this jitney Dwight L. Moody. I got home all tuckered out, and told my father (who was sitting up reading for the tenth or twentieth time a newspaper account of the hanging of two labor leaders) that the Y.M.C.A. fell a good deal short of what it was cracked up to be.

He bade me go back the next evening and try again, and I did so in filial duty. Indeed, I did so a dozen or more nights running, omitting Sundays, when the place was given over to spiritual exercises exclusively But each and every night that imbecile was in the reading-room, and each and every night he read from that revolting book to all within ear-shot. I gathered gradually that it was having a great run in devotional circles, and was, in fact, a sort of moral best-seller. The author, it appeared, was a Methodist bishop, and a great hand at inculcating righteousness. He not only knew by heart all the immemorial platitudes, stretching back to the days of Gog and Magog; he had also invented many more or less new ones, and it was these novelties that especially aroused the enthusiasm of his disciple. I wish I could recall some of them, but my memory has always had a humane faculty for obliterating the intolerable, and so I can't. But you may take my word for it that nothing in the subsequent writings of Dr. Orison Swett Marden or Dr. Frank Crane was worse.

In a little while my deliverance was at hand, for though my father had shown only irritation when I described to him the pulpit manner of the Professor, he was immediately sympathetic when I told him about the bishop's book, and the papuliferous exegete's laboring of it. "You had better quit," he said, "before you hit him with a spittoon, or go crazy. There ought to be a law against such roosters." *Rooster* was then his counter-word, and might signify anything from the most high-toned and elegant Shriner, bank cashier or bartender to the most scurvy and abandoned Socialist. This time he used it in its most opprobrious sense, and so my career in the Y.M.C.A. came to an end. I carried away from it, not only an indelible distrust of every sort of athlete, but also a loathing of Methodist bishops, and it was many years afterward before I could bring myself to admit any such right rev. father in God to my friendship. I have since learned that some of them are very pleasant and amusing fellows, despite their professional enmity to the human race, but the one who

wrote that book was certainly nothing of the sort. If, at
his decease, he escaped Hell, then moral theology is as
full of false alarms as secular law.

TEXT FOR NEWSPAPER DAYS

(FROM *Newspaper Days*, 1942)

★

At a time when the respectable bourgeois
youngsters of my generation were college freshmen, oppressed by simian sophomores and affronted with
balderdash daily and hourly by chalky pedagogues, I
was at large in a wicked seaport of half a million people, with a front seat at every public show, as free of
the night as of the day, and getting earfuls and eye-
fuls of instruction in a hundred giddy arcana, none of
them taught in schools. On my twenty-first birthday, by
all orthodox cultural standards, I probably reached my
all-time low, for the heavy reading of my teens had been
abandoned in favor of life itself, and I did not return
seriously to the lamp until a time near the end of this
record. But it would be an exaggeration to say that I
was ignorant, for if I neglected the humanities I was
meanwhile laying in all the worldly wisdom of a police
lieutenant, a bartender, a shyster lawyer, or a midwife.
And it would certainly be idiotic to say that I was not
happy. The illusion that swathes and bedizens journalism, bringing in its endless squads of recruits, was still
full upon me, and I had yet to taste the sharp teeth of responsibility. Life was arduous, but it was gay and carefree. The days chased one another like kittens chasing
their tails.

Whether or not the young journalists of today live so

spaciously is a question that I am not competent to answer, for my contacts with them, of late years, have been rather scanty. They undoubtedly get a great deal more money than we did in 1900, but their freedom is much less than ours was, and they somehow give me the impression, seen at a distance, of complacency rather than intrepidity. In my day a reporter who took an assignment was wholly on his own until he got back to the office, and even then he was little molested until his copy was turned in at the desk; today he tends to become only a homunculus at the end of a telephone wire, and the reduction of his observations to prose is commonly farmed out to literary castrati who never leave the office, and hence never feel the wind of the world in their faces or see anything with their own eyes. I well recall my horror when I heard, for the first time, of a journalist who had laid in a pair of what were then called bicycle pants and taken to golf: it was as if I had encountered a studhorse with his hair done up in frizzes, and pink bowknots peeking out of them. It seemed, in some vague way, ignominious, and even a bit indelicate.

★

FIRST APPEARANCE IN PRINT [*1899*]
(FROM the Baltimore *Morning Herald*)

★

A horse, a buggy and several sets of harness, valued in all at about $250, were stolen last night from the stable of Howard Quinlan, near Kingsville. The county police are at work on the case, but so far no trace of either thieves or booty has been found.

★

RECOLLECTIONS OF NOTABLE COPS
[1900–10]
(FROM *Newspaper Days*, 1942)

Some time ago I read in a New York paper that fifty or sixty college graduates had been appointed to the metropolitan police force, and were being well spoken of by their superiors. The news astonished me, for in my reportorial days there was simply no such thing in America as a book-learned cop, though I knew a good many who were very smart. The force was then recruited, not from the groves of Academe, but from the ranks of workingmen. The best police captain I ever knew in Baltimore was a meat-cutter by trade, and had lost one of his thumbs by a slip of his cleaver, and the next best was a former bartender. All the mounted cops were ex-hostlers passing as ex-cavalrymen, and all the harbor police had come up through the tugboat and garbage-scow branches of the merchant marine. It took a young reporter a little while to learn how to read and interpret the reports that cops turned in, for they were couched in a special kind of English, with a spelling peculiar to itself. If a member of what was then called "the finest" had spelled *larceny* in any way save *larsensy,* or *arson* in any way save *arsony,* or *fracture* in any way save *fraxr,* there would have been a considerable lifting of eyebrows. I well recall the horror of the Baltimore cops when the first board to examine applicants for places on the force was set up. It was a harmless body headed by a political dentist, and the hardest question in its first examination paper was "What is the plural of *ox?*," but all the cops in town predicted that it would quickly contaminate their craft with a great horde of what they called "professors," and reduce it to the level of letter-carrying or school-teaching.

But, as I have noted, their innocence of *literae humaniores* was not necessarily a sign of stupidity, and from some of them, in fact, I learned the valuable lesson that sharp wits can lurk in unpolished skulls. I knew cops who were matches for the most learned and unscrupulous lawyers at the Baltimore bar, and others who had made monkeys of the oldest and crabbedest judges on the bench, and were generally respected for it. Moreover, I knew cops who were really first-rate policemen, and loved their trade as tenderly as so many art artists or movie actors. They were badly paid, but they carried on their dismal work with unflagging diligence, and loved a long, hard chase almost as much as they loved a quick, brisk clubbing. Their one salient failing, taking them as a class, was their belief that any person who had been arrested, even on mere suspicion, was unquestionably and *ipso facto* guilty. But that theory, though it occasionally colored their testimony in a garish manner, was grounded, after all, on nothing worse than professional pride and *esprit de corps,* and I am certainly not one to hoot at it, for my own belief in the mission of journalism has no better support than the same partiality, and all the logic I am aware of stands against it.

In those days that pestilence of Service which torments the American people today was just getting under way, and many of the multifarious duties now carried out by social workers, statisticians, truant officers, visiting nurses, psychologists, and the vast rabble of inspectors, smellers, spies and bogus experts of a hundred different faculties either fell to the police or were not discharged at all. An ordinary flatfoot in a quiet residential section had his hands full. In a single day he might have to put out a couple of kitchen fires, arrange for the removal of a dead mule, guard a poor epileptic having a fit on the sidewalk, catch a runaway horse, settle a combat with table knives between husband and wife, shoot a cat for killing pigeons, rescue a dog or a baby from a sewer, bawl out a white-wings for spilling garbage, keep order on the sidewalk at two or three funerals, and flog half a dozen bad boys for throwing horse-apples at a blind man. The cops downtown, especially along the wharves and in the red-light districts, had even more curious and complicated jobs, and some of them attained to a high degree of virtuosity.

As my memory gropes backward I think, for example, of a strange office that an old-time roundsman named Charlie had to undertake every Spring. It was to pick up enough skilled workmen to effect the annual redecoration and refurbishing of the Baltimore City Jail. Along about May 1 the warden would telephone to police headquarters that he needed, say, ten head of painters, five plumbers, two blacksmiths, a tile-setter, a roofer, a bricklayer, a carpenter and a locksmith, and it was Charlie's duty to go out and find them. So far as I can recall, he never failed, and usually he produced two or three times as many craftsmen of each category as were needed, so that the warden had some chance to pick out good ones. His plan was simply to make a tour of the saloons and stews in the Marsh Market section of Baltimore, and look over the drunks in congress assembled. He had a trained eye, and could detect a plumber or a painter through two weeks' accumulation of beard and dirt. As he gathered in his candidates, he searched them on the spot, rejecting those who had no union cards, for he was a firm believer in organized labor. Those who passed were put into storage at a police-station, and there kept (less the unfortunates who developed delirium tremens and had to be handed over to the resurrection-men) until the whole convoy was ready. The next morning Gene Grannan, the police magistrate, gave them two weeks each for vagrancy, loitering, trespass, committing a nuisance, or some other plausible misdemeanor, the warden had his staff of master-workmen, and the jail presently bloomed out in all its vernal finery.

Some of these toilers returned year after year, and in the end Charlie recognized so many that he could accumulate the better part of his convoy in half an hour. Once, I remember, he was stumped by a call for two electricians. In those remote days there were fewer men of that craft in practise than today, and only one could be found. When the warden put on the heat Charlie sent him a trolley-car motorman who had run away from his wife and was trying to be shanghaied for the Chesapeake oyster-fleet. This poor man, being grateful for his security in jail, made such eager use of his meagre electrical knowledge that the warden decided to keep him, and even requested that his sentence be extended. Unhappily, Gene Grannan was a pretty good amateur lawyer, and knew that such an extension would be illegal. When the warden of the House of Correction, which was on a farm twenty miles from Baltimore, heard how well this system was working, he put in a requisition for six experienced milkers and a choir-leader, for he had a herd of cows and his colored prisoners loved to sing spirituals. Charlie found the choir-leader in no time, but he bucked at hunting for milkers, and got rid of the nuisance by sending the warden a squad of sailors who almost pulled the poor cows to pieces.

Gene had been made a magistrate as one of the first fruits of the rising reform movement in Baltimore, and was a man of the chastest integrity, but he knew too much about reformers to admire them, and lost no chance to afflict them. When, in 1900, or thereabout, a gang of snoopers began to tour the red-light districts, seeking to harass and alarm the poor working women there denizened, he instructed the gals to empty slops on them, and acquitted all who were brought in for doing it, usually on the ground that the complaining witnesses were disreputable persons, and could not be believed on oath. One day, sitting in his frowsy court-room, I saw him gloat in a positively indecent manner when a Methodist clergyman was led out from the cells by Mike Hogan, the turnkey. This holy man, believing that the Jews, unless they consented to be baptized, would all go to Hell, had opened a mission in what was then still called the Ghetto, and sought to save them. The adults, of course, refused to have anything to do with him, but he managed, after a while, to lure a number of *kosher* small boys into his den, chiefly by showing them magic-lantern pictures of the Buffalo Bill country and the Holy Land. When their fathers heard of this there was naturally an uproar, for it was a mortal sin in those days for an orthodox Jew to enter a *Goy Schul*. The ritual for delousing offenders was an arduous one, and cost both time and money. So the Jews came clamoring to Grannan, and he spent a couple of hours trying to figure out some charge to lay against the evangelist. Finally, he ordered him brought in, and entered him on the books for "annoying persons passing by and along a public highway, disorderly conduct, making loud and unseemly noises, and disturbing religious worship." He had to be acquitted, of course, but Gene scared him so badly with talk of the penitentiary that he shut down his mission forthwith, and left the Jews to their post-mortem sufferings.

As I have noted in Chapter II, Gene was a high favorite among us young reporters, for he was always good for copy, and did not hesitate to modify the course of justice in order to feed and edify us. One day an ancient German, obviously a highly respectable man, was brought in on the incredible charge of beating his wife. The testimony showed that they had been placidly married for more than 45 years, and seldom exchanged so much as a bitter word. But the night before, when the old man came home from the saloon where he played *Skat* every evening, the old woman accused him of having drunk more than his usual ration of eight beers, and in the course of the ensuing debate he gave her a gentle slap. Astounded, she let off an hysterical squawk, an officious neighbor rushed in, the cops came on his heels, and so the old man stood before the bar of justice, weeping copiously and with his wife weeping even more copiously beside him. Gene pondered the evidence with a frown on his face, and then announced his judgment. "The crime you are accused of committing," he said, "is a foul and desperate one, and the laws of all civilized countries prohibit it under heavy penalties. I could send you to prison for life, I could order you to the whipping-post [it still exists in Maryland, and for wife-beaters only], or I could sentence you to be hanged. [Here both parties screamed.] But inasmuch as this is your first offense I will be lenient. You will be taken hence to the House of Correction, and there confined for twenty years. In addition, you are fined $10,000." The old couple missed the fine, for at mention of the House of Correction both fainted. When the cops revived them, Gene told the prisoner that, on reflection, he had decided to strike out the sentence, and bade him go and sin no more. Husband and wife rushed out of the courtroom hand in hand, followed by a cop with the umbrella and market-basket that the old woman had forgotten. A week or two later news came in that she was ordering the old man about in a highly cavalier manner, and had cut down his evenings of *Skat* to four a week.

The cops liked and admired Gene, and when he was in good form he commonly had a gallery of them in his courtroom, guffawing at his whimsies. But despite his popularity among them he did not pal with them, for he was basically a very dignified, and even somewhat stiff fellow, and knew how to call them down sharply when their testimony before him went too far beyond the bounds of the probable. In those days, as in these, policemen led a social life almost as inbred as that of the justices of the Supreme Court of the United States, and outsiders were seldom admitted to their parties. But reporters were exceptions, and I attended a number of cop soirées of great elegance, with the tables piled mountain-high with all the delicacies of the season, and a keg of beer every few feet. The graft of these worthy men, at least in my time, was a great deal less than reformers alleged and the envious common people believed. Most of them, in my judgment, were very honest fellows, at least within the bounds of reason. Those who patrolled the fish-markets naturally had plenty of fish to eat, and those who manned the police-boats in the harbor took a certain toll from the pungy captains who brought up Baltimore's supplies of watermelons, cantaloupes, vegetables, crabs and oysters from the Eastern Shore of Maryland: indeed, this last impost amounted to a kind of *octroi,* and at one time the harbor force accumulated so much provender that they had to seize an empty warehouse on the waterfront to store it. But the pungy captains gave up uncomplainingly, for the pelagic cops protected them against the thieves and highjackers who swarmed in the harbor, and also against the land police. I never heard of cops getting anything that the donor was not quite willing and even eager to give. Every Italian who ran a peanut stand knew that making them free of it was good in stitutional promotion and the girls in the red-light districts liked to crochet neckties, socks and pulse-warmers for them. It was not unheard of for a cop to get mashed on such a girl, rescue her from her life of shame, and set her up as a more or less honest woman. I knew of several cases in which holy matrimony followed. But the more ambitious girls, of course, looked higher, and some of them, in my time, made very good marriages. One actually married a banker, and another died only a few years ago as the faithful and much respected wife of a prominent physician. The cop always laughed when reformers alleged that the wages of sin were death—specifically, that women who sold their persons always ended in the gutter, full of dope and despair. They knew that the overwhelming majority ended at the altar of God, and that nearly all of them married better men than they could have had any chance of meeting and roping if they had kept their virtue.

One dismal New Year's day I saw a sergeant lose an excellent chance to pocket $138.66 in cash money: I remember it brilliantly because I lost the same chance at the same moment. There had been the usual epidemic of suicides in the waterfront flop-houses, for the dawn of a new year turns the thoughts of homeless men to peace beyond the dissecting-room, and I accompanied the sergeant and a coroner on a tour of the fatal scenes. One of the dead men was lying on the fifth floor of a decaying warehouse that had been turned into ten-cent sleeping quarters, and we climbed up the long stairs to inspect him. All the other bums had cleared out, and the hophead clerk did not offer to go with us. We found the deceased stretched out in a peaceful attitude, with the rope with which he had hanged himself still around his neck. He had been cut down, but then abandoned.

The sergeant loosed the rope, and began a search of the dead man's pockets, looking for means to identify him. He found nothing whatever of that sort, but from a pants pocket he drew out a fat wad of bills, and a hasty count showed that it contained $416. A situation worthy of Scribe, or even Victor Hugo! Evidently the poor fellow was one of the Russell Sages that are occasionally found among bums. His money, I suppose, had been diminishing, and he had bumped himself off in fear that it would soon be all gone. The sergeant looked at the coroner, the coroner looked at me, and I looked at the sergeant. Then the sergeant wrapped up the money in a piece of newspaper lying nearby, and handed it to the coroner. "It goes," he said sadly, "to the

State of Maryland. The son-of-a-bitch died intestate, and with no heirs."

The next day I met the coroner, and found him in a low frame of mind. "It was a sin and a shame," he said, "to turn that money over to the State Treasury. What I could have done with $138.67! (I noticed he made a fair split, but collared one of the two odd cents.) Well, it's gone now—damn the luck! I never *did* trust that flatfoot."

THEODORE DREISER
(FROM *A Book of Prefaces*, 1916)

Out of the desert of American fictioneering, so populous and yet so dreary, Dreiser stands up—a phenomenon unescapably visible, but disconcertingly hard to explain. What forces combined to produce him in the first place, and how has he managed to hold out so long against the prevailing blasts—of disheartening misunderstanding and misrepresentation, of Puritan suspicion and opposition, of artistic isolation, of commercial seduction? There is something downright heroic in the way the man has held his narrow and perilous ground, disdaining all compromise, unmoved by the cheap success that lies so inviting around the corner. He has faced, in his day, almost every form of attack that a serious artist can conceivably encounter, and yet all of them together have scarcely budged him an inch. He still plods along in the laborious, cheerless way he first marked out for himself; he is quite as undaunted by baited praise as by bludgeoning, malignant abuse; his later novels are, if anything, more unyieldingly dreiserian than his earliest. As one who has long sought to entice him in this direction or that, fatuously

presuming to instruct him in what would improve and
profit him, I may well bear a reluctant and resigned sort
of testimony to his gigantic steadfastness. It is almost
as if any change in his manner, any concession to what
is usual and esteemed, any amelioration of his blind,
relentless exercises of *force majeure,* were a physical impossibility. One feels him at last to be authentically no
more than a helpless instrument (or victim) of that
inchoate flow of forces which he himself is so fond of
depicting as at once the answer to the riddle of life, and
a riddle ten times more vexing and accursed.

And his origins, as I say, are quite as mysterious as
his motive power. To fit him into the unrolling chart
of American, or even of English fiction is extremely
difficult. Save one thinks of H. B. Fuller (whose "With
the Procession" and "The Cliff-Dwellers" are still remembered by Huneker, but by whom else? [1]), he
seems to have had no fore-runner among us, and for all
the discussion of him that goes on, he has few avowed
disciples, and none of them gets within miles of him.
One catches echoes of him, perhaps, in Willa Sibert
Cather, in Mary S. Watts, in David Graham Phillips,
in Sherwood Anderson and in Joseph Medill Patterson,
but, after all, they are no more than echoes. In Robert
Herrick the thing descends to a feeble parody; in imitators further removed to sheer burlesque. All the latter-
day American novelists of consideration are vastly more
facile than Dreiser in their philosophy, as they are in
their style. In the fact, perhaps, lies the measure of
their difference. What they lack, great and small, is the
gesture of pity, the note of awe, the profound sense of
wonder—in a phrase, that "soberness of mind" which
William Lyon Phelps sees as the hallmark of Conrad
and Hardy, and which even the most stupid cannot es-

[1] Fuller's disappearance is one of the strangest phenomena of American letters. I was astonished some time ago to discover that he was
still alive. Back in 1899 he was already so far forgotten that William
Archer mistook his name, calling him Henry Y. Puller. *Vide* Archer's
pamphlet, The American Language; New York, 1899.

cape in Dreiser. The normal American novel, even in its most serious forms, takes colour from the national cocksureness and superficiality. It runs monotonously to ready explanations, a somewhat infantile smugness and hopefulness, a habit of reducing the unknowable to terms of the not worth knowing. What it cannot explain away with ready formulae, as in the later Winston Churchill,* it snickers over as scarcely worth explaining at all, as in the later Howells. Such a brave and tragic book as "Ethan Frome" is so rare as to be almost singular, even with Mrs. Wharton. There is, I daresay, not much market for that sort of thing. In the arts, as in the concerns of everyday, the American seeks escape from the insoluble by pretending that it is solved. A comfortable phrase is what he craves beyond all things —and comfortable phrases are surely not to be sought in Dreiser's stock.

I have heard argument that he is a follower of Frank Norris, and two or three facts lend it a specious probability. "McTeague" was printed in 1899; "Sister Carrie" a year later. Moreover, Norris was the first to see the merit of the latter book, and he fought a gallant fight, as literary advisor to Doubleday, Page & Co., against its suppression after it was in type. But this theory runs aground upon two circumstances, the first being that Dreiser did not actually read "McTeague," nor, indeed, grow aware of Norris, until after "Sister Carrie" was completed, and the other being that his development, once he began to write other books, was along paths far distant from those pursued by Norris himself. Dreiser, in truth, was a bigger man than Norris from the start; it is to the latter's unending honour that he recognized the fact instanter, and yet did all he could to help his rival. It is imaginable, of course, that Norris, living fifteen years longer, might have overtaken Dreiser, and even surpassed him; one finds an arrow pointing that way in "Vandover and the Brute"

* The American novelist, not Sir Winston. A.C.

(not printed until 1914). But it swings sharply around in "The Epic of the Wheat." In the second volume of that incomplete trilogy, "The Pit," there is an obvious concession to the popular taste in romance; the thing is so frankly written down, indeed, that a play has been made of it, and Broadway has applauded it. And in "The Octopus," despite some excellent writing, there is a descent to a mysticism so fantastic and preposterous that it quickly passes beyond serious consideration. Norris, in his day, swung even lower—for example, in "A Man's Woman" and in some of his short stories. He was a pioneer, perhaps only half sure of the way he wanted to go, and the evil lures of popular success lay all about him. It is no wonder that he sometimes seemed to lose his direction.

Émile Zola is another literary father whose paternity grows dubious on examination. I once printed an article exposing what seemed to me to be a Zolaesque attitude of mind, and even some trace of the actual Zola manner, in "Jennie Gerhardt"; there came from Dreiser the news that he had never read a line of Zola, and knew nothing about his novels. Not a complete answer, of course; the influence might have been exerted at second hand. But through whom? I confess that I am unable to name a likely medium. The effects of Zola upon Anglo-Saxon fiction have been almost *nil;* his only avowed disciple, George Moore, has long since recanted and reformed; he has scarcely rippled the prevailing romanticism. . . . Thomas Hardy? Here, I daresay, we strike a better scent. There are many obvious likenesses between "Tess of the D'Urbervilles" and "Jennie Gerhardt" and again between "Jude the Obscure" and "Sister Carrie." All four stories deal penetratingly and poignantly with the essential tragedy of women; all disdain the petty, specious explanations of popular fiction; in each one finds a poetical and melancholy beauty. Moreover, Dreiser himself confesses to an enchanted discovery of Hardy in 1896, three years before "Sister Carrie" was begun. But it is easy to push such a fact too hard, and to search for likenesses and parallels that are really not there. The truth is that Dreiser's points of contact with Hardy might be easily matched by many striking points of difference, and that the fundamental ideas in their novels, despite a common sympathy, are anything but identical. Nor does one apprehend any ponderable result of Dreiser's youthful enthusiasm for Balzac, which antedated his discovery of Hardy by two years. He got from both men a sense of the scope and dignity of the novel; they taught him that a story might be a good one, and yet considerably more than a story; they showed him the essential drama of the commonplace. But that they had more influence in forming his point of view, or even in shaping his technique, than any one of half a dozen other gods of those young days—this I scarcely find. In the structure of his novels, and in their manner of approach to life no less, they call up the work of Dostoyevsky and Turgenev far more than the work of either of these men—but of all the Russians save Tolstoi (as of Flaubert) Dreiser himself tells us that he was ignorant until ten years after "Sister Carrie." In his days of preparation, indeed, his reading was so copious and disorderly that antagonistic influences must have well-nigh neutralized one another, and so left the curious youngster to work out his own method and his own philosophy. Stevenson went down with Balzac, Poe with Hardy, Dumas *fils* with Tolstoi. There were even months of delight in Sienkiewicz, Lew Wallace and E. P. Roe! The whole repertory of the pedagogues had been fought through in school and college: Dickens, Thackeray, Hawthorne, Washington Irving, Kingsley, Scott. Only Irving and Hawthorne seem to have made deep impressions. "I used to lie under a tree," says Dreiser, "and read 'Twice Told Tales' by the hour. I thought "The Alhambra" was a perfect creation, and I still have a lingering affection for it." Add Bret Harte,

George Ebers, William Dean Howells, Oliver Wendell Holmes, and you have a literary stew indeed! . . . But for all its bubbling I see a far more potent influence in the chance discovery of Spencer and Huxley at twenty-three—the year of choosing! Who, indeed, will ever measure the effect of those two giants upon the young men of that era—Spencer with his inordinate meticulousness, his relentless pursuit of facts, his overpowering syllogisms, and Huxley with his devastating agnosticism, his insatiable questionings of the old axioms, above all, his brilliant style? Huxley, it would appear, has been condemned to the scientific hulks, along with bores innumerable and unspeakable; one looks in vain for any appreciation of him in treatises on beautiful letters.[1] And yet the man was a superb artist in works, a master-writer even more than a master-biologist, one of the few truly great stylists that England has produced since the time of Anne. One can easily imagine the effect of two such vigorous and intriguing minds upon a youth groping about for self-understanding and self-expression. They swept him clean, he tells us, of the lingering faith of his boyhood—a mediaeval, Rhenish Catholicism;—more, they filled him with a new and eager curiosity, an intense interest in the life that lay about him, a desire to seek out its hidden workings and underlying causes. A young man set afire by Huxley might perhaps make a very bad novelist, but it is a certainty that he could never make a sentimental and superficial one. There is no need to go further than this single moving adventure to find the genesis of Dreiser's disdain of the current platitudes, his sense of life as a complex biological phenomenon, only dimly comprehended, and his tenacious way of thinking

[1] For example, in The Cambridge History of English Literature, which runs to fourteen large volumes and a total of nearly 10,000 pages, Huxley receives but a page and a quarter of notice, and his remarkable mastery of English is barely mentioned in passing. His two debates with Gladstone, in which he did some of the best writing of the century, are not noticed at all.

things out, and of holding to what he finds good. Ah, that he had learned from Huxley, not only how to inquire, but also how to report! That he had picked up a talent for that dazzling style, so sweet to the ear, so damnably persuasive, so crystal-clear!

But the more one examines Dreiser, either as writer or as theorist of man, the more his essential isolation becomes apparent. He got a habit of mind from Huxley, but he completely missed Huxley's habit of writing. He got a view of woman from Hardy, but he soon changed it out of all resemblance. He got a certain fine ambition and gusto out of Balzac, but all that was French and characteristic he left behind. So with Zola, Howells, Tolstoi and the rest. The tracing of likenesses quickly becomes rabbinism, almost cabalism. The differences are huge and sprout up in all directions. Nor do I see anything save a flaming up of colonial passion in the current efforts to fit him into a German frame, and make him an agent of Prussian frightfulness in letters. Such bosh one looks for in the *Nation* and the Boston *Transcript,* and there is where one actually finds it. Even the *New Republic* has stood clear of it; it is important only as material for that treatise upon the patrioteer and his bawling which remains to be written. The name of the man, true enough, is obviously Germanic, and he has told us himself, in "A Traveler at Forty," how he sought out and found the tombs of his ancestors in some little town of the Rhine country. There are more of these genealogical revelations in "A Hoosier Holiday," but they show a Rhenish strain that was already running thin in boyhood. No one, indeed, who reads a Dreiser novel can fail to see the gap separating the author from these half-forgotten forebears. He shows even less of German influence than of English influence.

There is, as a matter of fact, little in modern German fiction that is intelligibly comparable to "Jennie Gerhardt" and "The Titan," either as a study of man or as a work of art. The naturalistic movement of the eighties was launched by men whose eyes were upon the theatre, and it is in that field that nine-tenths of its force has been spent.

★

In his manner, as opposed to his matter, he is more the Teuton, for he shows all of the racial patience and pertinacity and all of the racial lack of humour. Writing a novel is as solemn a business to him as trimming a beard is to a German barber. He blasts his way through his interminable stories by something not unlike main strength; his writing, one feels, often takes on the character of an actual siege operation, with tunnellings, drum fire, assaults in close order and hand-to-hand fighting. Once, seeking an analogy, I called him the Hindenburg of the novel. If it holds, then "The 'Genius'" is his Poland. The field of action bears the aspect, at the end, of a hostile province meticulously brought under the yoke, with every road and lane explored to its beginning, and every crossroads village laboriously taken, inventoried and policed. Here is the very negation of Gallic lightness and intuition, and of all forms of impressionism as well. Here is no series of illuminating flashes, but a gradual bathing of the whole scene with white light, so that every detail stands out.

And many of those details, of course, are trivial; even irritating. They do not help the picture; they muddle and obscure it; one wonders impatiently what their meaning is, and what the purpose may be of revealing them with such a precise, portentous air. . . . Turn to page 703 of "The 'Genius.'" By the time one gets there, one has hewn and hacked one's way through 702 large pages of fine print—97 long chapters, more than 250,000 words. And yet, at this hurried and impatient point, with the *coda* already begun, Dreiser halts the whole narrative to explain the origin, nature and inner meaning of Christian Science, and to make us privy to a lot of chatty stuff about Mrs. Althea

Jones, a professional healer, and to supply us with detailed plans and specifications of the apartment house in which she lives, works her tawdry miracles, and has her being. Here, in sober summary, are the particulars:

1. That the house is "of conventional design."
2. That there is "a spacious areaway" between its two wings.
3. That these wings are "of cream-coloured pressed brick."
4. That the entrance between them is "protected by a handsome wrought-iron door."
5. That to either side of this door is "an electric lamp support of handsome design."
6. That in each of these lamp supports there are "lovely cream-coloured globes, shedding a soft lustre."
7. That inside is "the usual lobby."
8 That in the lobby is "the usual elevator."
9. That in the elevator is the usual "uniformed negro elevator man."
10. That this negro elevator man (name not given) is "indifferent and impertinent."
11. That a telephone switchboard is also in the lobby.
12. That the building is seven stories in height.

In "The Financier" there is the same exasperating rolling up of irrelevant facts. The court proceedings in the trial of Cowperwood are given with all the exactness of a parliamentary report in the London *Times*. The speeches of the opposing counsel are set down nearly in full, and with them the remarks of the judge, and after that the opinion of the Appellate Court on appeal, with the dissenting opinions as a sort of appendix. In "Sister Carrie" the thing is less savagely carried out, but that is not Dreiser's fault, for the manuscript was revised by some anonymous hand, and the printed version is but little more than half the length of the original. In "The Titan" and "Jennie Gerhardt" no such brake upon exuberance is visible; both books are crammed with details that serve no purpose, and are as flat as ditch-water. Even in the two volumes of personal record, "A Traveler at Forty" and "A Hoosier Holiday," there is the same furious accumulation of trivialities. Consider the former. It is without structure, without selection, without reticence. One arises from it as from a great babbling, half drunken. On the one hand the author fills a long and gloomy chapter with the story of the Borgias, apparently under the impression that it is news, and on the other hand he enters into intimate and inconsequential confidences about all the persons he meets en route, sparing neither the innocent nor the obscure. The children of his English host at Bridgely Level strike him as fantastic little creatures, even as a bit uncanny—and he duly sets it down. He meets an Englishman on a French train who pleases him much, and the two become good friends and see Rome together, but the fellow's wife is "obstreperous" and "haughty in her manner" and so "loud-spoken in her opinions" that she is "really offensive"—and down it goes. He makes an impression on a Mlle. Marcelle in Paris, and she accompanies him from Monte Carlo to Ventimiglia, and there gives him a parting kiss and whispers, "*Avril-Fontainebleau*"—and lo, this sweet one is duly spread upon the minutes. He permits himself to be arrested by a fair privateer in Piccadilly, and goes with her to one of the dens of sin that suffragettes see in their nightmares, and cross-examines her at length regarding her ancestry, her professional ethics and ideals, and her earnings at her dismal craft—and into the book goes a full report of the proceedings. He is entertained by an eminent Dutch jurist in Amsterdam—and upon the pages of the chronicle it appears that the gentleman is "waxy" and "a little pedantic," and that he is probably the sort of "thin, delicate, well barbered" professor that Ibsen had in mind when he cast about for a husband for the daughter of General Gabler.

Such is the art of writing as Dreiser understands it and practises it—an endless piling up of minutiae, an almost ferocious tracking down of ions, electrons and molecules, an unshakable determination to tell it all. One is amazed by the mole-like diligence of the man, and no less by his exasperating disregard for the ease of his readers. A Dreiser novel, at least of the later canon, cannot be read as other novels are read—on a winter evening or summer afternoon, between meal and meal, travelling from New York to Boston. It demands the attention for almost a week, and uses up the faculties for a month. If, reading "The 'Genius,'" one were to become engrossed in the fabulous manner described in the publishers' advertisement, and so find oneself unable to put it down and go to bed before the end, one would get no sleep for three days and three nights.

Worse, there are no charms of style to mitigate the rigours of these vast steppes and pampas of narration. Joseph Joubert's saying that "words should stand out well from the paper" is quite incomprehensible to Dreiser; he never imitates Flaubert by writing for "*la respiration et l'oreille*." There is no painful groping for the inevitable wórd, or for what Walter Pater called "the gipsy phrase"; the common, even the commonplace, coin of speech is good enough. On the first page of "Jennie Gerhardt" one encounters "frank, open countenance," "diffident manner," "helpless poor," "untutored mind," "honest necessity," and half a dozen other stand-bys of the second-rate newspaper reporter. In "Sister Carrie" one finds "high noon," "hurrying throng," "unassuming restaurant," "dainty slippers," "high-strung nature," and "cool, calculating world"— all on a few pages. Carrie's sister, Minnie Hanson, "gets" the supper. Hanson himself is "wrapped up" in his child. Carrie decides to enter Storm and King's office, "no matter what." In "The Titan" the word "trig" is worked to death; it takes on, toward the end, the character of a banal and preposterous refrain. In the other books one encounters mates for it—words made to do duty in as many senses as the American verb "to fix" or the journalistic "to secure."

I often wonder if Dreiser gets anything properly describable as pleasure out of this dogged accumulation of threadbare, undistinguished, uninspiring nouns, adjectives, verbs, adverbs, pronouns, participles and conjunctions. To the man with an ear for verbal delicacies —the man who searches painfully for the perfect word, and puts the way of saying a thing above the thing said —there is in writing the constant joy of sudden discovery, of happy accident. A phrase springs up full blown, sweet and caressing. But what joy can there be in rolling up sentences that have no more life and beauty in them, intrinsically, than so many election bulletins? Where is the thrill in the manufacture of such a paragraph as that in which Mrs. Althea Jones' sordid habitat is described with such inexorable particularity? Or in the laborious confection of such stuff as this, from Book I, Chapter IV, of "The 'Genius'"?:

> The city of Chicago—who shall portray it! This vast ruck of life that had sprung suddenly into existence upon the dank marshes of a lake shore!

Or this from the epilogue to "The Financier":

> There is a certain fish whose scientific name is *Mycteroperca Bonaci,* and whose common name is Black Grouper, which is of considerable value as an afterthought in this connection, and which deserves much to be better known. It is a healthy creature, growing quite regularly to a weight of two hundred and fifty pounds, and living a comfortable, lengthy existence because of its very remarkable ability to adapt itself to conditions. . . .

Or this from his pamphlet, "Life, Art and America";[1]

Alas, alas! for art in America. It has a hard stubby row to hoe.

But I offer no more examples. Every reader of the Dreiser novels must cherish astounding specimens—of awkward, platitudinous marginalia, of whole scenes spoiled by bad writing, of phrases as brackish as so many lumps of sodium hyposulphite. Here and there, as in parts of "The Titan" and again in parts of "A Hoosier Holiday," an evil conscience seems to haunt him and he gives hard striving to his manner, and more than once there emerges something that is almost graceful. But a backsliding always follows this phosphorescence of reform. "The 'Genius,'" coming after "The Titan," marks the high tide of his bad writing. There are passages in it so clumsy, so inept, so irritating that they seem almost unbelievable; nothing worse is to be found in the newspapers. Nor is there any compensatory deftness in structure, or solidity of design, to make up for this carelessness in detail. The well-made novel, of course, can be as hollow as the well-made play of Scribe—but let us at least have a beginning, a middle and an end! Such a story as "The 'Genius'" is as gross and shapeless as Brünnhilde. It billows and bulges out like a cloud of smoke, and its internal organization is almost as vague. There are episodes that, with a few chapters added, would make very respectable novels. There are chapters that need but a touch or two to be excellent short stories. The thing rambles, staggers, trips, heaves, pitches, struggles, totters, wavers, halts, turns aside, trembles on the edge of collapse. More than once it seems to be foundering, both in the equine and in the maritime senses. The tale has been heard of a tree so tall that it took two men to see to the top of it.

[1] New York, 1917; reprinted from *The Seven Arts* for Feb. 1917.

Here is a novel so brobdingnagian that a single reader can scarcely read his way through it. . . .

Of the general ideas which lie at the bottom of all of Dreiser's work it is impossible to be in ignorance, for he has exposed them at length in "A Hoosier Holiday" and summarized them in "Life, Art and America." In their main outlines they are not unlike the fundamental assumptions of Joseph Conrad. Both novelists see human existence as a seeking without a finding; both reject the prevailing interpretations of its meaning and mechanism; both take refuge in "I do not know." Put "A Hoosier Holiday" beside Conrad's "A Personal Record," and you will come upon parallels from end to end. Or better still, put it beside Hugh Walpole's "Joseph Conrad," in which the Conradean metaphysic is condensed from the novels even better than Conrad has done it himself: at once you will see how the two novelists, each a worker in the elemental emotions, each a rebel against the current assurance and superficiality, each an alien to his place and time, touch each other in a hundred ways.

"Conrad," says Walpole, "is of the firm and resolute conviction that life is too strong, too clever and too remorseless for the sons of men." And then, in amplification: "It is as though, from some high window, looking down, he were able to watch some shore, from whose security men were forever launching little cockleshell boats upon a limitless and angry sea. . . . From his height he can follow their fortunes, their brave struggles, their fortitude to the very end. He admires their courage, the simplicity of their faith, but his irony springs from his knowledge of the inevitable end. . . ."

Substitute the name of Dreiser for that of Conrad, and you will have to change scarcely a word. Perhaps one, to wit, "clever." I suspect that Dreiser, writing so of his own creed, would be tempted to make it "stupid," or, at all events, "unintelligible." The struggle of man, as he sees it, is more than impotent; it is gratuitous and purposeless. There is, to his eye, no grand ingenuity, no skillful adaptation of means to end, no moral (or even dramatic) plan in the order of the universe. He can get out of it only a sense of profound and inexplicable *dis*order. The waves which batter the cockleshells change their direction at every instant. Their navigation is a vast adventure, but intolerably fortuitous and inept—a voyage without chart, compass, sun or stars. . . .

So at bottom. But to look into the blackness steadily, of course, is almost beyond the endurance of man. In the very moment that its impenetrability is grasped the imagination begins attacking it with pale beams of false light. All religions, I daresay, are thus projected from the questioning soul of man, and not only all religions, but also all great agnosticisms. Nietzsche, shrinking from the horror of that abyss of negation, revived the Pythagorean concept of *der ewigen Wiederkunft*—a vain and blood-curdling sort of comfort. To it, after a while, he added explanations almost Christian—a whole repertoire of whys and wherefores, aims and goals, aspirations and significances. The late Mark Twain, in an unpublished work, toyed with an equally daring idea; that men are to some unimaginably vast and incomprehensible Being what the unicellular organisms of his body are to man, and so on *ad infinitum*. Dreiser occasionally inclines to much the same hypothesis; he likens the endless reactions going on in the world we know, the myriadal creation, collision and destruction of entities, to the slow accumulation and organization of cells *in utero*. He would make us specks in the insentient embryo of some gigantic Presence whose form is still unimaginable and whose birth must wait for Eons and Eons. Again, he turns to something not easily distinguishable from philosophical idealism, whether out of Berkeley or Fichte it is hard to make out—that is, he would interpret the whole phenomenon of life as no more than an appearance, a nightmare of some unseen sleeper or of men themselves, an "uncanny blur of nothingness"—in Euripides' phrase, "a song sung by an idiot, dancing down the wind." Yet again, he talks vaguely of the intricate polyphony of a cosmic orchestra, cacophonous to our dull ears. Finally, he puts the observed into the ordered, reading a purpose in the displayed event: "life was intended to sting and hurt. . . ." But these are only gropings, and not to be read too critically. From speculations and explanations he always returns, Conrad-like, to the bald fact: to "the spectacle and stress of life." All he can make out clearly is "a vast compulsion which has nothing to do with the individual desires or tastes or impulses of individuals." That compulsion springs "from the settling processes of forces which we do not in the least understand, over which we have no control, and in whose grip we are as grains of dust or sand, blown hither and thither, for what purpose we cannot even suspect." [1] Man is not only doomed to defeat, but denied any glimpse or understanding of his antagonist. Here we come upon an agnosticism that has almost got beyond curiosity. What good would it do us, asks Dreiser, to know? In our ignorance and helplessness, we may at least get a slave's consolation out of cursing the unknown gods. Suppose we saw them striving blindly, too, and pitied them? . . .

But, as I say, this scepticism is often tempered by guesses at a possibly hidden truth, and the confession that this truth may exist reveals the practical unworkableness of the unconditioned system, at least for Dreiser. Conrad is far more resolute, and it is easy to see why. He is, by birth and training, an aristocrat. He has the gift of emotional detachment. The lures of facile doctrine do not move him. In his irony there is a disdain which plays about even the ironist himself. Dreiser is a product of far different forces and traditions, and is capable of no such escapement. Struggle as he may, and

[1] Life, Art and America, p. 5.

fume and protest as he may, he can no more shake off the chains of his intellectual and cultural heritage than he can change the shape of his nose. What that heritage is you may find out in detail by reading "A Hoosier Holiday," or in summary by glancing at the first few pages of "Life, Art and America." Briefly described, it is the burden of a believing mind, a moral attitude, a lingering superstition. One-half of the man's brain, so to speak, wars with the other half. He is intelligent, he is thoughtful, he is a sound artist—but there come moments when a dead hand falls upon him, and he is once more the Indiana peasant, snuffing absurdly over imbecile sentimentalities, giving a grave ear to quackeries, snorting and eye-rolling with the best of them. One generation spans too short a time to free the soul of man. Nietzsche, to the end of his days, remained a Prussian pastor's son, and hence two-thirds a Puritan; he erected his war upon holiness, toward the end, into a sort of holy war. Kipling, the grandson of a Methodist preacher, reveals the tin-pot evangelist with increasing clarity as youth and its ribaldries pass away and he falls back upon his fundamentals. And that other English novelist who springs from the servants' hall—let us not be surprised or blame him if he sometimes writes like a bounder.

The truth about Dreiser is that he is still in the transition stage between Christian Endeavour and civilization, between Warsaw, Indiana and the Socratic grove, between being a good American and being a free man, and so he sometimes vacillates perilously between a moral sentimentalism and a somewhat extravagant revolt. "The 'Genius,'" on the one hand, is almost a tract for rectitude, a Warning to the Young; its motto might be *Scheut die Dirnen!* And on the other hand, it is full of a laborious truculence that can only be explained by imagining the author as heroically determined to prove that he is a plain-spoken fellow and his own man, let the chips fall where they may. So, in spots, in "The

Financier" and "The Titan," both of them far better
books. There is an almost moral frenzy to expose and
riddle what passes for morality among the stupid. The
isolation of irony is never reached; the man is still
evangelical; his ideas are still novelties to him; he is as
solemnly absurd in some of his floutings of the Code
Américain as he is in his respect for Bouguereau, or in
his flirtings with the New Thought, or in his naif belief in the importance of novel-writing. Somewhere or
other I have called all this the Greenwich Village complex. It is not genuine artists, serving beauty reverently
and proudly, who herd in those cockroached cellars and
bawl for art; it is a mob of half-educated yokels and
cockneys to whom the very idea of art is still novel, and
intoxicating—and more than a little bawdy.

Not that Dreiser actually belongs to this ragamuffin
company. Far from it, indeed. There is in him, hidden
deep-down, a great instinctive artist, and hence the
makings of an aristocrat. In his muddled way, held
back by the manacles of his race and time, and his steps
made uncertain by a guiding theory which too often
eludes his own comprehension, he yet manages to produce works of art of unquestionable beauty and authority, and to interpret life in a manner that is poignant
and illuminating. There is vastly more intuition in him
than intellectualism; his talent is essentially feminine,
as Conrad's is masculine; his ideas always seem to be
deduced from his feelings. The view of life that got
into "Sister Carrie," his first book, was not the product
of a conscious thinking out of Carrie's problems. It
simply got itself there by the force of the artistic passion behind it; its coherent statement had to wait for
other and more reflective days. The thing began as a
vision, not as a syllogism. Here the name of Franz
Schubert inevitably comes up. Schubert was an ignoramus, even in music; he knew less about polyphony,
which is the mother of harmony, which is the mother
of music, than the average conservatory professor. But

nevertheless he had such a vast instinctive sensitiveness to musical values, such a profound and accurate feeling for beauty in tone, that he not only arrived at the truth in tonal relations, but even went beyond what, in his day, was known to be the truth, and so led an advance. Likewise, Giorgione de Castelfranco and Masaccio come to mind: painters of the first rank, but untutored, unsophisticated, uncouth. Dreiser, within his limits, belongs to this sabot-shod company of the elect. One thinks of Conrad, not as artist first, but as savant. There is something of the icy aloofness of the laboratory in him, even when the images he conjures up pulsate with the very glow of life. He is almost as self-conscious as the Beethoven of the last quartets. In Dreiser the thing is more intimate, more disorderly, more a matter of pure feeling. He gets his effects, one might almost say, not by designing them, but by living them.

But whatever the process, the power of the image evoked is not to be gainsaid. It is not only brilliant on the surface, but mysterious and appealing in its depths. One swiftly forgets his intolerable writing, his mirthless, sedulous, repellent manner, in the face of the Athenian tragedy he instils into his seduced and soulsick servant girls, his barbaric pirates of finances, his conquered and hamstrung supermen, his wives who sit and wait. He has, like Conrad, a sure talent for depicting the spirit in disintegration. Old Gerhardt, in "Jennie Gerhardt," is alone worth all the *dramatis personae* of popular American fiction since the days of "Rob o' the Bowl"; Howells could no more have created him, in his Rodinesque impudence of outline, than he could have created Tartuffe or Gargantua. Such a novel as "Sister Carrie" stands quite outside the brief traffic of the customary stage. It leaves behind it an unescapable impression of bigness, of epic sweep and dignity. It is not a mere story, not a novel in the customary American meaning of the word; it is at once a psalm of life and a criticism of life—and that criticism loses nothing by the fact that its burden is despair. Here, precisely, is the point of Dreiser's departure from his fellows. He puts into his novels a touch of the eternal *Weltschmerz*. They get below the drama that is of the moment and reveal the greater drama that is without end. They arouse those deep and lasting emotions which grow out of the recognition of elemental and universal tragedy. His aim is not merely to tell a tale; his aim is to show the vast ebb and flow of forces which sway and condition human destiny. One cannot imagine him consenting to Conan Doyle's statement of the purpose of fiction, quoted with characteristic approval by the New York *Times:* "to amuse mankind, to help the sick and the dull and the weary." Nor is his purpose to instruct; if he is a pedagogue it is only incidentally and as a weakness. The thing he seeks to do is to stir, to awaken, to move. One does not arise from such a book as "Sister Carrie" with a smirk of satisfaction; one leaves it infinitely touched.

★

Dreiser, like Mark Twain and Emerson before him, has been far more hospitably greeted in his first stage, now drawing to a close, in England than in his own country. The cause of this, I daresay, lies partly in the fact that "Sister Carrie" was in general circulation over there during the seven years that it remained suppressed on this side. It was during these years that such men as Arnold Bennett, Theodore Watts-Dunton, Frank Harris and H. G. Wells, and such critical journals as the *Spectator,* the *Saturday Review* and the *Athenaeum* became aware of him, and so laid the foundations of a sound appreciation of his subsequent work. Since the beginning of the war, certain English newspapers have echoed the alarmed American discovery that he is a literary agent of the Wilhelmstrasse, but it is to the honour of the English that this imbecility has got no countenance from reputable authority and has not injured his position.

At home, as I have shown, he is less fortunate. When criticism is not merely an absurd effort to chase him out of court because his ideas are not orthodox, as the Victorians tried to chase out Darwin and Swinburne, and their predecessors pursued Shelley and Byron, it is too often designed to identify him with some branch or other of "radical" poppycock, and so credit him with purposes he has never imagined. Thus Chautauqua pulls and Greenwich Village pushes. In the middle ground there proceeds the pedantic effort to dispose of him by labelling him. One faction maintains that he is a realist; another calls him a naturalist; a third argues that he is really a disguised romanticist. This debate is all sound and fury, signifying nothing, but out of it has come a valuation by Lawrence Gilman[1] which perhaps strikes very close to the truth. He is, says Mr. Gilman, "a sentimental mystic who employs the mimetic gestures of the realist." This judgment is apt in particular and sound in general. No such thing as a pure method is possible in the novel. Plain realism, as in Gorky's "Nachtasyl" and the war stories of Ambrose Bierce, simply wearies us by its vacuity; plain romance, if we ever get beyond our nonage, makes us laugh. It is their artistic combination, as in life itself, that fetches us— the subtle projection of the concrete muddle that is living against the ideal orderliness that we reach out for —the eternal war of experience and aspiration—the contrast between the world as it is and the world as it might be or ought to be. Dreiser describes the thing that he sees, laboriously and relentlessly, but he never forgets the dream that is behind it. "He gives you," continues Mr. Gilman, "a sense of actuality; but he gives you more than that: out of the vast welter and surge, the plethoric irrelevancies . . . emerges a sense

[1] The *North American Review*, February 1916.

of the infinite sadness and mystery of human life. . . ."[1]

"To see truly," said Renan, "is to see dimly." Dimness or mystery, call it what you will: it is in all these overgrown and formless, but profoundly moving books. Just what do they mean? Just what is Dreiser driving at? That such questions should be asked is only a proof of the straits to which pedagogy has brought criticism. The answer is simple: he is driving at nothing, he is merely trying to represent what he sees and feels. His moving impulse is no flabby yearning to teach, to expound, to make simple; it is that "obscure inner necessity" of which Conrad tells us, the irresistible creative passion of a genuine artist, standing spell-bound before the impenetrable enigma that is life, enamoured by the strange beauty that plays over its sordidness, challenged to a wondering and half-terrified sort of representation of what passes understanding. And *jenseits von Gut und Böse*. "For myself," says Dreiser, "I do not know what truth is, what beauty is, what love is, what hope is. I do not believe anyone absolutely and I do not doubt anyone absolutely. I think people are both evil and well-intentioned." The hatching of the Dreiser bugaboo is here; it is the flat rejection of the rubber-stamp formulae that outrages petty minds; not being "good," he must be "evil"—as William Blake said of Milton, a true poet is always "of the devil's party." But in that very groping toward a light but dimly seen there is a measure, it seems to me, of Dreiser's rank and consideration as an artist. "Now comes the public," says Hermann Bahr, "and demands that we explain what the poet is trying to say. The answer is this: If we knew exactly he would not be a poet. . . ."

[1] Another competent valuation, by Randolph Bourne, is in *The Dial*, June 14, 1917.

GORE IN THE CARIBBEES [*1917*]
(FROM *Heathen Days*, 1943)

No reporter of my generation, whatever his genius, ever really rated spats and a walking-stick until he had covered both a lynching and a revolution. The first, by the ill-favor of the gods, I always missed, usually by an inch. How often, alas, alas, did I strain and puff my way to some Christian hamlet of the Chesapeake Bay littoral, by buggy, farm-wagon or pack-mule, only to discover that an anti-social sheriff had spirited the blackamoor away, leaving nothing but a seething vacuum behind. Once, as I was on my travels, the same thing happened in the charming town of Springfield, Mo., the Paris and Gomorrah of the Ozarks. I was at dinner at the time with the late Edson K. Bixby, editor of the Springfield *Leader,* along with Paul Patterson and Henry M. Hyde, my colleagues of the Baltimore *Sunpapers.* When the alarm reached us we abandoned our victuals instantly, and leaped and galloped downtown to the jail. By the time we got there, though it was in less than three minutes, the cops had loaded the candidate—he was a white man—into their hurry-wagon and made off for Kansas City, and the lynching mob had been reduced to a hundred or so half-grown youths, a couple of pedlars selling hot-dogs and American flags, and a squawking herd of fascinated but disappointed children.

I had rather better luck with revolutions, though I covered only one, and that one I walked into by a sort of accident. The year was 1917 and I was returning from a whiff of World War I in a Spanish ship that had sailed from La Coruña, Spain, ten days before and was hoping, eventually, to get to Havana. It was, at the moment, somewhat in the maze of the Bahamas, but a wireless reached it nevertheless, and that wireless was directed to me and came from the *Sunpaper* office in Baltimore. It said, in brief, that a revolution had broken out in Cuba, that both sides were doing such rough lying that no one north of the Straits of Florida could make out what it was about, and that a series of succinct and illuminating dispatches describing its issues and personalities would be appreciated. I wirelessed back that the wishes of my superiors were commands, and then sent another wireless to a friend in Havana, Captain Asmus Leonhard, marine superintendent of the Munson Line, saying that I itched to see him the instant my ship made port. Captain Leonhard was a Dane of enormous knowledge but parsimonious speech, and I had a high opinion of his sagacity. He knew everyone worth knowing in Latin America, and thousands who were not, and his estimates of them seldom took more than three words. "A burglar," he would say, characterizing a general played up by all the North American newspapers as the greatest trans-Rio Grande hero since Bolívar, or "a goddam fraud," alluding to a new president of Colombia, El Salvador or Santo Domingo, and that was all. His reply to my wireless was in his usual manner. It said: "Sure."

When the Spanish ship, after groping about for two or three days in Exuma Sound, the North-East Providence Channel, the Tongue of Ocean and various other strangely-named Bahaman waterways, finally made Havana and passed the Morro, a smart young mulatto in Captain Leonhard's launch put out from shore, took me aboard his craft, and whisked me through the customs. The captain himself was waiting in front of the Pasaje Hotel in the Prado, eating a plate of Spanish bean-soup and simultaneously smoking a Romeo y Julieta cigar. "The issues in the revolution," he said, tackling the business in hand at once, "are simple. Menocal, who calls himself a Conservative, is president, and José Miguel Gómez, who used to be president and calls himself a Liberal, wants to make a come-back. That is the whole story. José Miguel says that when Menocal was reëlected last year the so-called Liberals were chased away from the so-called polls by the so-called army. On the other hand, Menocal says that José Miguel is a porch-climber and ought to be chased out of the island. Both are right."

It seemed clear enough, and I prepared to write a dispatch at once, but Captain Leonhard suggested that perhaps it might be a good idea for me to see Menocal first, and hear the official version in full. We were at the palace in three minutes, and found it swarming with dignitaries. Half of them were army officers in uniform, with swords, and the other half were functionaries of the secretariat. They pranced and roared all over the place, and at intervals of a few seconds more officers would dash up in motor-cars and muscle and whoop their way into the president's office. These last, explained Captain Leonhard, were couriers from the front, for José Miguel, having taken to the bush, was even now surrounded down in Santa Clara province, and there were high hopes that he would be nabbed anon. Despite all the hurly-burly it took only ten minutes for the captain to get me an audience with *el presidente*. I found His Excellency calm and amiable. He spoke English fluently, and was far from reticent. José Miguel, he said, was a fiend in human form who hoped by his treasons to provoke American intervention, and so upset the current freely-chosen and impeccably virtuous government. This foul plot would fail. The gallant Cuban army, which had never lost either a battle or a war, had the traitor cornered, and within a few days he would be chained up among the lizards in the fortress of La Cabaña, waiting for the firing-squad and trying in vain to make his peace with God.

So saying, *el presidente* bowed me out, at the same

time offering to put a motor-car and a secretary at my disposal. It seemed a favorable time to write my dispatch, but Captain Leonhard stayed me. "First," he said, "you had better hear what the revolutionists have to say." "The revolutionists!" I exclaimed. "I thought they were out in Santa Clara, surrounded by the army." "Some are," said the captain, "but some ain't. Let us take a hack." So we took a hack and were presently worming our way down the narrow street called Obispo. The captain called a halt in front of a bank, and we got out. "I'll wait here in the bank," he said, "and you go upstairs to Room 309. Ask for Dr. ——" and he whispered a name. "Who is this Dr. ——?" I whispered back. "He is the head of the revolutionary junta," replied the captain. "Mention my name, and he will tell you all about it."

I followed orders, and was soon closeted with the doctor—a very tall, very slim old man with a straggling beard and skin the color of cement. While we gabbled various persons rushed in and out of his office, most of them carrying papers which they slapped upon his desk. In a corner a young Cuban girl of considerable sightliness banged away at a typewriter. The doctor, like *el presidente,* spoke excellent English, and appeared to be in ebullient spirits. He had trustworthy agents, he gave me to understand, in the palace, some of them in high office. He knew what was going on in the American embassy. He got carbons of all official telegrams from the front. The progress of events there, he said, was extremely favorable to the cause of reform. José Miguel, though somewhat bulky for field service, was a military genius comparable to Joffre or Hindenburg, or even to Hannibal or Alexander, and would soon be making monkeys of the generals of the army. As for Menocal, he was a fiend in human form who hoped to provoke American intervention, and thereby make his corrupt and abominable régime secure.

All this naturally struck me as somewhat unusual,

though as a newspaper reporter I was supposed to be incapable of surprise. Here, in the very heart and gizzard of Havana, within sight and hearing of thousands, the revolutionists were maintaining what amounted to open headquarters, and their boss wizard was talking freely, and indeed in a loud voice, to a stranger whose only introduction had been, so to speak, to ask for Joe. I ventured to inquire of the doctor if there were not some danger that his gold-fish globe of a hideaway would be discovered. "Not much," he said. "The army is hunting for us, but the army is so stupid as to be virtually idiotic. The police know where we are, but they believe we are going to win, and want to keep their jobs afterward." From this confidence the doctor proceeded to boasting. "In ten days," he said, "we'll have Menocal jugged in La Cabaña. Shoot him? No; it would be too expensive. The New York banks that run him have plenty of money. If we let him live they will come across."

When I rejoined the captain downstairs I suggested again that it was high time for me to begin composing my dispatch, and this time he agreed. More, he hauled me down to the cable office, only a block or two away, and there left me. "If you get into trouble," he said, "call me up at the Pasaje. I'll be taking my nap, but the clerk will wake me if you need me." I found the cable office very comfortable and even luxurious. There were plenty of desks and typewriters, and when I announced myself I was invited to make myself free of them. Moreover, as I sat down and began to unlimber my prose a large brass spittoon was wheeled up beside me, apparently as a friendly concession to my nationality. At other desks a number of other gentlemen were in labor, and I recognized them at once as colleagues, for a newspaper reporter can always spot another, just as a Freemason can spot a Freemason, or a detective a detective. But I didn't know any of them, and fell to work without speaking to them. When my dispatch was finished I took it to the window, and was informed politely that it would have to be submitted to the censor, who occupied, it appeared, a room in the rear.

The censor turned out to be a young Cuban whose English was quite as good as Menocal's or the doctor's, but unhappily he had rules to follow, and I soon found that they were very onerous. While I palavered with him several of the colleagues came up with copy in their hands, and in two minutes an enormous debate was in progress. He was sworn, I soon gathered, to cut out everything even remotely resembling a fact. No names. No dates. Worse, no conjectures, prognostications, divinations. The colleagues, thus robbed of their habitual provender and full of outrage, put up a dreadful uproar, but the censor stood his ground, and presently I slipped away and called up Captain Leonhard. My respect for his influence was higher than ever now, and it had occurred to me that the revolutionists up the street might have a private cable, and that if they had he would undoubtedly be free of it. But when, in response to his order, I met him in front of the Pasaje, he said nothing about a cable, but heaved me instead into a hack. In ten minutes we were aboard an American ship just about to cast off from a wharf down in the region of the customs-house, and he was introducing me to one of the mates. "Tell him what to do," he said, "and he will do it." I told the mate to file my dispatch the instant his ship docked at Key West, he nodded silently and put the copy into an inside pocket, and that was that. Then the siren sounded and the captain and I returned to the pier.

It all seemed so facile that I became somewhat uneasy. Could the mate be trusted? The captain assured me that he could. But what of the ship? Certainly it did not look fit for wrestling with the notorious swells of the Straits of Florida. Its lines suggested that it had started out in life as an excursion boat on the Hudson, and it was plainly in the last stages of decrepitude. I knew that the run to Key West was rather more than a hundred miles, and my guess, imparted to the captain, was that no such craft could make it in less than forty-eight hours. But the captain only laughed. "That old hulk," he said, "is the fastest ship in the Caribbean. If it doesn't hit a log or break in two it will make Key West in five and a half hours." He was right as usual, for that night, just as I was turning in at the Pasaje I received a cable from the *Sunpaper* saying that my treatise on the revolution had begun to run, and was very illuminating and high-toned stuff.

Thereafter, I unloaded all my dissertations in the same manner. Every afternoon I would divert attention by waiting on the censor and filing a dispatch so full of contraband that I knew he would never send it, and then I would go down to the wharf and look up the mate. On the fourth day he was *non est* and I was in a panic, for the captain had gone on a business trip into Pinar del Rio and no one else could help me. But just as the lines were being cast off I caught sight of a likely-looking Americano standing at the gangway and decided to throw myself upon his Christian charity. He responded readily, and my dispatch went through as usual. Thereafter, though the mate never showed up again—I heard later that he was sick in Key West—I always managed to find an accommodating passenger. Meanwhile, the censor's copy-hook accumulated a fine crop of my rejected cablegrams, and mixed with them were scores by the colleagues. Every time I went to the cable office I found the whole corps raising hell, and threatening all sorts of reprisals and revenges. But they seldom got anything through save the official communiqués that issued from the palace at hourly intervals.

These communiqués were prepared by a large staff of press-agents, and were not only couched in extremely florid words but ran to great lengths. I had just come from Berlin, where all that the German General Staff had to say every day, though war was raging on two fronts, was commonly put into no more than 300 words, so this Latin exuberance rather astonished me. But the stuff made gaudy reading, and I sent a lot of it to the *Sunpaper* by mail, for the entertainment and instruction of the gentlemen of the copy-desk. The Cuban mails, of course, were censored like the cable, but the same Americano who carried my afternoon dispatch to Key West was always willing to mail a few long envelopes at the same place. Meanwhile, I hung about the palace, and picked up enough off-record gossip to give my dispatches a pleasant air of verisimilitude, soothing to editors if not to readers. Also, I made daily visits to the headquarters of the revolutionists, and there got a lot of information, some of it sound, to the same end. In three days, such is the quick grasp of the reportorial mind, I knew all the ins and outs of the revolution,* and in a week I was fit to write a history of Cuban politics from the days of Diego Velázquez. I was, of course, younger then than I am now, and reporters today are not what they used to be, but into that we need not go.

After a week it began to be plain, even on the evidence supplied by the revolutionists, that the uprising was making heavy weather of it, and when, a day or two later, the palace press-agents announced, in a communiqué running to 8,000 words, that José Miguel Gómez was about to be taken, I joined the colleagues in believing it. We all demanded, of course, to be let in on the final scene, and after a long series of conferences, with speeches by Menocal, half a dozen high army officers, all the press-agents and most of the correspondents, it was so ordered. According to both the palace and the

---

* Like many of Mencken's newspaper reports, this one reads like a parody, or a carefree fantasia on the truth. It was often so, but not if you were along with him on the same assignment. This apparently wild account is shrewdly close to the facts, as set down in hindsight by the *Encyclopædia Britannica*, 14th edition, p. 838. See also *The United States and the Caribbean*, by Dexter Perkins. A.C.

revolutionists, the front was down at Placetas in Santa Clara, 180 miles away, but even in those days there were plenty of Fords in Havana, and it was arranged that a fleet of them should start out the next morning, loaded with correspondents, typewriters and bottled beer. Unhappily, the trip was never made, for at the precise moment the order for it was being issued a dashing colonel in Santa Clara was leading his men in a grand assault upon José Miguel, and after ten minutes of terrific fire and deafening yells the Cuban Hindenburg hoisted his shirt upon the tip of his sword and surrendered. He did not have to take his shirt off for the purpose: it was already hanging upon a guava bush, for he had been preparing for a siesta in his hammock. Why he did not know of the projected attack I could never find out, for he was held incommunicado in La Cabaña until I left Cuba, and neither the palace nor the revolutionists seemed willing to discuss the subject.

The palace press-agents, you may be sure, spit on their hands when they heard the news, and turned out a series of communiqués perhaps unsurpassed in the history of war. Their hot, lascivious rhetoric was still flowing three or four days later, long after poor José Miguel was safely jugged among the lizards and scorpions. I recall one canto of five or six thousand words that included a minute autopsy on the strategy and tactics of the final battle, written by a gifted military pathologist on the staff of the victorious colonel. He described every move in the stealthy approach to José Miguel in the minutest detail, and pitched his analysis in highly graphic and even blood-curdling terms. More than once, it appeared, the whole operation was in dire peril, and a false step might have wrecked it, and thereby delivered Cuba to the wolves. Indeed, it might have been baffled at its very apex and apogee if only José Miguel had had his shirt on. As it was, he could not, according to Latin notions of decorum, lead his men, and in consequence they skedaddled, and he himself was forced to yield his sword to the agents of the New York banks.

The night of the victory was a great night in Havana, and especially at the palace. President Menocal kept open house in the most literal sense: his office door was wide open and anyone was free to rush in and hug him. Thousands did so, including scores of officers arriving home from the front. Some of these officers were indubitably Caucasians, but a great many were of darker shades, including saddle-brown and coffin-black. As they leaped out of their Fords in front of the palace the bystanders fell upon them with patriotic gloats and gurgles, and kissed them on both cheeks. Then they struggled up the grand staircase to *el presidente's* reception-room, and were kissed again by the superior public there assembled. Finally, they leaped into the inner office, and fell to kissing His Excellency and to being kissed by him. It was an exhilarating show, but full of strangeness to a Nordic. I observed two things especially. The first was that, for all the uproar, no one was drunk. The other was that the cops beat up no one.

José Miguel was brought to Havana the next morning, chained up in a hearse, and the palace press-agents announced in a series of ten or fifteen communiqués that he would be tried during the afternoon, and shot at sunrise the day following. The colleagues, robbed of their chance to see his capture, now applied for permission to see him put to death, and somewhat to their surprise it was granted readily. He was to be turned off, it appeared, at 6 a.m. promptly, so they were asked to be at the gate of La Cabaña an hour earlier. Most of them were on hand, but the sentry on watch refused to let them in, and after half an hour's wrangle a young officer came out and said that the execution had been postponed until the next day. But the next day it was put off again, and again the next, and after three or four days no more colleagues showed up at the gate. It was then announced by the palace literati that President

Menocal had commuted the sentence to solitary confinement for life in a dungeon on the Cayos de las Doce Leguas off the south coast, where the mosquitoes were as large as bullfrogs, along with confiscation of all the culprit's property, whether real, personal or mixed, and the perpetual loss of his civil rights, such as they were.

But even this turned out to be only tall talk, for President Menocal was a very humane man, and pretty soon he reduced José Miguel's sentence to fifty years, and then to fifteen, and then to six, and then to two. Soon after that he wiped out the jugging altogether, and substituted a fine—first of $1,000,000, then of $250,000, and then of $50,000. The common belief was that José Miguel was enormously rich, but this was found to be an exaggeration. When I left Cuba he was still protesting that the last and lowest fine was far beyond his means, and in the end, I believe, he was let off with the confiscation of his yacht, a small craft then laid up with engine trouble. When he died in 1921 he had resumed his old place among the acknowledged heroes of his country. Twenty years later Menocal joined him in Valhalla.

PATER PATRIÆ
(FROM *Damn! A Book of Calumny*, 1918)

If George Washington were alive today, what a shining mark he would be for the whole camorra of uplifters, forward-lookers and professional patriots! He was the Rockefeller of his time, the richest man in the United States, a promoter of stock companies, a land-grabber, an exploiter of mines and timber. He was a bitter opponent of foreign entanglements, and denounced their evils in harsh, specific terms. He had a liking for forthright and pugnacious men, and a contempt for lawyers, schoolmasters and all other such obscurantists. He was not pious. He drank whiskey whenever he felt chilly, and kept a jug of it handy. He knew far more profanity than Scripture, and used and enjoyed it more. He had no belief in the infallible wisdom of the common people, but regarded them as inflammatory dolts, and tried to save the Republic from them. He advocated no sure cure for all the sorrows of the world, and doubted that such a panacea existed. He took no interest in the private morals of his neighbors.

Inhabiting These States today, George would be ineligible for any office of honor or profit. The Senate would never dare confirm him; the President would not think of nominating him. He would be on trial in the newspapers for belonging to the Money Power. The Sherman Act would have him in its toils; he would be under indictment by every grand jury south of the Potomac; the Methodists of his native State would be denouncing him (he had a still at Mount Vernon) as a debaucher of youth, a recruiting officer for insane asylums, a poisoner of the home. And what a chance there would be for that ambitious young district attorney who thought to shadow him on his peregrinations—and grab him under the Mann Act!

QUID EST VERITAS?
(FROM *Damn! A Book of Calumny*, 1918)

All great religions, in order to escape absurdity, have to admit a dilution of agnosticism. It is only the savage, whether of the African bush or the American gospel tent, who pretends to know the will and intent of God exactly and completely. "For who hath known the mind of the Lord?" asked Paul of the Romans. "How unsearchable are His judgments, and His ways past finding out!" "It is the glory of God," said Solomon, "to conceal a thing." "Clouds and darkness," said David, "are around Him." "No man," said the Preacher, "can find out the work of God." . . . The difference between religions is a difference in their relative content of agnosticism. The most satisfying and ecstatic faith is almost purely agnostic. It trusts absolutely without professing to know at all.

THE ART ETERNAL
(FROM the New York *Evening Mail*, 1918)

One of the laudable by-products of the Freudian quackery is the discovery that lying, in most cases, is involuntary and inevitable—that the liar can no more avoid it than he can avoid blinking his eyes when a light flashes or jumping when a bomb goes off behind him. At its worst, indeed, this necessity takes on a downright pathological character, and is thus as innocent as sciatica. It is part of the morbid baggage of hysterics and neurasthenics: their lying is simply a symptom of their convulsive effort to adjust themselves to an environment which bears upon them too harshly for endurance. The rest of us are not quite so hard pushed, but pushed we all are. In us the thing works through the inferiority complex, which no man can escape. He who lacks it entirely is actually reckoned insane by the fact: his satisfaction with his situation in the world is indistinguishable from a delusion of grandeur. The great majority of us—all, in brief, who are normal—pass through life in constant revolt against our limitations, objective and subjective. Our conscious thought is largely devoted to plans and specifications for cutting a better figure in human society, and in our unconscious the business goes on much more steadily and powerfully. No healthy man, in his secret heart, is content with his destiny. He is tortured by dreams and images as a child is tortured by the thought of a state of existence in which it would live in a candy-store and have two stomachs.

Lying is the product of the unconscious yearning to realize such visions, and if the policeman, conscience, prevents the lie being put into plain words, then it is at least put into more or less plausible acts. We all play parts when we face our fellow-men, as even poets have noticed. No man could bring himself to reveal his true character, and, above all, his true limitations as a citizen and a Christian, his true meannesses, his true imbecilities, to his friends, or even to his wife. Honest autobiography is therefore a contradiction in terms: the moment a man considers himself, even *in petto,* he tries to gild and fresco himself. Thus a man's wife, however realistic her view of him, always flatters him in the end, for the worst she sees in him is appreciably better, by the time she sees it, than what is actually there. What she sees, even at times of the most appalling domestic revelation and confidence, is not the authentic man at all, but a compound made up in part of the authentic man and in part of his projection of a gaudy ideal. The man who is most respected by his wife is the one who makes this projection most vivid—that is, the one who is the most daring and ingratiating liar. He can never, of course, deceive her utterly, but if he is skillful he may at least deceive her enough to make her happy.

Omnis homo mendax: thus the Psalmist. So far the Freudians merely parrot him. What is new in their gospel is the doctrine that lying is instinctive, normal, and unavoidable—that a man is forced into it by his very will-to-live. This doctrine purges the business of certain ancient embarrassments, and restores innocence to the heart. Think of a lie as a compulsion neurosis, and you think of it more kindly. I need not add, I hope, that this transfer of it from the department of free will to that of determinism by no means disposes of the penalty that traditionally pursues it, supposing it to be detected and resented. The proponents of free will always make the mistake of assuming that the determinists are simply evil fellows looking for a way to escape the just consequences of their transgressing. No sense is in that assumption. If I lie on the witness-stand and am detected by the judge, I am jailed for perjury forthwith, regardless of my helplessness under compulsion. Here justice refuses absolutely to distinguish between a misfortune and a tort: the overt act is all it is concerned with. But as jurisprudence grows more intelligent and more civilized it may change its tune, to the benefit of liars, which is to say, to the benefit of humanity. Science is unflinchingly deterministic, and it has begun to force its determinism into morals. On some shining tomorrow a psychoanalyst may be put into the box to prove that perjury is simply a compulsion neurosis, like beating time with the foot at a concert or counting the lampposts along the highway.

However, I have but small faith in millenniums, and do not formally predict this one. Nor do I pronounce any moral judgment, pro or con: moral judgments, as old Friedrich used to say, are foreign to my nature. But let us not forget that lying, *per se,* is not forbidden by the moral code of Christendom. Holy Writ dismisses it cynically, and the statutes of all civilized states are silent about it. Only the Chinese, indeed, make it a penal offense. Perjury, of course, is prohibited everywhere, and also any mendacity which amounts to fraud and deprives a fellow-man of his property. But that far more common form of truth-stretching which has only the lesser aim of augmenting the liar's personal dignity and consequence is looked upon with a very charitable eye. So is that form which has the aim of helping another person in the same way. In the latter direction lying may even take on the stature of a positive virtue. The late King Edward VII, when Prince of Wales, attained to great popularity throughout Christendom by venturing into downright perjury. Summoned into a court of law to give expert testimony regarding some act of adultery, he lied like a gentleman, as the phrase goes, to protect a woman. The lie, to be sure, was intrinsically useless; no one believed that the lady was innocent. Nevertheless, every decent Christian applauded the perjurer for his good intentions, including even the judge on the bench, sworn to combat false witness by every resource of forensics. All of us, worms that we are, occasionally face the alternatives that confronted Edward. On the one hand, we may tell the truth, regardless of consequences, and on the other hand we may mellow it and sophisticate it to make it humane and tolerable.

For the habitual truth-teller and truth-seeker, indeed, the world has very little liking. He is always unpopular, and not infrequently his unpopularity is so excessive that it endangers his life. Run your eye back over the list of martyrs, lay and clerical: nine-tenths of them, you will find, stood accused of nothing worse than honest efforts to find out and announce the truth. Even today, with the scientific passion become familiar in the world, the general view of such fellows is highly unfavorable. The typical scientist, the typical critic of institutions, the typical truth-seeker in every field is held under suspicion by the great majority of men, and variously beset by posses of relentless foes. If he tries to find out the truth about arteriosclerosis, or surgical shock, or cancer, he is denounced as a scoundrel by the Christian Scientists, the osteopaths and the anti-vivisectionists. If he tries to tell the truth about the government, its agents seek to silence him and punish him. If he turns to fiction and endeavors to depict his fellow men accurately, he has the Comstocks on his hands. In no field can he count upon a friendly audience, and freedom from assault. Especially in the United States is his whole enterprise viewed with bilious eye. The men the American people admire most extravagantly are the most daring liars; the men they detest most violently are those who try to tell them the truth. A Galileo could no more be elected President of the United States than he could be elected Pope of Rome. Both high posts are reserved for men favored by God with an extraordinary genius for swathing the bitter facts of life in bandages of soft illusion.

★

THE SKEPTIC
(FROM the *Smart Set,* May 1919)

No man ever quite believes in any other man. One may believe in an idea absolutely, but not in a man. In the highest confidence there is always a flavor of doubt—a feeling, half instinctive and half logical, that, after all, the scoundrel *may* have something up his sleeve. This doubt, it must be obvious, is always more than justified, for no man is worthy of unlimited reliance—his treason, at best, only waits for sufficient temptation. The trouble with the world is not that men are too suspicious in this direction, but that they tend to be too confiding—that they still trust themselves too far to other men, even after bitter experience. Women, I believe, are measurably less sentimental, in this as in other things. No married woman ever trusts her husband absolutely, nor does she ever act as if she *did* trust him. Her utmost confidence is as wary as an American pickpocket's confidence that the policeman on the beat will stay bought.

THE INCOMPARABLE BUZZ-SAW
(FROM the *Smart Set*, May 1919)

The allurement that women hold out to men is precisely the allurement that Cape Hatteras holds out to sailors: they are enormously dangerous and hence enormously fascinating. To the average man, doomed to some banal drudgery all his life long, they offer the only grand hazard that he ever encounters. Take them away and his existence would be as flat and secure as that of a moo-cow. Even to the unusual man, the adventurous man, the imaginative and romantic man, they offer the adventure of adventures. Civilization tends to dilute and cheapen all other hazards. Even war has been largely reduced to caution and calculation; already, indeed, it employs almost as many press-agents, letter-openers and generals as soldiers. But the duel of sex continues to be fought in the Berserker manner. Whoso approaches women still faces the immemorial dangers. Civilization has not made them a bit more safe than they were in Solomon's time; they are still inordinately menacing, and hence inordinately provocative, and hence inordinately charming.

The most disgusting cad in the world is the man who, on grounds of decorum and morality, avoids the game of love. He is one who puts his own ease and security above the most laudable of philanthropies. Women have a hard time of it in this world. They are oppressed by man-made laws, man-made social customs, masculine egoism, the delusion of masculine superiority.

Their one comfort is the assurance that, even though it may be impossible to prevail against man, it is always possible to enslave and torture a man. This feeling is fostered when one makes love to them. One need not be a great beau, a seductive catch, to do it effectively. Any man is better than none. To shrink from giving so much happiness at such small expense, to evade the business on the ground that it has hazards—this is the act of a puling and tacky fellow.

A BLIND SPOT
(FROM the *Smart Set*, April 1920)

No doubt my distaste for democracy as a political theory is, like every other human prejudice, due to an inner lack—to a defect that is a good deal less in the theory than in myself. In this case it is very probably my incapacity for envy. That emotion, or weakness, or whatever you choose to call it, is quite absent from my make-up; where it ought to be there is a vacuum. In the face of another man's good fortune I am as inert as a curb broker before Johann Sebastian Bach. It gives me neither pleasure nor distress. The fact, for example, that John D. Rockefeller had more money than I have is as uninteresting to me as the fact that he believed in total immersion and wore detachable cuffs. And the fact that some half-anonymous ass or other has been elected President of the United States, or appointed a professor at Harvard, or married to a rich wife, or even to a beautiful and amiable one: this fact is as meaningless to me as the latest piece of bogus news from eastern Europe.

The reason for all this does not lie in any native nobility or acquired virtue. Far from it, indeed. It lies in the accidental circumstance that the business I pursue in the world seldom brings me into very active competition with other men. I have, of course, rivals, but they do not rival me directly and exactly, as one delicatessen dealer or clergyman or lawyer or politician rivals another. It is only rarely that their success costs me anything, and even then the fact is usually concealed. I have always had enough money to meet my modest needs, and have always found it easy to get more than I actually want. A skeptic as to all ideas, including especially my own, I have never suffered a pang when the ideas of some other imbecile prevailed.

Thus I am never envious, and so it is impossible for me to feel any sympathy for men who are. *Per corollary,* it is impossible for me to get any glow out of such hallucinations as democracy and Puritanism, for if you pump envy out of them you empty them of their very life blood: they are all immovably grounded upon the inferior man's hatred of the man who is having a better time. One often hears them accounted for, of course, in other ways. Puritanism is represented as a lofty sort of obedience to God's law. Democracy is depicted as brotherhood, even as altruism. All such notions are in error. There is only one honest impulse at the bottom of Puritanism, and that is the impulse to punish the man with a superior capacity for happiness —to bring him down to the miserable level of "good" men *i.e.,* of stupid, cowardly and chronically unhappy men. And there is only one sound argument for democracy, and that is the argument that it is a crime for any man to hold himself out as better than other men, and, above all, a most heinous offense for him to prove it.

What I admire most in any man is a serene spirit, a steady freedom from moral indignation, an all-embracing tolerance—in brief, what is commonly called good sportsmanship. Such a man is not to be mistaken for one who shirks the hard knocks of life. On the contrary, he is frequently an eager gladiator, vastly enjoying opposition. But when he fights he fights in the manner of a gentleman fighting a duel, not in that of a longshoreman cleaning out a waterfront saloon. That is to say, he carefully guards his *amour propre* by assuming that his opponent is as decent· a man as he is, and just as honest—and perhaps, after all, right. Such an attitude is palpably impossible to a democrat. His distinguishing mark is the fact that he always attacks his opponents, not only with all arms, but also with snorts and objurgations—that he is always filled with moral indignation—that he is incapable of imagining honor in an antagonist, and hence incapable of honor himself. Such fellows I do not like. I do not share their emotion. I can't understand their indignation, their choler. In particular, I can't fathom their envy. And so I am against them.

ABRAHAM LINCOLN
(FROM the *Smart Set*, May 1920)

Some time ago a publisher told me that there are four kinds of books that seldom, if ever, lose money in the United States—first, murder stories; secondly, novels in which the heroine is forcibly overcome by the hero; thirdly, volumes on spiritualism, occultism and other such claptrap, and fourthly, books on Lincoln. But despite all the vast mass of Lincolniana and the constant discussion of old Abe in other ways, even so elemental a problem as that of his religious ideas— surely an important matter in any competent biography —is yet but half solved. Was he a Christian? Did he believe in the Divinity of Jesus? I am left in doubt. He was very polite about it, and very cautious, as befitted a

H. L. MENCKEN

politician in need of Christian votes, but how much
genuine conviction was in that politeness? And if his
occasional references to Jesus were thus open to question, what of his rather vague avowals of belief in a
personal God and in the immortality of the soul?
Herndon and some of his other early friends always
maintained that he was an atheist, but the Rev. William
E. Barton, one of the best of the later Lincolnologists,
argues that this atheism was simply disbelief in the idiotic Methodist and Baptist dogmas of his time—that
nine Christian churches out of ten, if he were alive today, would admit him to their high privileges and prerogatives without anything worse than a few warning
coughs. As for me, I still wonder.

Lincoln becomes the American solar myth, the chief
butt of American credulity and sentimentality. Washington, of late years, has been perceptibly humanized;
every schoolboy now knows that he used to swear a
good deal, and was a sharp trader, and had a quick eye
for a pretty ankle. But meanwhile the varnishers and
veneerers have been busily converting Abe into a plas-
ter saint, thus making him fit for adoration in the
Y.M.C.A.'s. All the popular pictures of him show him in
his robes of state, and wearing an expression fit for a
man about to be hanged. There is, so far as I know, not
a single portrait of him showing him smiling—and yet
he must have cackled a good deal, first and last: who
ever heard of a storyteller who didn't? Worse, there is
an obvious effort to pump all his human weaknesses
out of him, and so leave him a mere moral apparition,
a sort of amalgam of John Wesley and the Holy
Ghost. What could be more absurd? Lincoln, in point
of fact, was a practical politician of long experience and
high talents, and by no means cursed with idealistic superstitions. Until he emerged from Illinois they always
put the women, children and clergy to bed when he got
a few gourds of corn aboard, and it is a matter of unescapable record that his career in the State Legisla-

ture was indistinguishable from that of a Tammany Nietzsche. Even his handling of the slavery question was that of a politician, not that of a messiah. Nothing alarmed him more than the suspicion that he was an Abolitionist, and Barton tells of an occasion when he actually fled town to avoid meeting the issue squarely. An Abolitionist would have published the Emancipation Proclamation the day after the first battle of Bull Run. But Lincoln waited until the time was more favorable—until Lee had been hurled out of Pennsylvania, and more important still, until the political currents were safely running his way. Even so, he freed the slaves in only a part of the country: all the rest continued to clank their chains until he himself was an angel in Heaven.

Like William Jennings Bryan, he was a dark horse made suddenly formidable by fortunate rhetoric. The Douglas debate launched him, and the Cooper Union speech got him the Presidency. His talent for emotional utterance was an accomplishment of late growth. His early speeches were mere empty fireworks—the hollow rhodomontades of the era. But in middle life he purged his style of ornament and it became almost baldly simple—and it is for that simplicity that he is remembered today. The Gettysburg speech is at once the shortest and the most famous oration in American history. Put beside it, all the whoopings of the Websters, Sumners and Everetts seem gaudy and silly. It is eloquence brought to a pellucid and almost gem-like perfection—the highest emotion reduced to a few poetical phrases. Nothing else precisely like it is to be found in the whole range of oratory. Lincoln himself never even remotely approached it. It is genuinely stupendous.

But let us not forget that it is poetry, not logic; beauty, not sense. Think of the argument in it. Put it into the cold words of everyday. The doctrine is simply this: that the Union soldiers who died at Gettysburg sacrificed their lives to the cause of self-determination

—"that government of the people, by the people, for the people," should not perish from the earth. It is difficult to imagine anything more untrue. The Union soldiers in that battle actually fought *against* self-determination; it was the Confederates who fought for the right of their people to govern themselves. What was the practical effect of the battle of Gettysburg? What else than the destruction of the old sovereignty of the States, *i.e.*, of the people of the States? The Confederates went into battle free; they came out with their freedom subject to the supervision and veto of the rest of the country—and for nearly twenty years that veto was so effective that they enjoyed scarcely more liberty, in the political sense, than so many convicts in the penitentiary.

LODGE

(FROM the Baltimore *Evening Sun,* June 15, 1920. Written on my return from the Republican National Convention in Chicago, which nominated Warren G. Harding for the Presidency. Henry Cabot Lodge, then a Senator from Massachusetts and one of the leaders of the Republican party, was permanent chairman of the convention. I came back from Chicago on the same train that carried him, and in fact had the compartment next to his. The weather was very hot and there was no air-conditioning. In the morning coming into Washington he astounded humanity by appearing in the corridor in his shirt-sleeves. Harding died on August 2, 1923, and Lodge on November 9, 1924.)

What Lodge thinks of it, viewing all that ghastly combat of mountebanks in ironical retrospect, would make an interesting story—perhaps the most interesting about the convention that could be told, or even imagined. He presided over the sessions from a sort of aloof intellectual balcony, far above the swarming and bawling of the common herd. He was there in the flesh, but his soul was in some remote and esoteric

Cathay. Perhaps even the presence of the flesh was no more than an optical delusion, a mirage due to the heat. At moments when the whole infernal hall seemed bathed in a steam produced by frying delegates and alternates alive, he was as cool as an undertaker at a hanging. He did not sweat like the general. He did not puff. He did not fume. If he put on a fresh collar every morning it was mere habit and foppishness—a sentimental concession to the Harvard tradition. He might have worn the same one all week.

It was delightful to observe the sardonic glitter in his eye, his occasional ill-concealed snort, his general air of detachment from the business before him. For a while he would watch the show idly, letting it get more and more passionate, vociferous and preposterous. Then, as if suddenly awakened, he would stalk into it with his club and knock it into decorum in half a minute. I call the thing a club; it was certainly nothing properly describable as a gavel. The head of it was simply a large globe of hard wood, as big as an ordinary cantaloupe. The handle was perhaps two feet long. The weight of it I can't estimate. It must have been light, else so frail a man would have found it too much for him. But it made a noise like the breaking in a door, and before that crash whole delegations went down.

Supporting it was the Lodge voice, and behind the voice the Lodge sneer. That voice seemed quite extraordinary in so slim and ancient a man. It had volume, resonance, even a touch of music: it was pleasant to hear, and it penetrated that fog of vaporized humanity to great depth. No man who spoke from the platform spoke more clearly, more simply or more effectively. Lodge's keynote speech, of course, was bosh, but it was bosh delivered with an air—bosh somehow dignified by the manner of its emission. The same stuff, shoveled into the atmosphere by any other statesman on the platform, would have simply driven the crowd out of the hall, and perhaps blown up the convention then and there. But Lodge got away with it because he was Lodge—because there was behind it his unescapable confidence in himself, his disarming disdain of discontent below, his unapologetic superiority.

This superiority was and is quite real. Lodge is above the common level of his party, his country and his race, and he knows it very well, and is not disposed toward the puerile hypocrisy of denying it. He has learning. He has traditions behind him. He is absolutely sure of himself in all conceivable American societies. There was a profound irony in the rôle that he had to play at Chicago, and it certainly did not escape him. One often detected him snickering into his beard as the obscene farce unrolled itself before him. He was a nurse observing sucklings at their clumsy play, a philosopher shooing chickens out of the corn. His delight in the business visibly increased as the climax was approached. It culminated in a colossal chuckle as the mob got out of hand, and the witches of crowd folly began to ride, and the burlesque deliberations of five intolerable days came to flower in the half-frightened, half-defiant nomination of Harding—a tin-horn politician with the manner of a rural corn doctor and the mien of a ham actor.

I often wonder what such a man as Lodge thinks secretly of the democracy he professes to cherish. It must interest him enormously, at all events as spectacle, else he would not waste his time upon it. He might have given over his days to the writing of bad history —an avocation both amusing and respectable, with a safe eminence as its final reward. He might have gone in for diplomacy and drunk out of the same jug with kings. He might have set up general practise as a Boston intellectual, groaning and sniffing an easy way through life in the lofty style of the Adams brothers. Instead he dedicated himself to politics, and spent years mastering its complex and yet fundamentally childish technique.

Well, what reward has it brought him? At 73 he is a boss in the Senate, holding domination over a herd of miscellaneous mediocrities by a loose and precarious tenure. He has power, but men who are far beneath him have more power. At the great quadrennial pow-wow of his party he plays the part of bellwether and chief of police. Led by him, the rabble complains bitterly of lack of leadership. And when the glittering prize is fought for, he is shouldered aside to make way for a gladiator so bogus and so preposterous that the very thought of him must reduce a scion of the Cabots to sour and sickly mirth.

A superior fellow? Even so. But superior enough to disdain even the Presidency, so fought for by fugitives from the sewers? I rather doubt it. My guess is that the gaudy glamor of the White House has intrigued even Henry Cabot—that he would leap for the bauble with the best of them if it were not clearly beyond his reach. The blinding rays, reflected from the brazen front of Roosevelt, bathed him for a while; he had his day on the steps of the throne, and I suspect that he was not insensitive to the thrill of it. On what other theory can one account for his sober acceptance of the whole Roosevelt hocus-pocus save on this theory of bedazzlement? Imagine the prince of cynics actually bamboozled by the emperor of mountebanks! Think of Swift reading Nick Carter, Edward Bok and Harold Bell Wright!

He came back from Chicago on the same train that carried Harding. Harding traveled in one car and Lodge in another. So far as I could observe their communications were confined to a few politenesses. Lodge sat in a compartment all alone, gazing out of the window with his inscrutable ghost of a smile. He breakfasted alone. He lunched alone. He dined alone. His job was done, and he was once more serenely out of it.

CAVIA COBAYA
(FROM the *Smart Set*, August 1920)

I find the following in Theodore Dreiser's "Hey-Rub-a-Dub-Dub":

Does the average strong, successful man confine himself to one woman? Has he ever?

The first question sets an insoluble problem. How are we, in such intimate matters, to say what is the average and what is not the average? But the second question is easily answered, and the answer is, He has. Here Dreiser's curious sexual obsession simply led him into absurdity. His view of the traffic of the sexes remained the naïve one of an ex-Baptist nymph in Greenwich Village. Did he argue that Otto von Bismarck was not a "strong, successful man"? If not, then he should have known that Bismarck was a strict monogamist—a man full of sin, but always faithful to his Johanna. Again, there was Thomas Henry Huxley. Again, there was William Ewart Gladstone. Yet again, there were Robert Schumann, Felix Mendelssohn, Johann Sebastian Bach, Ulysses S. Grant, Andrew Jackson, Louis Pasteur, Martin Luther, Helmuth von Moltke, Stonewall Jackson, Robert Browning, William T. Sherman, Sam Adams, . . . I could extend the list to pages. . . . Perhaps I am unfair to Dreiser. His notion of a "strong, successful man" may have been, not such a genuinely superior fellow as Bismarck or Bach, but such a mere brigand as Yerkes or Jim Fisk. If so, he was still wrong. If so, he ran aground on John D. Rockefeller.

THE NATIONAL LETTERS

(FROM *Prejudices: Second Series*, 1920)

It is convenient to begin, like the gentlemen of God, with a glance at a text or two. The first, a short one, is from Ralph Waldo Emerson's celebrated oration, "The American Scholar," delivered before the Phi Beta Kappa Society at Cambridge on August 31st, 1837. Emerson was then thirty-four years old and almost unknown in his own country, though he had already published "Nature" and established his first contacts with Landor and Carlyle. But "The American Scholar" brought him into instant notice at home, partly as man of letters but more importantly as seer and prophet, and the fame thus founded has endured without much diminution, at all events in New England, to this day. Oliver Wendell Holmes, giving words to what was undoubtedly the common feeling, hailed the address as the intellectual declaration of independence of the American people, and that judgment, amiably passed on by three generations of pedagogues, still survives in the literature books. I quote from the first paragraph:

> Our day of dependence, our long apprenticeship to the learning of other lands, draws to a close. . . . Events, actions arise, that must be sung, that will sing themselves. Who can doubt that poetry will revive and lead in a new age, as the star in the constellation Harp, which now flames in our zenith, astronomers announce, shall one day be the pole-star for a thousand years?

This, as I say, was in 1837. Thirty-three years later, in 1870, Walt Whitman echoed the prophecy in his even more famous "Democratic Vistas." What he saw in his vision and put into his gnarled and gasping prose was

> a class of native authors, literatuses, far different, far higher in grade, than any yet known, sacerdotal, modern, fit to cope with our occasions, lands, permeating the whole mass of American morality, taste, belief, breathing into it a new breath of life, giving it decision, affecting politics far more than the popular superficial suffrage, with results inside and underneath the elections of Presidents or Congress—radiating, begetting appropriate teachers, schools, manners, and, as its grandest result, accomplishing, (what neither the schools nor the churches and their clergy have hitherto accomplished, and without which this nation will no more stand, permanently, soundly, than a house will stand without a substratum,) a religious and moral character beneath the political and productive and intellectual bases of the States. The promulgation and belief in such a class or order—a new and greater literatus order—its possibility, (nay, certainly,) underlies these entire speculations. . . . Above all previous lands, a great original literature is sure to become the justification and reliance, (in some respects the sole reliance,) of American democracy.

Thus Whitman in 1870, the time of the first draft of "Democratic Vistas." He was of the same mind, and said so, in 1888, four years before his death. I could bring up texts of like tenor in great number, from the years before 1837, from those after 1888, and from every decade between. The dream of Emerson, though the eloquence of its statement was new and arresting, embodied no novel projection of the fancy; it merely gave a sonorous *Waldhorn* tone to what had been dreamed and said before. You will find almost the same high hope, the same exuberant confidence in the essays of the elder Channing and in the "Lectures on American Literature" of Samuel Lorenzo Knapp, L.L.D., the first native critic of beautiful letters—the primordial tadpole of all our later Mores, Brownells, Phelpses, Mabies, Brander Matthewses and other such grave and glittering fish. Knapp believed, like Whitman long after him, that the sheer physical grandeur of the New World would inflame a race of bards to unprecedented utterance. "What are the Tibers and Scamanders," he demanded, "measured by the Missouri and the Amazon? Or what the loveliness of Illysus or Avon by the Connecticut or the Potomack? Whenever a nation wills it, prodigies are born." That is to say, prodigies literary and ineffable as well as purely material—prodigies aimed, in his own words, at "the olympick crown" as well as at mere railroads, ships, wheatfields, droves of hogs, factories and money. Nor were Channing and Knapp the first of the haruspices. Noah Webster, the lexicographer, who "taught millions to spell but not one to sin," had seen the early starlight of the same Golden Age so early as 1789, as the curious will find by examining his "Dissertations on the English Language," a work fallen long since into undeserved oblivion. Nor was Whitman, taking sober second thought exactly a century later, the last of them. Out of many brethren of our own day, extravagantly articulate in print and among the chautauquas, I choose one—not because his hope is of purest water, but precisely because, like Emerson, he dilutes it with various discreet whereases. He is Van Wyck Brooks, a young man far more intelligent, penetrating and hospitable to fact than any of the reigning professors—a critic who is sharply differentiated from them, indeed, by the simple circumstance that he has information and sense. Yet this extraordinary Mr. Brooks, in his "Letters and Leadership," published in 1918, rewrites "The American Scholar" in terms borrowed almost bodily from "Democratic Vistas"—that is to say, he prophesies with Emerson and exults with Whitman. First there is the Emersonian doctrine of the soaring individual made articulate by freedom and realizing "the responsibility that lies upon us, each in the measure of his own gift." And then there is Whitman's vision of a self-interpretative democracy, forced into high literary adventures by Joseph Conrad's "obscure inner necessity," and so achieving a "new synthesis adaptable to the unique conditions of our life." And finally there is the specific prediction, the grandiose, Adam Forepaugh mirage: "We shall become a luminous people, dwelling in the light and sharing our light. . . ."

As I say, the roll of such soothsayers might be almost endlessly lengthened. There is, in truth, scarcely a formal discourse upon the national letters (forgetting, perhaps, Barrett Wendell's sour threnody upon the New England *Aufklarung*) that is without some touch of this previsional exultation, this confident hymning of glories to come, this fine assurance that American literature, in some future always ready to dawn, will burst into so grand a flowering that history will cherish its loveliest blooms even above such salient American gifts to culture as the moving-picture, the phonograph, the New Thought and the bichloride tablet. If there was ever a dissenter from the national optimism, in this as in other departments, it was surely Edgar Allan Poe—without question the bravest and most original, if perhaps also the least orderly and judicious, of all the critics that we have produced. And yet even Poe, despite his general habit of disgust and dismay, caught a flash or two of that engaging picture —even Poe, for an instant, in 1846, thought that he saw the beginnings of a solid and autonomous native literature, its roots deep in the soil of the republic—as you will discover by turning to his forgotten essay on J. G. C. Brainard, a thrice-forgotten doggereleer of Jackson's time. Poe, of course, was too cautious to let his imagination proceed to details; one feels that a certain doubt, a saving peradventure or two, played about the unaccustomed vision as he beheld it. But, nevertheless, he unquestionably beheld it. . . .

★

Now for the answering fact. How has the issue replied to these visionaries? It has replied in a way that is manifestly to the discomfiture of Emerson as a prophet, to the dismay of Poe as a pessimist disarmed by transient optimism, and to the utter collapse of Whitman. We have, as everyone knows, produced no such "new and greater literatus order" as that announced by old Walt. We have given a gaping world no books that "radiate," and surely none intelligibly comparable to stars and constellations. We have achieved no prodigies of the first class, and very few of the second class, and not many of the third and fourth classes. Our literature, despite several false starts that promised much, is chiefly remarkable, now as always, for its respectable mediocrity. Its typical great man, in our own time, has been Howells, as its typical great man a generation ago was Lowell, and two generations ago, Irving. Viewed largely, its salient character appears as a sort of timorous flaccidity, an amiable hollowness. In bulk it grows more and more formidable, in ease and decorum it makes undoubted progress, and on the side of mere technic, of the bald capacity to write, it shows an ever-widening competence. But when one proceeds from such agencies and externals to the intrinsic substance, to the creative passion within, that substance quickly reveals itself as thin and watery, and that passion fades to something almost puerile. In all that mass of suave and often highly diverting writing there is no visible movement toward a distinguished and singular excellence, a signal national quality, a ripe and stimulating flavor, or, indeed, toward any other describable goal. What one sees is simply a general irresolution, a pervasive superficiality. There is no sober grappling with fundamentals, but only a shy sporting on the surface;

there is not even any serious approach, such as Whitman dreamed of, to the special experiences and emergencies of the American people. When one turns to any other national literature—to Russian literature, say, or French, or German or Scandinavian—one is conscious immediately of a definite attitude toward the primary mysteries of existence, the unsolved and ever-fascinating problems at the bottom of human life, and of a definite preoccupation with some of them, and a definite way of translating their challenge into drama. These attitudes and preoccupations raise a literature above mere poetizing and tale-telling; they give it dignity and importance; above all, they give it national character. But it is precisely here that the literature of America, and especially the later literature, is most colorless and inconsequential. As if paralyzed by the national fear of ideas, the democratic distrust of whatever strikes beneath the prevailing platitudes, it evades all resolute and honest dealing with what, after all, must be every healthy literature's elementary materials. One is conscious of no brave and noble earnestness in it, of no generalized passion for intellectual and spiritual adventure, of no organized determination to think things out. What is there is a highly self-conscious and insipid correctness, a bloodless respectability, a submergence of matter in manner—in brief, what is there is the feeble, uninspiring quality of German painting and English music.

It was so in the great days and it is so today. There has always been hope and there has always been failure. Even the most optimistic prophets of future glories have been united, at all times, in their discontent with the here and now. "The mind of this country," said Emerson, speaking of what was currently visible in 1837, "is taught to aim at low objects. . . . There is no work for any but the decorous and the complaisant. . . . Books are written . . . by men of talent . . . who start wrong, who set out from accepted dogmas, not from their own sight of principles." And then, turning to the way out: "The office of the scholar (*i.e.*, of Whitman's 'literatus') is to cheer, to raise and to guide men by showing them *facts amid appearances*." Whitman himself, a full generation later, found that office still unfilled. "Our fundamental want to-day in the United States," he said, "with closest, amplest reference to present conditions, and to the future, is of a class, and the clear idea of a class, of native authors, literatuses, far different, far higher in grade, than any yet known"—and so on, as I have already quoted him. And finally, to make an end of the prophets, there is Brooks, with nine-tenths of his book given over, not to his prophecy —it is crowded, indeed, into the last few pages—but to a somewhat heavy mourning over the actual scene before him. On the side of letters, the aesthetic side, the side of ideas, we present to the world at large, he says, "the spectacle of a vast, undifferentiated herd of good-humored animals"—Knights of Pythias, Presbyterians, standard model Ph.D's, readers of the *Saturday Evening Post,* admirers of Richard Harding Davis and O. Henry, devotees of Hamilton Wright Mabie's "white list" of books, members of the Y.M.C.A. or the Drama League, weepers at chautauquas, wearers of badges, 100 per cent. patriots, children of God. Poe I pass over; I shall turn to him again later on. Nor shall I repeat the parrotings of Emerson and Whitman in the jeremiads of their innumerable heirs and assigns. What they all establish is what is already obvious: that American thinking, when it concerns itself with beautiful letters as when it concerns itself with religious dogma or political theory, is extraordinarily timid and superficial— that it evades the genuinely serious problems of life and art as if they were stringently taboo—that the outward virtues it undoubtedly shows are always the virtues, not of profundity, not of courage, not of originality, but merely those of an emasculated and often very trashy dilettantism.

★

The current scene is surely depressing enough. What one observes is a literature in three layers, and each inordinately doughy and uninspiring—each almost without flavor or savor. It is hard to say, with much critical plausibility, which layer deserves to be called the upper, but for decorum's sake the choice may be fixed upon that which meets with the approval of the reigning Lessings. This is the layer of the novels of the late Howells, Judge Grant, Alice Brown and the rest of the dwindling survivors of New England *Kultur,* of the brittle, academic poetry of Woodberry and the elder Johnson, of the tea-party essays of Crothers, Miss Repplier and company, and of the solemn, highly judicial, coroner's inquest criticism of More, Brownell, Babbitt and their imitators. Here we have manner, undoubtedly. The thing is correctly done; it is never crude or gross; there is in it a faint perfume of college-town society. But when this highly refined and attenuated manner is allowed for what remains is next to nothing. One never remembers a character in the novels of these aloof and de-Americanized Americans; one never encounters an idea in their essays; one never carries away a line out of their poetry. It is literature as an academic exercise for talented grammarians, almost as a genteel recreation for ladies and gentlemen of fashion—the exact equivalent, in the field of letters, of eighteenth-century painting and German *Augenmusik.*

What ails it, intrinsically, is a dearth of intellectual audacity and of aesthetic passion. Running through it, and characterizing the work of almost every man and woman producing it, there is an unescapable suggestion of the old Puritan suspicion of the fine arts as such—of the doctrine that they offer fit asylum for good citizens only when some ulterior and superior purpose is carried into them. This purpose, naturally enough, most commonly shows a moral tinge. The aim of poetry, it appears, is to fill the mind with lofty thoughts—not to give it joy, but to give it a grand and somewhat gaudy sense of virtue. The essay is a weapon against the degenerate tendencies of the age. The novel, properly conceived, is a means of uplifting the spirit; its aim is to inspire, not merely to satisfy the low curiosity of man in man. The Puritan, of course, is not entirely devoid of aesthetic feeling. He has a taste for good form; he responds to style; he is even capable of something approaching a purely aesthetic emotion. But he fears this aesthetic emotion as an insinuating distraction from his chief business in life: the sober consideration of the all-important problem of conduct. Art is a temptation, a seduction, a Lorelei, and the Good Man may safely have traffic with it only when it is broken to moral uses—in other words, when its innocence is pumped out of it, and it is purged of gusto. It is precisely this gusto that one misses in all the work of the New England school, and in all the work of the formal schools that derive from it. One observes in such a fellow as Dr. Henry Van Dyke an excellent specimen of the whole clan. He is, in his way, a genuine artist. He has a hand for pretty verses. He wields a facile rhetoric. He shows, in indiscreet moments, a touch of imagination. But all the while he remains a sound Presbyterian, with one eye on the devil. He is a Presbyterian first and an artist second, which is just as comfortable as trying to be a Presbyterian first and a chorus girl second. To such a man it must inevitably appear that a Molière, a Wagner, a Goethe or a Shakespeare was more than a little bawdy.

The criticism that supports this decaying caste of literary Brahmins is grounded almost entirely upon ethical criteria. You will spend a long while going through the works of such typical professors as More, Phelps, Boynton, Burton, Perry, Brownell and Babbitt before ever you encounter a purely aesthetic judgment upon an aesthetic question. It is almost as if a man estimating daffodils should do it in terms of artichokes.

Phelps' whole body of "we church-goers" criticism—
the most catholic and tolerant, it may be said in passing, that the faculty can show—consists chiefly of a
plea for correctness, and particularly for moral correctness; he never gets very far from "the axiom of the
moral law." Brownell argues eloquently for standards
that would bind an imaginative author as tightly as
a Sunday-school superintendent is bound by the Ten
Commandments and the Mann Act. Sherman tries to
save Shakespeare for the right-thinking by proving
that he was an Iowa Methodist—a member of his local
Chamber of Commerce, a contemner of Reds, an advocate of democracy and the League of Nations, a patriotic dollar-a-year-man during the Armada scare. Elmer
More devotes himself, year in and year out, to denouncing the Romantic movement, *i.e.*, the effort to
emancipate the artist from formulae and categories,
and so make him free to dance with arms and legs.
And Babbitt, to make an end, gives over his days and
his nights to deploring Rousseau's anarchistic abroga-
tion of "the veto power" over the imagination, leading
to such "wrongness" in both art and life that it threatens "to wreck civilization." In brief, the alarms of
schoolmasters. Not many of them deal specifically with
the literature that is in being. It is too near to be quite
nice. To More or Babbitt only death can atone for the
primary offense of the artist. But what they preach
nevertheless has its echoes contemporaneously, and
those echoes, in the main, are woefully falsetto. I often
wonder what sort of picture of These States is conjured
up by foreigners who read, say, Crothers, Van Dyke,
Babbitt, the later Winston Churchill, and the old maids
of the Freudian suppression school. How can such a
foreigner, moving in those damp, asthmatic mists,
imagine such phenomena as Roosevelt, Billy Sunday,
Bryan, the Becker case, the I.W.W., Newport, Palm
Beach, the University of Chicago, Chicago itself—the
whole, gross, glittering, excessively dynamic, infinitely

grotesque, incredibly stupendous drama of American life?

As I have said, it is not often that the *ordentlichen Professoren* deign to notice contemporary writers, even of their own austere kidney. In all the Shelburne Essays there is none on Howells, or on Churchill, or on Mrs. Wharton; More seems to think of American literature as expiring with Longfellow and Donald G. Mitchell. He has himself hinted that in the department of criticism of criticism there enters into the matter something beyond mere aloof ignorance. "I soon learned (as editor of the pre-Bolshevik *Nation*)," he says, "that it was virtually impossible to get fair consideration for a book written by a scholar not connected with a university from a reviewer so connected." This class-consciousness, however, should not apply to artists, who are admittedly inferior to professors, and it surely does not show itself in such men as Phelps and Spingarn, who seem to be very eager to prove that they are not professorial. Yet Phelps, in the course of a long work on the novel, pointedly omits all mention of such men as Dreiser, and Spingarn, as the aforesaid Brooks has said, "appears to be less inclined even than the critics with whom he is theoretically at war to play an active, public part in the secular conflict of darkness and light." When one comes to the *Privat-Dozenten* there is less remoteness, but what takes the place of it is almost as saddening. To Sherman and Percy Boynton the one aim of criticism seems to be the enforcement of correctness—in Emerson's phrase, the upholding of "some great decorum, some fetish of a government, some ephemeral trade, or war, or man"—*e.g.*, Puritanism, democracy, monogamy, the League of Nations, the Wilsonian piffle. Even among the critics who escape the worst of this schoolmastering frenzy there is some touch of the heavy "culture" of the provincial schoolma'm. For example, consider Clayton Hamilton, M.A., vice-president of the National Institute of Arts and Letters. Here are the tests he proposes for dramatic critics, *i.e.*, for gentlemen chiefly employed in reviewing such characteristic American compositions as the Ziegfeld Follies, "Up in Mabel's Room," "Ben-Hur" and "The Witching Hour":

1. Have you ever stood bareheaded in the nave of Amiens?
2. Have you ever climbed to the Acropolis by moonlight?
3. Have you ever walked with whispers into the hushed presence of the Frari Madonna of Bellini?

What could more brilliantly evoke an image of the eternal Miss Birch, blue veil flying and Baedeker in hand, plodding along faithfully through the interminable corridors and catacombs of the Louvre, the while bands are playing across the river, and young bucks in three-gallon hats are sparking the gals, and the Jews and harlots uphold the traditions of French *hig leef* at Longchamps, and American deacons are frisked and debauched up on martyrs' hill? The banality of it is really too exquisite to be borne; the lack of humor is almost that of a Fifth Avenue divine. One seldom finds in the pronunciamentoes of these dogged professors, indeed, any trace of either Attic or Gallic salt. When they essay to be jocose, the result is usually simply an elephantine whimsicality, by the chautauqua out of the *Atlantic Monthly*. Their satire is mere ill-nature. One finds it difficult to believe that they have ever read Lewes, or Hazlitt, or, above all, Saintsbury. I often wonder, in fact, how Saintsbury would fare, an unknown man, at the hands of, say, Brownell or More. What of his iconoclastic gayety, his boyish weakness for tweaking noses and pulling whiskers, his obscene delight in slang? . . .

★

So far, the disease. As to the cause, I have delivered a few hints. I now describe it particularly. It is, in brief, a defect in the general culture of the country—one reflected, not only in the national literature, but also in the national political theory, the national attitude toward religion and morals, the national habit in all departments of thinking. It is the lack of a civilized aristocracy, secure in its position, animated by an intelligent curiosity, skeptical of all facile generalizations, superior to the sentimentality of the mob, and delighting in the battle of ideas for its own sake.

The word I use, despite the qualifying adjective, has got itself meanings, of course, that I by no means intend to convey. Any mention of an aristocracy, to a public fed upon democratic fustian, is bound to bring up images of stockbrokers' wives lolling obscenely in opera boxes, or of haughty Englishmen slaughtering whole generations of grouse in an inordinate and incomprehensible manner, or of Junkers with tight waists elbowing American schoolmarms off the sidewalks of German beer towns, or of perfumed Italians coming over to work their abominable magic upon the daughters of breakfast-food and bathtub kings. Part of this misconception, I suppose, has its roots in the gaudy imbecilities of the yellow press, but there is also a part that belongs to the general American tradition, along with the oppression of minorities and the belief in political panaceas. Its depth and extent are constantly revealed by the naïve assumption that the so-called fashionable folk of the large cities—chiefly wealthy industrials in the interior-decorator and country-club stage of culture—constitute an aristocracy, and by the scarcely less remarkable assumption that the peerage of England is identical with the gentry—that is, that such men as Lord Northcliffe, Lord Iveagh and even Lord Reading are English gentlemen, and of the ancient line of the Percys.

Here, as always, the worshiper is the father of the gods, and no less when they are evil than when they are benign. The inferior man must find himself superiors, that he may marvel at his political equality with them, and in the absence of recognizable superiors *de facto* he creates superiors *de jure*. The sublime principle of one man, one vote must be translated into terms of dollars, diamonds, fashionable intelligence; the equality of all men before the law must have clear and dramatic proofs. Sometimes, perhaps, the thing goes further and is more subtle. The inferior man needs an aristocracy to demonstrate not only his mere equality, but also his actual superiority. The society columns in the newspapers may have some such origin: they may visualize once more the accomplished journalist's understanding of the mob mind that he plays upon so skillfully, as upon some immense and cacophonous organ, always going *fortissimo*. What the inferior man and his wife see in the sinister revels of those amazing first families, I suspect, is often a massive witness to their own higher rectitude—to their relative innocence of cigarette-smoking, poodle-coddling, child-farming and the more abstruse branches of adultery—in brief, to their firmer grasp upon the immutable axioms of Christian virtue, the one sound boast of the nether nine-tenths of humanity in every land under the cross.

But this bugaboo aristocracy, as I hint, is actually bogus, and the evidence of its bogusness lies in the fact that it is insecure. One gets into it only onerously, but out of it very easily. Entrance is effected by dint of a long and bitter struggle, and the chief incidents of that struggle are almost intolerable humiliations. The aspirant must school and steel himself to sniffs and sneers; he must see the door slammed upon him a hundred times before ever it is thrown open to him. To get in at all he must show a talent for abasement—and abasement makes him timorous. Worse, that timorousness is not cured when he succeeds at last. On the contrary, it is made even more tremulous, for what he faces within the gates is a scheme of things made up almost wholly of harsh and often unintelligible taboos, and the penalty for violating even the least of them is swift and disastrous. He must exhibit exactly the right social habits, appetites and prejudices, public and private. He must harbor exactly the right political enthusiasms and indignations. He must have a hearty taste for exactly the right sports. His attitude toward the fine arts must be properly tolerant and yet not a shade too eager. He must read and like exactly the right books, pamphlets and public journals. He must put up at the right hotels when he travels. His wife must patronize the right milliners. He himself must stick to the right haberdashery. He must live in the right neighborhood. He must even embrace the right doctrines of religion. It would ruin him, for all opera box and society column purposes, to set up a plea for justice to the Bolsheviki, or even for ordinary decency. It would ruin him equally to wear celluloid collars, or to move to Union Hill, N.J., or to serve ham and cabbage at his table. And it would ruin him, too, to drink coffee from his saucer, or to marry a chambermaid with a gold tooth, or to join the Seventh Day Adventists. Within the boundaries of his curious order he is worse fettered than a monk in a cell. Its obscure conception of propriety, its nebulous notion that this or that is honorable, hampers him in every direction, and very narrowly. What he resigns when he enters, even when he makes his first deprecating knock at the door, is every right to attack the ideas that happen to prevail within. Such as they are, he must accept them without question. And as they shift and change in response to great instinctive movements (or perhaps, now and then, to the punished but not to be forgotten revolts of extraordinary rebels) he must shift and change with them, silently and quickly. To hang back, to challenge and dispute, to preach reforms and revolutions—these are crimes against the brummagem Holy Ghost of the order.

Obviously, that order cannot constitute a genuine

aristocracy, in any rational sense. A genuine aristocracy is grounded upon very much different principles. Its first and most salient character is its interior security, and the chief visible evidence of that security is the freedom that goes with it—not only freedom in act, the divine right of the aristocrat to do what he jolly well pleases, so long as he does not violate the primary guarantees and obligations of his class, but also and more importantly freedom in thought, the liberty to try and err, the right to be his own man. It is the instinct of a true aristocracy, not to punish eccentricity by expulsion, but to throw a mantle of protection about it—to safeguard it from the suspicions and resentments of the lower orders. Those lower orders are inert, timid, inhospitable to ideas, hostile to changes, faithful to a few maudlin superstitions. All progress goes on on the higher levels. It is there that salient personalities, made secure by artificial immunities, may oscillate most widely from the normal track. It is within that entrenched fold, out of reach of the immemorial certainties of the mob, that extraordinary men of the lower orders may find their city of refuge, and breathe a clear air. This, indeed, is at once the hall-mark and the justification of an aristocracy—that it is beyond responsibility to the general masses of men, and hence superior to both their degraded longings and their no less degraded aversions. It is nothing if it is not autonomous, curious, venturesome, courageous, and everything if it is. It is the custodian of the qualities that make for change and experiment; it is the class that organizes danger to the service of the race; it pays for its high prerogatives by standing in the forefront of the fray.

No such aristocracy, it must be plain, is now on view in the United States. The makings of one were visible in the Virginia of the later eighteenth century, but with Jefferson and Washington the promise died. In New England, it seems to me, there was never any aristocracy, either in being or in nascency: there was only a theocracy that degenerated very quickly into a plutocracy on the one hand and a caste of sterile *Gelehrten* on the other—the passion for God splitting into a lust for dollars and a weakness for mere words. Despite the common notion to the contrary—a notion generated by confusing literacy with intelligence —New England has never shown the slightest sign of a genuine enthusiasm for ideas. It began its history as a slaughter-house of ideas, and it is to-day not easily distinguishable from a cold-storage plant. Its celebrated adventures in mysticism, once apparently so bold and significant, are now seen to have been little more than an elaborate hocus-pocus—respectable Unitarians shocking the peasantry and scaring the horned cattle in the fields by masquerading in the robes of Rosicrucians. The ideas that it embraced in those austere and far-off days were stale, and when it had finished with them they were dead: to-day one hears of Jakob Bohme almost as rarely as one hears of Allen G. Thurman. So in politics. Its glory is Abolition—an English invention, long under the interdict of the native plutocracy. Since the Civil War its six states have produced fewer political ideas, as political ideas run in the Republic, than any average county in Kansas or Nebraska. Appomattox seemed to be a victory for New England idealism. It was actually a victory for the New England plutocracy, and that plutocracy has dominated thought above the Housatonic ever since. The sect of professional idealists has so far dwindled that it has ceased to be of any importance, even as an opposition. When the plutocracy is challenged now, it is challenged by the proletariat.

Well, what is on view in New England is on view in all other parts of the nation, sometimes with ameliorations, but usually with the colors merely exaggerated. What one beholds, sweeping the eye over the land, is a culture that, like the national literature, is in three layers—the plutocracy on top, a vast mass of undifferentiated human blanks at the bottom, and a forlorn *intelligentsia* gasping out a precarious life between. I need not set out at any length, I hope, the intellectual deficiencies of the plutocracy—its utter failure to show anything even remotely resembling the makings of an aristocracy. It is badly educated, it is stupid, it is full of low-caste superstitions and indignations, it is without decent traditions or informing vision; above all, it is extraordinarily lacking in the most elemental independence and courage. Out of this class comes the grotesque fashionable society of our big towns, already described. Imagine a horde of peasants incredibly enriched and with almost infinite power thrust into their hands, and you will have a fair picture of its habitual state of mind. It shows all the stigmata of inferiority—moral certainty, cruelty, suspicion of ideas, fear. Never did it function more revealingly than in the late *pogrom* against the so-called Reds, *i.e.*, against humorless idealists who, like Andrew Jackson, took the platitudes of democracy quite seriously. The machinery brought to bear upon these feeble and scattered fanatics would have almost sufficed to repel an invasion by the united powers of Europe. They were hunted out of their sweat-shops and coffee-houses as if they were so many Carranzas or Ludendorffs, dragged to jail to the tooting of horns, arraigned before quaking judges on unintelligible charges, condemned to deportation without the slightest chance to defend themselves, torn from their dependent families, herded into prison-ships, and then finally dumped in a snow waste, to be rescued and fed by the Bolsheviki. And what was the theory at the bottom of all these astounding proceedings? So far as it can be reduced to comprehensible terms it was much less a theory than a fear—a shivering, idiotic, discreditable fear of a mere banshee—an overpowering, paralyzing dread that some extra-eloquent Red, permitted to emit his balderdash unwhipped, might eventually convert a couple of courageous men, and that the courageous men, filled with indignation against the plutocracy, might take to the highroad, burn down a nail-factory or two, and slit the throat of some virtuous profiteer. In order to lay this fear, in order to ease the jangled nerves of the American successors to the Hapsburgs and Hohenzollerns, all the constitutional guarantees of the citizen were suspended, the statute-books were burdened with laws that surpass anything heard of in the Austria of Maria Theresa, the country was handed over to a frenzied mob of detectives, informers and *agents provocateurs*—and the Reds departed laughing loudly, and were hailed by the Bolsheviki as innocents escaped from an asylum for the criminally insane.

Obviously, it is out of reason to look for any hospitality to ideas in a class so extravagantly fearful of even the most palpably absurd of them. Its philosophy is firmly grounded upon the thesis that the existing order must stand forever free from attack, and not only from attack, but also from mere academic criticism, and its ethics are as firmly grounded upon the thesis that every attempt at any such criticism is a proof of moral turpitude. Within its own ranks, protected by what may be regarded as the privilege of the order, there is nothing to take the place of this criticism. A few feeble platitudes by Andrew Carnegie and a book of moderate merit by John D. Rockefeller's press-agent constitute almost the whole of the interior literature of ideas. In other countries the plutocracy has often produced men of reflective and analytical habit, eager to rationalize its instincts and to bring it into some sort of relationship to the main streams of human thought. The case of David Ricardo at once comes to mind. There have been many others: John Bright, Richard Cobden, George Grote, and, in our own time, Walther von Rathenau. But in the United States no such phenomenon has been visible. There was a day, not long ago, when certain young men of wealth gave signs of an unaccustomed interest in ideas on the political side, but the most they managed to achieve was a banal sort of Socialism, and even this was abandoned in sudden terror when the war came, and Socialism fell under suspicion of being genuinely international—in brief, of being honest under the skin. Nor has the plutocracy of the country ever fostered an inquiring spirit among its intellectual valets and footmen, which is to say, among the gentlemen who compose headlines and leading articles for its newspapers. What chiefly distinguishes the daily press of the United States from the press of all other countries pretending to culture is not its lack of truthfulness or even its lack of dignity and honor, for these deficiencies are common to the newspapers everywhere, but its incurable fear of ideas, its constant effort to evade the discussion of fundamentals by translating all issues into a few elemental fears, its incessant reduction of all reflection to mere emotion. It is, in the true sense, never well-informed. It is seldom intelligent, save in the arts of the mob-master. It is never courageously honest. Held harshly to a rigid correctness of opinion by the plutocracy that controls it with less and less attempt at disguise, and menaced on all sides by censorships that it dare not flout, it sinks rapidly into formalism and feebleness. Its yellow section is perhaps its most respectable section for there the only vestige of the old free journalist survives. In the more conservative papers one finds only a timid and petulant animosity to all questioning of the existing order, however urbane and sincere—a pervasive and ill-concealed dread that the mob now heated up against the orthodox hobgoblins may suddenly begin to unearth hobgoblins of its own, and so run amok. For it is upon the emotions of the mob, of course, that the whole comedy is played. Theoretically the mob is the repository of all political wisdom and virtue; actually it is the ultimate source of all political power. Even the plutocracy cannot make war upon it openly, or forget the least of its weaknesses.

The business of keeping it in order must be done discreetly, warily, with delicate technique. In the main that business consists of keeping alive its deep-seated fears—of strange faces, of unfamiliar ideas, of unhackneyed gestures, of untested liberties and responsibilities. The one permanent emotion of the inferior man, as of all the simpler mammals, is fear—fear of the unknown, the complex, the inexplicable. What he wants beyond everything else is safety. His instincts incline him toward a society so organized that it will protect him at all hazards, and not only against perils to his hide but also against assaults upon his mind—against the need to grapple with unaccustomed problems, to weigh ideas, to think things out for himself, to scrutinize the platitudes upon which his everyday thinking is based. Content under kaiserism so long as it functions efficiently, he turns, when kaiserism falls, to some other and perhaps worse form of paternalism, bringing to its benign tyranny only the docile tribute of his pathetic allegiance. In America it is the newspaper that is his boss. From it he gets support for his elemental illusions. In it he sees a visible embodiment of his own wisdom and consequence. Out of it he draws fuel for his simple moral passion, his congenital suspicion of heresy, his dread of the unknown. And behind the newspaper stands the plutocracy, ignorant, unimaginative and timorous.

Thus at the top and at the bottom. Obviously, there is no aristocracy here. One finds only one of the necessary elements, and that only in the plutocracy, to wit, a truculent egoism. But where is intelligence? Where are ease and surety of manner? Where are enterprise and curiosity? Where, above all, is courage, and in particular, moral courage—the capacity for independent thinking, for difficult problems, for what Nietzsche called the joys of the labyrinth? As well look for these things in a society of half-wits. Democracy, obliterating the old aristocracy, has left only a vacuum in its place; in a century and a half it has failed either to lift up the mob to intellectual autonomy and dignity or to purge the plutocracy of its inherent stupidity and swinishness. It is precisely here, the first and favorite scene of the Great Experiment, that the culture of the individual has been reduced to the most rigid and absurd regimentation. It is precisely here, of all civilized countries, that eccentricity in demeanor and opinion has come to bear the heaviest penalties. The whole drift of our law is toward the absolute prohibition of all ideas that diverge in the slightest from the accepted platitudes, and behind that drift of law there is a far more potent force of growing custom, and under that custom there is a national philosophy which erects conformity into the noblest of virtues and the free functioning of personality into a capital crime against society.

STAR-SPANGLED MEN

FROM the *New Republic,* September 1920. This piece belongs to my private archeology. It is dated beyond repair, but I print it because it is full of my view of the issues and leaders of World War I. In World War II I took a similar line, but by that time I had ceased to write on public matters and so not much indication of it got on paper. In World War I, as I indicate, there were no gauds for civilians, but that lack was remedied in a wholesale manner in World War II.)

I open the memoirs of General Grant, Volume II, at the place where he is describing the surrender of General Lee, and find the following:

I was without a sword, as I usually was when on horseback on the field, and wore a soldier's blouse for a coat, with the shoulder straps of my rank to indicate to the army who I was.

Anno 1865. I look out of my window and observe an officer of the United States Army passing down the street. Anno 1922. Like General Grant, he is without a sword. Like General Grant, he wears a sort of soldier's blouse for a coat. Like General Grant, he employs shoulder straps to indicate to the Army who he is. But there is something more. On the left breast of this officer, apparently a major, there blazes so brilliant a mass of color that, as the sun strikes it and the flash bangs my eyes, I wink, catch my breath and sneeze. There are two long strips, each starting at the sternum and disappearing into the shadows of the axilla—every hue in the rainbow, the spectroscope, the kaleidoscope—imperial purples, *sforzando* reds, wild Irish greens, romantic blues, loud yellows and oranges, rich maroons, sentimental pinks, all the half-tones from ultra-violet to infrared, all the vibrations from the impalpable to the unendurable. A gallant *Soldat* indeed! How he would shame a circus ticket-wagon if he wore all the medals and badges, the stars and crosses, the pendants and lavallières, that go with those ribbons! . . . I glance at his sleeves. A simple golden stripe on the one—six months beyond the raging main. None on the other— the Kaiser's cannon missed him.

Just what all these ribbons signify I am sure I don't know; probably they belong to campaign medals and tell the tale of butcheries in foreign and domestic parts—mountains of dead Filipinos, Mexicans, Haitians, Dominicans, West Virginia miners, perhaps even Prussians. But in addition to campaign medals and the Distinguished Service Medal there are now certainly enough foreign orders in the United States to give a distinct brilliance to the national scene, viewed, say, from Mars. The Frederician tradition, borrowed by the ragged Continentals and embodied in Article I, Section 9, of the Constitution, lasted until 1918, and then suddenly blew up; to mention it today is a sort of indecorum, and tomorrow, no doubt, will be a species

of treason. Down with Frederick; up with John Philip
Sousa! Imagine what Sir John Pershing would look
like at a state banquet of his favorite American order,
the Benevolent and Protective one of Elks, in all the
Byzantine splendor of his casket of ribbons, badges,
stars, garters, sunbursts and cockades—the lordly Bath
of the grateful motherland, with its somewhat disconcerting "Ich dien"; the gorgeous tricolor baldrics,
sashes and festoons of the Légion d'Honneur; the
grand cross of SS. Maurizio e Lazzaro of Italy; the
Danilo of Montenegro, with its cabalistic monogram of
Danilo I and its sinister hieroglyphics; the breastplate
of the Paulownia of Japan, with its rising sun of thirty-
two white rays, its blood-red heart, its background of
green leaves and its white ribbon edged with red; the
mystical St. Saviour of Greece, with its Greek motto
and its brilliantly enameled figure of Christ; above all,
the Croix de Guerre of Czecho-Slovakia, a new one
and hence not listed in the books, but surely no shrinking violet.

Alas, Pershing was on the wrong side—that is, for
one with a fancy for gauds of that sort. The most
blinding of all known orders is the Medijie of Turkey,
which not only entitles the holder to four wives, but
also requires him to wear a red fez and a frozen star
covering his whole façade. I was offered this order by
Turkish spies during the war, and it wobbled me a
good deal. The Alexander of Bulgaria is almost as seductive. The badge consists of an eight-pointed white
cross, with crossed swords between the arms and a red
Bulgarian lion over the swords. The motto is "Za
Chrabrost!" Then there are the Prussian orders—the
Red and Black Eagles, the Pour le Mérite, the Prussian
Crown, the Hohenzollern and the rest. And the Golden
Fleece of Austria—the noblest of them all. Think of
the Golden Fleece on a man born in Linn County, Missouri. . . . I begin to doubt that the General would
have got it, even supposing him to have taken the other

side. The Japs, I note, gave him only the grand cordon of the Paulownia, and the Belgians and Montenegrins were similarly cautious. There are higher classes. The highest of the Paulownia is only for princes, which is to say, only for non-Missourians.

Pershing is the champion, with General March a bad second. March is a K.C.M.G., and entitled to wear a large cross of white enamel bearing a lithograph of the Archangel Michael and the motto, "Auspicium Melioris Aevi," but he is not a K.C.B.[1] Admirals Benson and Sims are also grand crosses of Michael and George, and like most other respectable Americans, members of the Legion of Honor, but they seem to have been forgotten by the Greeks and Montenegrins.[2] British-born and extremely Anglomaniacal Sims[3] refused the Distinguished Service Medal of his adopted country, but is careful to mention in "Who's Who in America" that his grand cross of Michael and George was conferred upon him, not by some servile gold-stick, but by "King George of England";[4] Benson omits mention of His Majesty, as do Pershing and March. It would be hard to think of any other American officers, real or bogus, who would refuse the D.S.M., or, failing it, the grand decoration of chivalry of the Independent Order of Odd Fellows. I once saw the latter hung, with ceremonies of the utmost

[1] March went to the Philippines as commander of the forgotten Astor Battery and saw long and hard service here. He was a commander of the artillery in the A.E.F. and later its chief of staff. He retired from the Army in 1921. He had many decorations besides the grand cross of the order of St. Michael and St. George, including the grand cordon of the Chia Ho of China and that of Polonia Restituta.

[2] Benson was chief of naval operations in World War I. He had the order of the Rising Sun of Japan, the order of St. Gregory the Great, conferred by the Pope, and a gold medal struck in his honor by New Mexico. He died in 1932.

[3] Sims was born in Canada. He was commander of the naval forces in European waters throughout World War I. He had Japanese, Belgian and Italian orders, and was a LL.D. of Yale, Harvard, Tufts, Pennsylvania, Columbia, Williams, Juniata, Stevens, McGill, Queen's, California, Union, Wesleyan, and Cambridge (England). He died in 1936.

[4] From 1922 onward he struck this out.

magnificence, upon a bald-headed tinner who had served the fraternity long and faithfully; as he marched down the hall toward the throne of the Supreme Exalted Pishposh a score of scared little girls, the issue of other tinners, strewed his pathway with roses, and around the stem of each rose was a piece of glittering tinfoil. The band meanwhile played "The Rosary," and, at the conclusion of the spectacle, as fried oysters were served, "Wien Bleibt Wien."

It was, I suspect, by way of the Odd Fellows and other such gaudy heirs to the Deutsche Ritter and the Rosicrucians that the lust to gleam and jingle got into the arteries of the American people. For years the austere tradition of Washington's day served to keep the military bosom bare of spangles, but all the while a weakness for them was growing in the civil population. Rank by rank, they became Knights of Pythias, Odd Fellows, Red Men, Nobles of the Mystic Shrine, Knights Templar, Patriarchs Militant, Elks, Moose, Woodmen of the World, Foresters, Hoo-Hoos, Ku Kluxers—and in every new order there were thirty-two degrees, and for every degree there was a badge, and for every badge there was a yard of ribbon. The Nobles of the Mystic Shrine, chiefly paunchy wholesalers of the Rotary Club species, are not content with swords, baldrics, stars, garters, jewels; they also wear red fezzes. The Elks run to rubies. The Red Men array themselves like Sitting Bull. The patriotic ice-wagon drivers and Methodist deacons of the Ku Klux Klan carry crosses set with incandescent lights. An American who is forced by his profession to belong to many such orders —say a life insurance solicitor, an undertaker or a dealer in oil stock—accumulates a trunk full of decorations, many of them weighing a pound. There is a mortician in Hagerstown, Md., who has been initiated eighteen times. When he robes himself to plant a fellow joiner he weighs three hundred pounds and sparkles and flashes like the mouth of Hell itself. He is entitled to bear seven swords, all jeweled, and to hang his watch chain with the golden busts of nine wild animals, all with precious stones for eyes. Put beside this lowly washer of the dead, Pershing newly polished would seem almost like a Trappist.

But even so the civil arm is robbed of its just dues in the department of gauds and radioactivity, no doubt by the direct operation of military vanity and jealousy. Despite a million proofs (and perhaps a billion eloquent arguments) to the contrary, it is still the theory at the official ribbon counter that the only man who serves in a war is the man who serves in uniform. This is soft for the Bevo officer,[5] who at least has his service stripes and the spurs that gnawed into his desk, but it is hard upon his brother Elmer, the dollar-a-year man, who worked twenty hours a day for fourteen months buying soap-powder, canned asparagus and raincoats for the army of God. Elmer not only labored with inconceivable diligence; he also faced hazards of no mean order, for on the one hand was his natural prejudice in favor of a very liberal rewarding of commercial enterprise, and on the other hand were his patriotism and his fear of Atlanta Penitentiary. I daresay that many and many a time, after working his twenty hours, he found it difficult to sleep the remaining four hours. I know, in fact, survivors of that obscure service who are far worse wrecks today than Pershing is. Their reward is —what? Winks, sniffs, innuendoes. If they would indulge themselves in the now almost univesal American yearning to go adorned, they must join the Knights of Pythias. Even the American Legion fails them, for though it certainly does not bar non-combatants, it insists that they shall have done their non-combating in uniform.

What I propose is a variety of the Distinguished

---

[5] A Bevo officer was one who fought the wicked Hun from a desk in Washington. The name derived from that of a near-beer of the time.

Service Medal for civilians—perhaps, better still, a distinct order for civilians, closed to the military and with badges of different colors and areas, to mark off varying services to democracy. Let it run, like the Japanese Paulownia, from high to low—the lowest class for the patriot who sacrificed only time, money and a few nights' sleep; the highest for the great martyr who hung his country's altar with his dignity, his decency and his sacred honor. For Elmer and his nervous insomnia, a simple rosette, with an iron badge bearing the national motto, "Safety First"; for the university president who prohibited the teaching of the enemy language in his learned grove, heaved the works of Goethe out of the university library, cashiered every professor unwilling to support Woodrow for the first vacancy in the Trinity, took to the stump for the National Security League,[6] and made two hundred speeches in moving picture theaters—for this giant of loyal endeavor let no 100 per cent. American speak of anything less than the grand cross of the order, with a gold badge in stained glass, a baldric of the national colors, a violet plug hat with a sunburst on the side, the privilege of the floor of Congress, and a pension of $10,000 a year. After all, the cost would not be excessive; there are not many of them. Such prodigies of patriotism are possible only to rare and gifted men. For the grand cordons of the order, *e.g.*, college professors who spied upon and reported the seditions of their associates, state presidents of the American Protective League,[7] alien property custodians, judges whose sen-

[6] A band of patriots which made a deafening uproar in the 1914–1918 era. Its fronts were Elihu Root and Alton B. Parker.

[7] An organization of amateur detectives working under the ægis of the Department of Justice. In 1917 its operatives reported that I was an intimate associate and agent of "the German monster, Nietzsky," and I was solemnly investigated. But I was a cunning fellow in those days and full of a malicious humor, so I not only managed to throw off the charge but even to write the report upon myself. I need not say that it gave me a clean bill of health—and I still have a carbon to prove it. As a general rule the American Protective League confined itself to easier victims. Its specialty was harassing German waiters.

tences of conscientious objectors mounted to more than 50,000 years, members of George Creel's herd of 2,000 American historians, the authors of the Sisson documents,[8] etc.—pensions of $10 a day would be enough, with silver badges and no plug hats. For the lower ranks, bronze badges and the legal right to the title of "The Hon.," already every true American's by courtesy.

Not, of course, that I am insensitive to the services of the gentlemen of those lower ranks, but in such matters one must go by rarity rather than by intrinsic value. If the grand cordon or even the nickel-plated eagle of the third class were given to every patriot who bored a hole through the floor of his flat to get evidence against his neighbors, the Krausmeyers, and to everyone who visited the Hofbräuhaus nightly, denounced the Kaiser in searing terms, and demanded assent from Emil and Otto, the waiters, and to everyone who notified the catchpolls of the Department of Justice when the wireless plant was open in the garret of the Arion Liedertafel, and to all who took a brave and forward part in slacker raids, and to all who lent their stenographers funds at 6 per cent. to buy Liberty bonds at 4¼ per cent., and to all who sold out at 99 and then bought in again at 83.56, and to all who served as jurors or perjurers in cases against members and ex-members of the I.W.W., and to the German-American members of the League for German Democracy, and to all the Irish who snitched upon the Irish—if decorations were thrown about with any such lavishness, then there would be no nickel left for our bathrooms. On the civilian side as on the military side the great re-

[8] Creel served as chairman of what was called the Committee on Public Information from 1917 to 1919. Its chief business was to propagate the official doctrine as to the causes and issues of the war. To that end Creel recruited his horde of college historians and they solemnly certified to the truth of everything that emanated from Washington and London. The Sisson documents were supposed to show a sinister conspiracy of the Russian Communists, but what the specifications were I forget. Creel's committee was also in charge of newspaper censorship during the war.

wards of war go, not to mere dogged industry and fidelity, but to originality—to the unprecedented, the arresting, the bizarre. The New York *Tribune* liar who invented the story about the German plant for converting the corpses of the slain into soap did more for democracy and the Wilsonian idealism, and hence deserves a more brilliant recognition, than a thousand uninspired hawkers of atrocity stories supplied by Viscount Bryce and his associates. For that great servant of righteousness the grand cordon, with two silver badges and the chair of history at Columbia, would be scarcely enough; for the ordinary hawkers any precious metal would be too much.

Whether or not the Y.M.C.A. has decorated its chocolate peddlers and soul-snatchers I do not know; since the chief Y.M.C.A. lamasery in my town of Baltimore became the scene of a homosexual scandal I have ceased to frequent evangelical society. If not, then there should be some governmental recognition of these highly characteristic heroes of the war for democracy. The veterans of the line, true enough, dislike them excessively, and have a habit of denouncing them obscenely when the corn-juice flows. They charged too much for cigarettes; they tried to discourage the amiability of the ladies of France; they had a habit of being absent when the shells burst in air. Well, some say this and some say that. A few, at least, of the pale and oleaginous brethren must have gone into the Master's work because they thirsted to save souls, and not simply because they desired to escape the trenches. And a few, I am told, were anything but unpleasantly righteous, as a round of Wassermanns would show. If, as may be plausibly argued, these Soldiers of the Double Cross deserve to live at all, then they surely deserve to be hung with white enameled stars of the third class, with gilt dollar marks superimposed. Motto: "Glory, glory, hallelujah!"

But what of the vaudeville actors, the cheer leaders, the doughnut fryers, the camp librarians, the press agents? I am not forgetting them. Let them be distributed among all the classes from the seventh to the eighth, according to their sufferings for the holy cause. And the agitators against Beethoven, Bach, Brahms, Wagner, Richard Strauss, all the rest of the cacophonous Huns? And the specialists in the crimes of the German professors? And the collectors for the Belgians, with their generous renunciation of all commissions above 80 per cent. And the pathologists who denounced Johannes Müller as a fraud, Karl Ludwig as an imbecile, and Paul Ehrlich as a thief? And the patriotic chemists who discovered arsenic in dill pickles, ground glass in pumpernickel, bichloride tablets in Bismarck herring, pathogenic organisms in aniline dyes? And the inspired editorial writers of the New York *Times* and *Tribune,* the Boston *Transcript,* the Philadelphia *Ledger,* the Mobile *Register,* the Jones Corners *Eagle?* And the headline writers? And the Columbia, Yale and Princeton professors? And the authors of books describing how the Kaiser told them the whole plot in 1913, while they were pulling his teeth or shining his shoes? And the ex-ambassadors? And the *Nietzschefresser?* And the chautauqua orators? And the four-minute men? [9] And the Methodist pulpit pornographers who switched so facilely from vice-crusading to German atrocities? And Dr. Newell Dwight Hillis? And Dr. Henry van Dyke? [10] And the Vigilantes? [11] Let

[9] These were bores who visited the movie parlors of the time and broke in upon The Perils of Pauline with brief but rousing speeches. How many were in practise first and last I do not know, but there must have been hundreds of thousands. They were chiefly recruited from the ranks of Rotarians, Kiwanians, chautauquans, evangelical clergymen, and minor political aspirants.

[10] Hillis was a Presbyterian clergyman, but went over to the Congregationalists and spent most of his life in the old pulpit of Henry Ward Beecher in Brooklyn. He brought out a book called German Atrocities in 1918, in which all of the most fantastic inventions of the English propaganda bureau were treated gravely. Such horrors apparently fascinated him, and he wallowed in them in a really obscene manner. He died in 1929. Van Dyke, another Presbyterian, took the same line, though less violently. He had been pastor of the Brick

no grateful heart forget them!

Palmer and Burleson I leave for special legislation.[12] If mere university presidents, such as Nicholas Murray Butler, are to have the grand cross, then Palmer deserves to be rolled in malleable gold from head to foot, and polished until he blinds the cosmos—then Burleson must be hung with diamonds like Mrs. Warren and bathed in spotlights like Gaby Deslys. . . . Finally, I reserve a special decoration, to be conferred *in camera* and worn only in secret chapter, for husbands who took chances and refused to read anonymous letters from Paris: the somber badge of the Ordre de la Cuculus Canorus, first and only class.

THE ARCHANGEL WOODROW

(FROM the *Smart Set,* January 1921)

Wilson was a typical Puritan—of the better sort, perhaps, for he at least toyed with the ambition to appear as a gentleman, but nevertheless a true Puritan. Magnanimity was simply beyond him. Confronted, on his death-bed, with the case of poor Debs, all his instincts compelled him to keep Debs in jail. I daresay

Presbyterian Church in New York, but in the war era was professor of English literature at Princeton. He was taken gravely as a poet and essayist in his day, and rose to be president of the National Institute of Arts and Letters, but his writings were hollow and he is now pretty well forgotten. He died in 1933.

[11] An organization of professional patriots analogous to the American Protective League, but even worse. Its heroic members specialized in daubing yellow paint on the houses of persons suspected of having doubts about the Wilson idealism. In some regions they also resorted to assault, always at odds of at least 10 to 1.

[12] A. Mitchell Palmer, a Quaker, was Attorney-General under Wilson. He was the superintendent of many ferocious spy-hunts. He died in 1936. Albert Sidney Burleson was Wilson's Postmaster General. He specialized in the censorship of the mails. He died in 1937.

that, as a purely logical matter, he saw clearly that the old fellow ought to be turned loose; certainly he must have known that Washington would not have hesitated, or Lincoln. But Calvinism triumphed as his intellectual faculties decayed. In the full bloom of health, with a plug hat on his head, he aped the gentry of his wistful adoration very cleverly, but lying in bed, stripped like Thackeray's Louis XIV, he reverted to his congenital Puritanism, which is to say, bounderism.

There is a truly devastating picture of him in "The Story of a Style," by Dr. William Bayard Hale. Hale was peculiarly equipped for the business, for he was at one time high in the literary and philosophical confidence of the late Messiah, and learned to imitate his gaudy rhetoric with great skill—so perfectly, indeed, that he was delegated to write one of the Woodrovian books, to wit, "The New Freedom," once a favorite text of *New Republic* Liberals, deserving Democrats, and the tender-minded in general. But in the end he revolted against both the new Euphuism and its eminent pa, and when he wrote his book he tackled both with considerable ferocity, and, it must be added, vast effect. His analysis of the whole Wilsonian buncombe, in fact, is appallingly cruel. He shows its ideational hollowness, its ludicrous strutting and bombast, its heavy dependence upon greasy and meaningless words, its frequent descents to mere sound and fury, signifying nothing. In particular, he devotes himself to a merciless study of what, after all, must remain the deceased Moses's chief contribution to both history and beautiful letters, *viz.*, his biography of Washington. This incredible work is an almost inexhaustible mine of bad writing, faulty generalizing, childish pussyfooting, ludicrous posturing, and naïve stupidity. To find a match for it one must try to imagine a biography of the Duke of Wellington by his barber. Well, Hale spreads it out on his operating table, sharpens his snickersnee upon his bootleg, and proceeds to so harsh an anatomizing that it nearly makes me sympathize with the author. Not many of us—writers, and hence vain and artificial fellows—could undergo so relentless an examination without damage. But not many of us, I believe, would suffer quite so horribly as Woodrow. The book is a mass of puerile affectations, and as Hale unveils one after the other he performs a sound service for American scholarship and American letters.

I say that his book is cruel, but I must add that his laparotomies are carried on with every decorum—that he by no means rants and rages against his victim. On the contrary, he keeps his temper even when there is strong temptation to lose it, and his inquiry maintains itself upon the literary level as much as possible, without needless descents to political and personal matters. More than once, in fact, he says very kind things about Woodrow—a man probably quite as mellow and likable within as the next man, despite his strange incapacity for keeping his friends. The Woodrovian style, at the height of the Wilson hallucination, was much praised by cornfed connoisseurs. I read editorials, in those days, comparing it to the style of the Biblical prophets, and arguing that it vastly exceeded the manner of any living literatus. Looking backward, it is not difficult to see how that doctrine arose. Its chief sponsors, first and last, were not men who actually knew anything about writing English, but simply editorial writers on party newspapers, *i.e.*, men who related themselves to literary artists in much the same way that an Episcopal bishop relates himself to Paul of Tarsus. What intrigued such gentlemen was the plain fact that Wilson was their superior in their own special field—that he accomplished with a great deal more skill than they did themselves the great task of reducing all the difficulties of the hour to a few sonorous and unintelligible phrases, often with theological overtones—that he knew better than they did how to arrest and enchant the boobery with words that were simply words, and nothing else. The vulgar like and respect that sort of balderdash. A discourse packed with valid ideas, accurately expressed, is quite incomprehensible to them. What they want is the sough of vague and comforting words—words cast into phrases made familiar to them by the whooping of their customary political and ecclesiastical rabble-rousers, and by the highfalutin style of the newspapers that they read. Woodrow knew how to conjure up such words. He knew how to make them glow, and weep. He wasted no time upon the heads of his dupes, but aimed directly at their ears, diaphragms and hearts.

But reading his speeches in cold blood offers a curious experience. It is difficult to believe that even idiots ever succumbed to such transparent contradictions, to such gaudy processions of mere counter-words, to so vast and obvious a nonsensicality. Hale produces sentence after sentence that has no apparent meaning at all —stuff quite as bad as the worst bosh of Warren Gamaliel Harding. When Wilson got upon his legs in those days he seems to have gone into a sort of trance, with all the peculiar illusions and delusions that belong to a pedagogue gone *mashugga*. He heard words giving three cheers; he saw them race across a blackboard like Marxians pursued by the *Polizei;* he felt them rush up and kiss him. The result was the grand series of moral, political, sociological and theological maxims which now lodges imperishably in the cultural heritage of the American people, along with Lincoln's "government of the people, by the people," etc., Perry's "We have met the enemy, and they are ours," and Vanderbilt's "The public be damned." The important thing is not that a popular orator should have uttered such vaporous and preposterous phrases, but that they should have been gravely received, for weary years, by a whole race of men, some of them intelligent. Here is a matter that deserves the sober inquiry of competent psychologists.

119

The boobs took fire first, but after a while even college presidents—who certainly ought to be cynical men, if ladies of joy are cynical women—were sending up sparks, and for a long while anyone who laughed was in danger of the calaboose.

THE LIBERTINE
(FROM *In Defense of Women*, 1922)

★

The average man of our time and race is far more virtuous than his wife's imaginings make him out—far less schooled in sin, far less enterprising in amour. I do not say, of course, that he is pure in heart, for the chances are that he isn't; what I do say is that, in the overwhelming majority of cases, he is pure in act, even in the face of temptation. And why? For several main reasons, not to go into minor ones. One is that he lacks the courage. Another is that he lacks the money. Another is that he is fundamentally moral, and has a conscience. It takes more sinful initiative than he has to plunge into any affair save the most casual and sordid; it takes more ingenuity and intrepidity than he has to carry it off; it takes more money than he can conceal from his consort to finance it. A man may force his actual wife to share the direst poverty, but even the least vampirish woman of the third part demands to be courted in what, considering his station in life, is the grand manner, and the expenses of that grand manner scare off all save a small minority of specialists in deception. So long, indeed, as a wife knows her husband's income accurately, she has a sure means of holding him to his oaths.

Even more effective than the fiscal barrier is the barrier of poltroonery. The one character that distinguishes man from the other higher vertebrata is his excessive timorousness, his easy yielding to alarms, his incapacity for adventure without a crowd behind him.

★

The moment a concrete Temptress rises before him, her nose talced, her lips scarlet, her eyelashes dropping provokingly—the moment such an abandoned wench has at him, and his lack of ready funds begins to conspire with his lack of courage to assault and wobble him—at that precise moment his conscience flares into function, and so finishes his business. First he sees difficulty, then he sees danger, then he sees wrong. The result? The result is that he slinks off in trepidation, and another vampire is baffled of her prey. It is, indeed, the secret scandal of Christendom, at least in the Protestant regions, that most men are faithful to their wives. You will travel a long way before you find a married man who will admit that *he* is, but the facts are the facts. For one American husband who maintains a chorus girl in levantine luxury around the corner, there are hundreds who are as true to their oaths, year in and year out, as so many convicts in the deathhouse, and would be no more capable of any such loathsome malpractice, even in the face of free opportunity, than they would be of cutting off the ears of their young.[1]

---

[1] I see nothing in the Kinsey Report to change my conclusions here. All that humorless document really proves is (*a*) that all men lie when they are asked about their adventures in amour, and (*b*) that pedagogues are singularly naïve and credulous creatures.

THE LURE OF BEAUTY
(FROM *In Defense of Women*, 1922)

★

Save on the stage, the handsome fellow has no appreciable advantage in amour over his more Gothic brother. In real life, indeed, he is viewed with the utmost suspicion by all women save the most stupid. A ten-cent-store girl, perhaps, may plausibly fall in love with a movie actor, and a half-idiotic old widow may succumb to a gigolo with shoulders like the Parthenon, but no woman of poise and self-respect, even supposing her to be transiently flustered by a lovely buck, would yield to that madness for an instant, or confess it to her dearest friend.

This disdain of the pretty fellow is often accounted for by amateur psychologists on the ground that women are anesthetic to beauty—that they lack the quick and delicate responsiveness of man. Nothing could be more absurd. Women, in point of fact, commonly have a far keener esthetic sense than men. Beauty is more important to them; they give more thought to it; they crave more of it in their immediate surroundings. The average man, at least in England and America, takes a bovine pride in his indifference to the arts; he can think of them only as sources of somewhat discreditable amusement; one seldom hears of him showing half the enthusiasm for any beautiful thing that his wife displays in the presence of a fine fabric, an effective color, or a graceful form. Women are resistant to so-called beauty in men for the simple and sufficient reason that such beauty is chiefly imaginary.

A truly beautiful man, indeed, is as rare as a truly beautiful piece of jewelry.

What men mistake for beauty in themselves is usually nothing save a certain hollow gaudiness, a revolting flashiness, the superficial splendor of a prancing animal. The most lovely movie actor, considered in the light of genuine esthetic values, is no more than a study in vulgarity; his like is to be found, not in the Uffizi gallery or among the harmonies of Brahms, but among the plush sofas, rococo clocks and hand-painted oil-paintings of a third-rate auction-room. All women, save the least intelligent, penetrate this imposture with sharp eyes. They know that the human body, except for a brief time in childhood, is not a beautiful thing, but a hideous thing. Their own bodies give them no delight; it is their constant effort to disguise and conceal them; they never expose them esthetically, but only as an act of the grossest sexual provocation. If it were advertised that a troupe of men of easy virtue were to do a strip-tease act upon a public stage, the only women who would go to the entertainment would be a few delayed adolescents, a psychopathic old maid or two, and a guard of indignant members of the parish Ladies Aid Society.

Men show no such sagacious apprehension of the relatively feeble loveliness of the human frame. The most effective lure that a woman can hold out to a man is the lure of what he fatuously conceives to be her beauty. This so-called beauty, of course, is almost always a pure illusion. The female body, even at its best, is very defective in form; it has harsh curves and very clumsily distributed masses; compared to it the average milk-jug, or even cuspidor, is a thing of intelligent and gratifying design—in brief, an *objet d'art*. Below the neck by the bow and below the waist astern there are two masses that simply refuse to fit into a balanced composition. Viewed from the side, a woman presents an exaggerated S bisected by an imperfect straight line, and so she inevitably suggests a drunken dollar-mark.

Moreover, it is extremely rare to find a woman who shows even the modest sightliness that her sex is theoretically capable of; it is only the rare beauty who is even tolerable. The average woman, until art comes to her aid, is ungraceful, misshapen, badly calved and crudely articulated, even for a woman. If she has a good torso, she is almost sure to be bow-legged. If she has good legs, she is almost sure to have bad hair. If she has good hair, she is almost sure to have scrawny hands, or muddy eyes, or no chin. A woman who meets fair tests all round is so uncommon that she becomes a sort of marvel, and usually gains a livelihood by exhibiting herself as such, either on the stage, in the half-world, or as the private jewel of some wealthy connoisseur.

But this lack of genuine beauty in women lays on them no practical disadvantage in the primary business of their sex, for its effects are more than overborne by the emotional suggestibility, the herculean capacity for illusion, the almost total absence of critical sense in men. Men do not demand genuine beauty, even in the most modest doses; they are quite content with the mere appearance of beauty. That is to say, they show no talent whatever for differentiating between the artificial and the real. A film of face powder, skillfully applied, is as satisfying to them as an epidermis of damask. The hair of a dead Chinaman, artfully dressed and dyed, gives them as much delight as the authentic tresses of Venus. False bosoms intrigue them as effectively as the soundest of living fascia. A pretty frock fetches them quite as surely and securely as lovely legs, shoulders, hands or eyes.

In brief, they estimate women, and hence acquire their wives, by reckoning up purely superficial aspects, which is just as intelligent as estimating an egg by purely superficial aspects. They never go behind the returns; it never occurs to them to analyze the impressions they receive. The result is that many a man, deceived by such paltry sophistications, never really sees his wife—that is, as our Heavenly Father is supposed to see her, and as the embalmer will see her—until they have been married for years. All the tricks may be infantile and obvious, but in the face of so naïve a spectator the temptation to continue practising them is irresistible. A trained nurse tells me that even when undergoing the extreme discomfort of parturition the great majority of women continue to modify their complexions with pulverized magnesium silicate, and to give thought to the arrangement of their hair. Such transparent devices reduce the psychologist to a sour sort of mirth, yet it must be plain that they suffice to entrap and make fools of men, even the most discreet.

And what esthetic deafness, dumbness and blindness thus open the way for, vanity instantly reinforces. That is to say, once a normal man has succumbed to the meretricious charms of a definite fair one (or, more accurately, once a definite fair one has marked him out and grabbed him by the nose), he defends his choice with all the heat and steadfastness appertaining to the defense of a point of honor. To tell a man flatly that his wife is not beautiful is so harsh and intolerable an insult that even an enemy seldom ventures upon it. One would offend him far less by arguing that his wife is an idiot. One would, relatively speaking, almost caress him by spitting into his eye. The ego of the male is simply unable to stomach such an affront. It is a weapon as discreditable as the poison of the Borgias.

Thus, on humane grounds, a conspiracy of silence surrounds the delusion of female beauty, and its victim is permitted to get quite as much delight out of it as if if were sound. The baits he swallows most are not edible and nourishing ones, but simply bright and gaudy ones. He succumbs to a pair of well-managed eyes, a graceful twist of the body, a synthetic complexion or a skillful display of legs without giving the slightest

thought to the fact that a whole woman is there, and that within the cranial cavity of the woman lies a brain, and that the idiosyncrasies of that brain are of vastly more importance than all imaginable physical stigmata combined. But not many men, lost in the emotional maze preceding, are capable of any very clear examination of such facts. They dodge those facts, even when they are favorable, and lay all stress upon the surrounding and concealing superficialities. The average stupid and sentimental man, if he has a noticeably sensible wife, is almost apologetic about it. The ideal of his sex is always a pretty wife, and the vanity and coquetry that so often go with prettiness are erected into charms.
★

THE GOOD MAN
(FROM the *Smart Set*, 1923)

Man, at his best, remains a sort of one-lunged animal, never completely rounded and perfect, as a cockroach, say, is perfect. If he shows one valuable quality, it is almost unheard of for him to show any other. Give him a head, and he lacks a heart. Give him a heart of a gallon capacity, and his head holds scarcely a pint. The artist, nine times out of ten, is a dead-beat and given to the debauching of virgins, so-called. The patriot is a bigot, and, more often than not, a bounder and a poltroon. The man of physical bravery is often on a level, intellectually, with a Baptist clergyman. The intellectual giant has bad kidneys and cannot thread a needle. In all my years of search in this world, from the Golden Gate in the West to the Vistula in the East, and from the Orkney Islands in the North to the Spanish Main in the South, I have never met a thoroughly moral man who was honorable.

THE ANGLO-SAXON
(FROM the Baltimore *Evening Sun*, July 1923)

★

When I speak of Anglo-Saxons, of course, I speak inexactly and in the common phrase. Even within the bounds of that phrase the American of the dominant stock is Anglo-Saxon only partially, for there is probably just as much Celtic blood in his veins as Germanic, and his norm is to be found, not south of the Tyne and west of the Severn, but on the two sides of the northern border. Among the first English colonists there were many men of almost pure Teutonic stock from the east and south of England, and their influence is yet visible in many characteristic American folkways, in certain traditional American ideas—some of them now surviving only in national hypocrisies—and, above all, in the fundamental peculiarities of the American dialect of English. But their Teutonic blood was early diluted by Celtic strains from Scotland, from the north of Ireland, from Wales, and from the west of England, and today those Americans who are regarded as being most thoroughly Anglo-Saxons—for example, the mountaineers of the Appalachian slopes from Pennsylvania to Georgia—are obviously far more Celtic than Teutonic, not only physically but also mentally. They are leaner and taller than the true English, and far more given to moral obsessions and religious fanaticism. A Methodist revival is not an English phenomenon; it is Welsh. So is the American tendency, marked by every foreign student of our history, to turn all political combats into moral crusades. The English themselves, of course, have been greatly polluted by Scotch, Irish and Welsh blood during the past three centuries, and for years past their government has been largely in the hands of Celts, but though this fact, by making them more like Americans, has tended to conceal the difference that I am discussing, it has certainly not sufficed to obliterate it altogether. The English notion of humor remains different from the American notion, and so does the English view of personal liberty, and on the same level of primary ideas there are many other obvious differences.

But though I am thus convinced that the American Anglo-Saxon wears a false label, and grossly libels both of the great races from which he claims descent, I can imagine no good in trying to change it. Let him call himself whatever he pleases. Whatever he calls himself, it must be plain that the term he uses designates a genuinely distinct and differentiated race—that he is separated definitely, in character and habits of thought, from the men of all other recognizable strains—that he represents, among the peoples of the earth, almost a special species, and that he runs true to type. The traits that he developed when the first mixture of races took place in colonial days are the traits that he still shows; despite the vast changes in his material environment, he is almost precisely the same, in the way he thinks and acts, as his forefathers were. Some of the other great races of men, during the past two centuries, have changed very noticeably, but the American Anglo-Saxon has stuck to his hereditary guns. Moreover, he tends to show much less variation than other races between man and man. No other race, save it be the Chinese, is so thoroughly regimented.

The good qualities of this so-called Anglo-Saxon are many, and I am certainly not disposed to question them, but I here pass them over without apology, for he devotes practically the whole of his literature and fully a half of his oral discourse to celebrating them himself, and so there is no danger that they will ever be disregarded. No other known man, indeed, is so violently the blowhard, save it be his English kinsman. In this fact lies the first cause of the ridiculous figure he commonly cuts in the eyes of other people: he brags and blusters so incessantly that, if he actually had the combined virtues of Socrates, the Cid and the Twelve Apostles, he would still go beyond the facts, and so appear a mere Bombastes Furioso. This habit, I believe, is fundamentally English, but it has been exaggerated in the Americano by his larger admixture of Celtic blood. In late years in America it has taken on an almost pathological character, and is to be explained, perhaps, only in terms of the Freudian necromancy. Braggadocio, in the 100% American—"we won the war," "it is our duty to lead the world," and so on—is probably no more than a protective mechanism erected to conceal an inescapable sense of inferiority.

That this inferiority is real must be obvious to any impartial observer. Whenever the Anglo-Saxon, whether of the English or of the American variety, comes into sharp conflict with men of other stocks, he tends to be worsted, or, at best, to be forced back upon extraneous and irrelevant aids to assist him in the struggle. Here in the United States his defeat is so palpable that it has filled him with vast alarms, and reduced him to seeking succor in grotesque and extravagant devices. In the fine arts, in the sciences and even in the more complex sorts of business the children of the later immigrants are running away from the descendants of the early settlers. To call the roll of Americans eminent in almost any field of human endeavor above the most elemental is to call a list of strange and often outlandish names; even the panel of Congress presents a startling example. Of the Americans who have come into notice during the past fifty years as poets, as novelists, as critics, as painters, as sculptors and in the minor arts, less than half bear Anglo-Saxon names, and in this minority there are few of pure Anglo-Saxon blood. So in the sciences. So in the higher reaches of engineering and technology. So in philosophy and its branches. So even in industry and agriculture. In those areas where the competition between the new and the old bloodstreams is most sharp and clearcut, say in New York, in seaboard New England and in the farming States of the upper Middle West, the defeat of the so-called Anglo-Saxon is overwhelming and unmistakable. Once his predominance everywhere was actual and undisputed; today, even where he remains superior numerically, it is largely sentimental and illusory.

The descendants of the later immigrants tend generally to move upward; the descendants of the first settlers, I believe, tend plainly to move downward, mentally, spiritually and even physically. Civilization is at its lowest mark in the United States precisely in those areas where the Anglo-Saxon still presumes to rule. He runs the whole South—and in the whole South there are not as many first-rate men as in many a single city of the mongrel North. Wherever he is still firmly in the saddle, there we look for such pathological phenomena as Fundamentalism, Prohibition and Ku Kluxery, and there they flourish. It is not in the northern cities, with their mixed population, that the death-rate is highest, and politics most corrupt, and religion nearest to voodooism, and every decent human aspiration suspect; it is in the areas that the recent immigrations have not penetrated, where "the purest Anglo-Saxon blood in the world" still flows. I could pile up evidences, but they are not necessary. The fact is too plain to be challenged. One testimony will be sufficient: it comes from two inquirers who made an exhaustive survey of a region in southeastern Ohio, where "the people are more purely Americans than in the rest of the State":

> Here gross superstition exercises strong control over the thought and action of a large proportion of the people. Syphilitic and other venereal diseases are common and increasing over whole counties, while in some communities nearly every family is afflicted with inherited or infectious disease. Many cases of incest are known; inbreeding is rife. Imbeciles, feeble-minded, and delinquents are numerous, politics is corrupt, and selling of votes is common, petty crimes abound, the schools have been badly managed and poorly attended. Cases of rape, assault, and robbery are of almost weekly occurrence within five minutes' walk of the corporation limits of one of the county seats, while in another county political control is held by a self-confessed criminal. Alcoholic intemperance is excessive. Gross immorality and its evil results are by no means confined to the hill districts, but are extreme also in the towns.[1]

As I say, the American of the old stock is not unaware of this steady, and, of late, somewhat rapid deterioration—this gradual loss of his old mastery in the land his ancestors helped to wring from the Indian and the wildcat. He senses it, indeed, very painfully, and, as if in despair of arresting it in fact, makes desperate efforts to dispose of it by denial and concealment. These efforts often take grotesque and extravagant forms. Laws are passed to hobble and cage the citizen of newer stocks in a hundred fantastic ways. It is made difficult and socially dangerous for him to teach his children the speech of his fathers, or to maintain the cultural attitudes that he has inherited from them. Every divergence from the norm of the low-cast Anglo-

[1] Since the above was written there has been unqualified confirmation of it by a distinguished English authority, to wit, Arnold J. Toynbee. See his Study of History, Vol. I, pp. 466–67, and Vol. II, pp. 311–12.

Saxon is treated as an *attentat* against the commonwealth, and punished with eager ferocity.

It so happens that I am myself an Anglo-Saxon—one of far purer blood, indeed, than most of the half-bleached Celts who pass under the name in the United States and England. I am in part Angle and in part Saxon, and what else I am is safely white, Nordic, Protestant and blond. Thus I feel free, without risk of venturing into bad taste, to regard frankly the *soi-disant* Anglo-Saxon of this incomparable Republic and his rather less dubious cousin of the Motherland. How do the two appear to me, after years spent largely in accumulating their disfavor? What are the characters that I discern most clearly in the so-called Anglo-Saxon type of man? I may answer at once that two stick out above all others. One is his curious and apparently incurable incompetence—his congenital inability to do any difficult thing easily and well, whether it be isolating a bacillus or writing a sonata. The other is his astounding susceptibility to fears and alarms—in short, his hereditary cowardice.

To accuse so enterprising and successful a race of cowardice, of course, is to risk immediate derision; nevertheless, I believe that a fair-minded examination of its history will bear me out. Nine-tenths of the great feats of derring-do that its sucklings are taught to venerate in school—that is, its feats as a race, not the isolated exploits of its extraordinary individuals, most of them at least partly of other stocks—have been wholly lacking in even the most elementary gallantry. Consider, for example, the events attending the extension of the two great empires, English and American. Did either movement evoke any genuine courage and resolution? The answer is plainly no. Both empires were built up primarily by swindling and butchering unarmed savages, and after that by robbing weak and friendless nations. Neither produced a hero above the average run of those in the movies; neither exposed the folks at home to any serious danger of reprisal. Almost always, indeed, mercenaries have done the Anglo-Saxon's fighting for him—a high testimony to his common sense, but scarcely flattering, I fear, to the truculence he boasts of. The British empire was won mainly by Irishmen, Scotchmen and native allies, and the American empire, at least in large part, by Frenchmen and Spaniards. Moreover, neither great enterprise cost any appreciable amount of blood; neither presented grave and dreadful risks; neither exposed the conqueror to the slightest danger of being made the conquered. The British won most of their vast dominions without having to stand up in a single battle against a civilized and formidable foe, and the Americanos won their continent at the expense of a few dozen puerile skirmishes with savages. The total cost of conquering the whole area from Plymouth Rock to the Golden Gate and from Lake George to the Everglades, including even the cost of driving out the French, Dutch, English and Spaniards, was less than the cost of defending Verdun.

So far as I can make out there is no record in history of any Anglo-Saxon nation entering upon any great war without allies. The French have done it, the Dutch have done it, the Germans have done it, the Japs have done it, and even such inferior nations as the Danes, the Spaniards, the Boers and the Greeks have done it, but never the English or Americans. Can you imagine the United States resolutely facing a war in which the odds against it were as huge as they were against Spain in 1898? The facts of history are wholly against any such fancy. The Anglo-Saxon always tries to take a gang with him when he goes into battle, and even when he has it behind him he is very uneasy, and prone to fall into panic at the first threat of genuine danger. Here I put an unimpeachably Anglo-Saxon witness on the stand, to wit, the late Charles W. Eliot. I find him saying, in an article quoted with approbation by the

Congressional Record, that during the Revolutionary War the colonists now hymned so eloquently in the school-books "fell into a condition of despondency from which nothing but the steadfastness of Washington and the Continental army *and the aid from France* saved them," and that "when the War of 1812 brought grave losses a considerable portion of the population experienced a moral collapse, from which they were rescued only by the exertions of a few thoroughly patriotic statesmen and the exploits of three or four American frigates on the seas"—to say nothing of an enterprising Corsican gentleman, Bonaparte by name.

In both these wars the Americans had enormous and obvious advantages, in terrain, in allies and in men; nevertheless, they fought, in the main, very badly, and from the first shot to the last a majority of them stood in favor of making peace on almost any terms. The Mexican and Spanish Wars I pass over as perhaps too obscenely ungallant to be discussed at all; of the former, U. S. Grant, who fought in it, said that it was "the most unjust war ever waged by a stronger against a weaker nation." Who remembers that, during the Spanish War, the whole Atlantic Coast trembled in fear of the Spaniards' feeble fleet—that all New England had hysterics every time a strange coal-barge was sighted on the sky-line, that the safe-deposit boxes of Boston were emptied and their contents transferred to Worcester, and that the Navy had to organize a patrol to save the coast towns from depopulation? Perhaps those Reds, atheists and pro-Germans remember it who also remember that during World War I the entire country went wild with fear of an enemy who, without the aid of divine intervention, obviously could not strike it a blow at all—and that the great moral victory was gained at last with the assistance of twenty-one allies and at odds of eight to one.[2]

[2] The case of World War II was even more striking. The two enemies that the United States tackled had been softened by years of a hard

But the American Civil War remains? Does it, indeed? The almost unanimous opinion of the North, in 1861, was that it would be over after a few small battles; the first soldiers were actually enlisted for but three months. When, later on, it turned unexpectedly into a severe struggle, recruits had to be driven to the front by force, and the only Northerners remaining in favor of going on were Abraham Lincoln, a few ambitious generals and the profiteers. I turn to Dr. Eliot again. "In the closing year of the war," he says, "large portions of the Democratic party in the North *and of the Republican party,* advocated surrender to the Confederacy, *so downhearted were they.*" Downhearted at odds of three to one! The South was plainly more gallant, but even the gallantry of the South was largely illusory. The Confederate leaders, when the war began, adopted at once the traditional Anglo-Saxon device of seeking allies. They tried and expected to get the aid of England, and they actually came very near succeeding. When hopes in that direction began to fade (*i.e.,* when England concluded that tackling the North would be dangerous), the common people of the Confederacy threw up the sponge, and so the catastrophe, when it came at last, was mainly internal. The South failed to bring the quaking North to a standstill because, to borrow a phrase that Dr. Eliot uses in another connection, it "experienced a moral collapse of unprecedented depth and duration." The folks at home failed to support the troops in the field, and the troops in the field began to desert. Even so early as Shiloh, indeed, many Confederate regiments were already refusing to fight.

This reluctance for desperate chances and hard odds, so obvious in the military record of the English-speaking nations, is also conspicuous in times of peace. What

---

struggle with desperate foes, and those foes continued to fight on. Neither enemy could muster even a tenth of the materials that the American forces had the use of. And at the end both were outnumbered in men by odds truly enormous.

a man of another and superior stock almost always notices, living among so-called Anglo-Saxons, is (*a*) their incapacity for prevailing in fair rivalry, either in trade, in the fine arts or in what is called learning—in brief, their general incompetence, and (*b*) their invariable effort to make up for this incapacity by putting some inequitable burden upon their rivals, usually by force. The Frenchman, I believe, is the worst of chauvinists, but once he admits a foreigner to his country he at least treats that foreigner fairly, and does not try to penalize him absurdly for his mere foreignness. The Anglo-Saxon American is always trying to do it; his history is a history of recurrent outbreaks of blind rage against peoples who have begun to worst him. Such movements would be inconceivable in an efficient and genuinely self-confident people, wholly assured of their superiority, and they would be equally inconceivable in a truly gallant and courageous people, disdaining unfair advantages and overwhelming odds. Theoretically launched against some imaginary inferiority in the non-Anglo-Saxon man, either as patriot, as democrat or as Christian, they are actually launched at his general superiority, his greater fitness to survive in the national environment. The effort is always to penalize him for winning in fair fight, to handicap him in such a manner that he will sink to the general level of the Anglo-Saxon population, and, if possible, even below it. Such devices, of course, never have the countenance of the Anglo-Saxon minority that is authentically superior, and hence self-confident and tolerant. But that minority is pathetically small, and it tends steadily to grow smaller and feebler. The communal laws and the communal *mores* are made by the folk, and they offer all the proof that is necessary, not only of its general inferiority, but also of its alarmed awareness of that inferiority. The normal American of the "pure-blooded" majority goes to rest every night with an uneasy feeling that there is a burglar under the bed, and he gets up every morning with a sickening fear that his underwear has been stolen.

This Anglo-Saxon of the great herd is, in many important respects, the least civilized of white men and the least capable of true civilization. His political ideas are crude and shallow. He is almost wholly devoid of esthetic feeling. The most elementary facts about the visible universe alarm him, and incite him to put them down. Educate him, make a professor of him, teach him how to express his soul, and he still remains palpably third-rate. He fears ideas almost more cravenly than he fears men. His blood, I believe, is running thin; perhaps it was not much to boast of at the start; in order that he may exercise any functions above those of a trader, a pedagogue or a mob orator, it needs the stimulus of other and less exhausted strains. The fact that they increase is the best hope of civilization in America. They shake the old race out of its spiritual lethargy, and introduce it to disquiet and experiment. They make for a free play of ideas. In opposing the process, whether in politics, in letters or in the ages-long struggle toward the truth, the prophets of Anglo-Saxon purity and tradition only make themselves ridiculous.

★

HOLY WRIT
(FROM the *Smart Set*, October 1923)

Whoever it was who translated the Bible into excellent French prose is chiefly responsible for the collapse of Christianity in France. Contrariwise, the men

who put the Bible into archaic, sonorous and often unintelligible English gave Christianity a new lease of life
wherever English is spoken. They did their work at
a time of great theological blather and turmoil, when
men of all sorts, even the least intelligent, were beginning to take a vast and unhealthy interest in exegetics
and apologetics. They were far too shrewd to feed this
disconcerting thirst for ideas with a Bible in plain English; the language they used was deliberately artificial
even when it was new. They thus dispersed the mob by
appealing to its emotions, as a mother quiets a baby by
crooning to it. The Bible that they produced was so
beautiful that the great majority of men, in the face of
it, could not fix their minds upon the ideas in it. To
this day it has enchanted the English-speaking peoples
so effectively that, in the main, they remain Christians,
at least sentimentally. Paine has assaulted them, Darwin and Huxley have assaulted them, and a multitude
of other merchants of facts have assaulted them, but
they still remember the twenty-third Psalm when the
doctor begins to shake his head, they are still moved
beyond compare (though not, alas, to acts!) by the
Sermon on the Mount, and they still turn once a year
from their sordid and degrading labors to immerse
themselves unashamed in the story of the manger. It is
not much, but it is something. I do not admire the
general run of American Bible-searchers—Methodists,
United Brethren, Baptists, and such vermin. But try
to imagine what the average low-browed Methodist
would be if he were not a Methodist but an atheist!

The Latin Church, which I constantly find myself
admiring, despite its frequent astounding imbecilities,
has always kept clearly before it the fact that religion is
not a syllogism, but a poem. It is accused by Protestant
dervishes of withholding the Bible from the people. To
some extent this is true; to the same extent the church
is wise; again to the same extent it is prosperous. Its

toying with ideas, in the main, have been confined to its clergy, and they have commonly reduced the business to a harmless play of technicalities—the awful concepts of Heaven and Hell brought down to the level of a dispute of doctors in long gowns, eager only to dazzle other doctors. Its greatest theologians remain unknown to 99% of its adherents. Rome, indeed, has not only preserved the original poetry in Christianity; it has also made capital additions to that poetry—for example, the poetry of the saints, of Mary, and of the liturgy itself. A solemn high mass must be a thousand times as impressive, to a man with any genuine religious sense in him, as the most powerful sermon ever roared under the big-top by a Presbyterian auctioneer of God. In the face of such overwhelming beauty it is not necessary to belabor the faithful with logic; they are better convinced by letting them alone.

Preaching is not an essential part of the Latin ceremonial. It was very little employed in the early church, and I am convinced that good effects would flow from abandoning it today, or, at all events, reducing it to a few sentences, more or less formal. In the United States the Latin brethren have been seduced by the example of the Protestants, who commonly transform an act of worship into a puerile intellectual exercise; instead of approaching God in fear and wonder these Protestants settle back in their pews, cross their legs, and listen to an ignoramus try to prove that he is a better theologian than the Pope. This folly the Romans now slide into. Their clergy begin to grow argumentative, doctrinaire, ridiculous. It is a pity. A bishop in his robes, playing his part in the solemn ceremonial of the mass, is a dignified spectacle, even though he may sweat freely; the same bishop, bawling against Darwin half an hour later, is seen to be simply an elderly Irishman with a bald head, the son of a respectable saloon-keeper in South Bend, Ind. Let the reverend fathers go back to

Bach. If they keep on spoiling poetry and spouting ideas, the day will come when some extra-bombastic deacon will astound humanity and insult God by proposing to translate the liturgy into American, that all the faithful may be convinced by it.

AFTERTHOUGHTS

MASTERS OF TONE
(FROM the *Smart Set*, May 1912)

Wagner—The rape of the Sabines . . . a *kommers* in Olympus.

Beethoven—The glory that was Greece . . . the grandeur that was Rome . . . a laugh.

Haydn—A seidel on the table . . . a girl on your knee . . . another and different girl in your heart.

Chopin—Two embalmers at work upon a minor poet . . . the scent of tuberoses . . . Autumn rain.

Richard Strauss—Old Home Week in Gomorrah.

Johann Strauss—Forty couples dancing . . . one by one they slip from the hall . . . sounds of kisses . . . the lights go out.

Puccini—Silver macaroni, exquisitely tangled.

Debussy—A pretty girl with one blue eye and one brown one.

Bach—Genesis I, I.

THE NOBLE EXPERIMENT [*1920–33*]

(FROM *Heathen Days*, 1943)

★

I once came so near going dry in Pennsylvania, and in the very midst of a huge fleet of illicit breweries, that the memory of it still makes me shiver. This was at Bethlehem in the Lehigh Valley, in 1924. I had gone to the place with my publisher, Alfred Knopf, to hear the celebrated Bach Choir, and we were astounded after the first day's sessions to discover that not a drop of malt liquor was to be had in the local pubs. This seemed strange and unfriendly, for it is well known to every musicologist that the divine music of old Johann Sebastian cannot be digested without the aid of its natural solvent. But so far as we could make out there was absolutely none on tap in the Lehigh Valley, though we searched high and low, and threw ourselves upon the mercy of cops, taxi-drivers, hotel clerks, the Elks, the rev. clergy, and half the tenors and basses of the choir. All reported that Prohibition agents had been sighted in the mountains a few days before, and that as a result hundreds of kegs had been buried and every bartender was on the alert. How we got through the second day's sessions I don't know; the music was magnificent, but our tonsils became so parched that we could barely join in the final Amen. Half an hour before our train was scheduled to leave for New York we decided to go down to the Lehigh station and telegraph to a bootician in the big city, desiring him to start westward at once and meet us at Paterson, N.J. On the way to the station we discussed this madcap scheme dismally, and the taxi-driver overheard us. He was a compassionate man, and his heart bled for us.

"Gents," he said, "I hate to horn in on what ain't none of my business, but if you feel that bad about it I think I know where some stuff is to be had. The point is, can you get it?"

We at once offered him money to introduce us, but he waived us off.

"It wouldn't do you no good," he said. "These Pennsylvania Dutch never trust a hackman."

"But where is the place?" we breathed.

"I'm taking you to it," he replied, and in a moment we were there.

It was a huge, blank building that looked like a forsaken warehouse, but over a door that appeared to be tightly locked there was the telltale sign, "Sea Food"—the universal euphemism for beerhouse in Maryland and Pennsylvania throughout the thirteen awful years. We rapped on the door and presently it opened about half an inch, revealing an eye and part of a mouth. The ensuing dialogue was *sotto voce* but *staccato* and *appassionata*. The eye saw that we were famished, but the mouth hesitated.

"How do I know," it asked, "that you ain't two of them agents?"

The insinuation made us boil, but we had to be polite.

"*Agents!*" hissed Knopf. "What an idea! Can't you *see* us? Take a good look at us."

The eye looked, but the mouth made no reply.

"Can't you tell musicians when you see them?" I broke in. "Where did you ever see a Prohibition agent who looked so innocent, so moony, so dumb? We are actually fanatics. We came here to hear Bach. Is this the way Bethlehem treats its guests? We came a thousand miles, and now—"

"*Three* thousand miles," corrected Knopf.

"*Five* thousand," I added, making it round numbers.

Suddenly I bethought me that the piano score of the B minor mass had been under my arm all the while. What better introduction? What more persuasive proof of our *bona fides*? I held up the score and pointed to the title on the cover. The eye read:

J. S. Bach
Mass in B Minor

The eye flicked for an instant or two, and then the mouth spoke. "Come in, gents," it said. As the door opened our natural momentum carried us into the bar in one leap, and there we were presently immersed in two immense *Humpen*. The quality we did not pause to observe; what we mainly recalled later was the astounding modesty of the bill, which was sixty-five cents for five *Humpen*—Knopf had two and I had three—and two sandwiches. We made our train just as it was pulling out.

It was a narrow escape from death in the desert, and we do not forget all these years afterward that we owed it to Johann Sebastian Bach, that highly talented and entirely respectable man, and especially to his mass in B minor. In the great city of Cleveland, Ohio, a few months later, I had much worse luck. I went there, in my capacity of newspaper reporter, to help cover the Republican national convention which nominated Calvin Coolidge, and I assumed like everyone else that the Prohibition agents would lay off while the job was put through, if only as a mark of respect to their commander-in-chief. This assumption turned out to be erroneous. The agents actually clamped down on Cleveland with the utmost ferocity, and produced a drought that was virtually complete. Even the local cops and newspaper reporters were dry, and many of the latter spent a large part of their time touring the quarters of the out-of-town correspondents, begging for succor. But the supplies brought in by the correspondents were gone in a few days, and by the time the convention actually opened a glass of malt liquor was as hard to come by in Cleveland as an honest politician.

The news of this horror quickly got about, and one morning I received a dispatch in cipher from a Christian friend in Detroit, saying that he was loading a motor-launch with ten cases of bottled beer and ale, and sending it down the Detroit river and across Lake Erie in charge of two of his goons. They were instructed, he said, to notify me the instant they arrived off the Cleveland breakwater. Their notice reached me the next afternoon, but by that time the boys were nominating Cal, so I could not keep the rendezvous myself, but had to send an agent. This agent was Paul de Kruif, then a young man of thirty-four, studying the literary art under my counsel. Paul was a fellow of high principles and worthy of every confidence; moreover, he was dying of thirst himself. I started him out in a rowboat, and he was gone three hours. When he got back he was pale and trembling, and I could see at a glance that some calamity had befallen. When he got his breath he gasped out the story.

The two goons, it appeared, had broken into their cargo on the way down from Detroit, for the weather was extremely hot. By the time they anchored off the Cleveland breakwater they had got down three cases, and while they were waiting for de Kruif they knocked off two more. This left but five—and they figured that it was just enough to get them back to Detroit, for the way was uphill all the way, as a glance at a map will show. De Kruif, who was a huge and sturdy Dutchman with a neck like John L. Sullivan, protested violently and even undertook to throw them overboard and pirate the launch and cargo, but they pulled firearms on him, and the best he could do was to get six bottles. These he drank on his return in the rowboat, for the heat, as I have said, was extreme. As a result, I got nothing whatsoever; indeed, not a drop of malt touched my throat until the next night at 11.57, when the ex-

press for Washington and points East crossed the fron-
tier of the Maryland Free State.

This was my worst adventure during Prohibition,
and in many ways it remains the worst adventure of my
whole life, though I have been shot at four times and
my travels have taken me to Albania, Trans-Jordan and
Arkansas.

THE ARTIST
(FROM the Baltimore *Evening Sun*, April 7, 1924)

It is almost as safe to assume that an artist
of any dignity is against his country, *i.e.*, against the
environment in which God hath placed him, as it is to
assume that his country is against the artist. The special
quality which makes an artist of him might almost be
defined, indeed, as an extraordinary capacity for irritation, a pathological sensitiveness to environmental
pricks and stings. He differs from the rest of us mainly
because he reacts sharply and in an uncommon manner
to phenomena which leave the rest of us unmoved, or,
at most, merely annoy us vaguely. He is, in brief, a
more delicate fellow than we are, and hence less fitted
to prosper and enjoy himself under the conditions of
life which he and we must face alike. Therefore, he
takes to artistic endeavor, which is at once a criticism
of life and an attempt to escape from life.

So much for the theory of it. The more the facts are
studied, the more they bear it out. In those fields of art,
at all events, which concern themselves with ideas as
well as with sensations it is almost impossible to find
any trace of an artist who was not actively hostile to
his environment, and thus an indifferent patriot. From

Dante to Tolstoy and from Shakespeare to Mark Twain the story is ever the same. Names suggest themselves instantly: Goethe, Heine, Shelley, Byron, Thackeray, Balzac, Rabelais, Cervantes, Swift, Dostoevsky, Carlyle, Molière, Pope—all bitter critics of their time and nation, most of them piously hated by the contemporary 100 percenters, some of them actually fugitives from rage and reprisal.

Dante put all of the patriotic Italians of his day into Hell, and showed them boiling, roasting and writhing on hooks. Cervantes drew such a devastating picture of the Spain that he lived in that it ruined the Spaniards. Shakespeare made his heroes foreigners and his clowns Englishmen. Goethe was in favor of Napoleon. Rabelais, a citizen of Christendom rather than of France, raised a cackle against it that Christendom is still trying in vain to suppress. Swift, having finished the Irish and then the English, proceeded to finish the whole human race. The exceptions are few and far between, and not many of them will bear examination. So far as I know, the only eminent writer in English history who was also a 100% Englishman, absolutely beyond suspicion, was Samuel Johnson. The Ku Klux of his day gave him a clean bill of health; he was the Roosevelt of the Eighteenth Century. But was Johnson actually an artist? If he was, then a cornet-player is a musician. He employed the materials of one of the arts, to wit, words, but his use of them was hortatory, not artistic. Johnson was the first Rotarian: living today, he would be a United States Senator, or a university president. He left such wounds upon English prose that it was a century recovering from them.

CHIROPRACTIC
(FROM the Baltimore *Evening Sun*, December 1924)

This preposterous quackery flourishes lushly in the back reaches of the Republic, and begins to conquer the less civilized folk of the big cities. As the old-time family doctor dies out in the country towns, with no competent successor willing to take over his dismal business, he is followed by some hearty blacksmith or ice-wagon driver, turned into a chiropractor in six months, often by correspondence. In Los Angeles the Damned there are probably more chiropractors than actual physicians, and they are far more generally esteemed. Proceeding from the Ambassador Hotel to the heart of the town, along Wilshire boulevard, one passes scores of their gaudy signs; there are even many chiropractic "hospitals." The mormons who pour in from the prairies and deserts, most of them ailing, patronize these "hospitals" copiously, and give to the chiropractic pathology the same high respect that they accord to the theology of the town sorcerers. That pathology is grounded upon the doctrine that all human ills are caused by the pressure of misplaced vertebræ upon the nerves which come out of the spinal cord—in other words, that every disease is the result of a pinch. This, plainly enough, is buncombe. The chiropractic therapeutics rest upon the doctrine that the way to get rid of such pinches is to climb upon a table and submit to a heroic pummeling by a retired piano-mover. This, obviously, is buncombe doubly damned.

Both doctrines were launched upon the world by an old quack named Andrew T. Still, the father of osteopathy. For years the osteopaths merchanted them, and made money at the trade. But as they grew opulent they grew ambitious, *i.e.*, they began to study anatomy and physiology. The result was a gradual abandonment of Papa Still's ideas. The high-toned osteopath of today is a sort of eclectic. He tries anything that promises to work, from tonsillectomy to the X-rays. With four years' training behind him, he probably knows more anatomy than the average graduate of the Johns Hopkins Medical School, or at all events, more osteology. Thus enlightened, he seldom has much to say about pinched nerves in the back. But as he abandoned the Still revelation it was seized by the chiropractors, led by another quack, one Palmer. This Palmer grabbed the pinched nerve nonsense and began teaching it to ambitious farm-hands and out-at-elbow Baptist preachers in a few easy lessons. Today the backwoods swarm with chiropractors, and in most States they have been able to exert enough pressure on the rural politicians to get themselves licensed.[1] Any lout with strong hands and arms is perfectly equipped to become a chiropractor. No education beyond the elements is necessary. The takings are often high, and so the profession has attracted thousands of recruits—retired baseball players, work-weary plumbers, truck-drivers, longshoremen, bogus dentists, dubious preachers, cashiered school superintendents. Now and then a quack of some other school—say homeopathy—plunges into it. Hundreds of promising students come from the intellectual ranks of hospital orderlies.

Such quackeries suck in the botched, and help them on to bliss eternal. When these botched fall into the hands of competent medical men they are very likely to be patched up and turned loose upon the world, to beget their kind. But massaged along the backbone to cure their lues, they quickly pass into the last stages,

---

[1] It is not altogether a matter of pressure. Large numbers of rustic legislators are themselves believers in chiropractic. So are many members of Congress.

and so their pathogenic heritage perishes with them. What is too often forgotten is that nature obviously intends the botched to die, and that every interference with that benign process is full of dangers. That the labors of quacks tend to propagate epidemics and so menace the lives of all of us, as is alleged by their medical opponents—this I doubt. The fact is that most infectious diseases of any seriousness throw out such alarming symptoms and so quickly that no sane chiropractor is likely to monkey with them. Seeing his patient breaking out in pustules, or choking, or falling into a stupor, he takes to the woods at once, and leaves the business to the nearest medical man. His trade is mainly with ambulant patients; they must come to his studio for treatment. Most of them have lingering diseases; they tour all the neighborhood doctors before they reach him. His treatment, being nonsensical, is in accord with the divine plan. It is seldom, perhaps, that he actually kills a patient, but at all events he keeps many a worthy soul from getting well.

The osteopaths, I fear, are finding this new competition serious and unpleasant. As I have said, it was their Hippocrates, the late Dr. Still, who invented all of the thrusts, lunges, yanks, hooks and bounces that the lowly chiropractors now employ with such vast effect, and for years the osteopaths had a monopoly of them. But when they began to grow scientific and ambitious their course of training was lengthened until it took in all sorts of tricks and dodges borrowed from the regular doctors, or resurrection men, including the plucking of tonsils, adenoids and appendices, the use of the stomach-pump, and even some of the legerdemain of psychiatry. They now harry their students furiously, and turn them out ready for anything from growing hair on a bald head to frying a patient with the x-rays. All this new striving, of course, quickly brought its inevitable penalties. The osteopathic graduate, having sweated so long, was no longer willing to take a case of delirium tremens for $2, and in consequence he lost patients. Worse, very few aspirants could make the long grade. The essence of osteopathy itself could be grasped by any lively farm-hand or night watchman in a few weeks, but the borrowed magic baffled him. Confronted by the phenomenon of gastrulation, or by the curious behavior of heart muscle, or by any of the current theories of immunity, he commonly took refuge, like his brother of the orthodox faculty, in a gulp of laboratory alcohol, or fled the premises altogether. Thus he was lost to osteopathic science, and the chiropractors took him in; nay, they welcomed him. He was their meat. Borrowing that primitive part of osteopathy which was comprehensible to the meanest understanding, they threw the rest overboard, at the same time denouncing it as a sorcery invented by the Medical Trust. Thus they gathered in the garage mechanics, ash-men and decayed welter-weights, and the land began to fill with their graduates. Now there is a chiropractor at every cross-roads.

I repeat that it eases and soothes me to see them so prosperous, for they counteract the evil work of the so-called science of public hygiene, which now seeks to make imbeciles immortal. If a man, being ill of a pus appendix, resorts to a shaved and fumigated longshoreman to have it disposed of, and submits willingly to a treatment involving balancing him on McBurney's spot and playing on his vertebræ as on a concertina, then I am willing, for one, to believe that he is badly wanted in Heaven. And if that same man, having achieved lawfully a lovely babe, hires a blacksmith to cure its diphtheria by pulling its neck, then I do not resist the divine will that there shall be one less radio fan later on. In such matters, I am convinced, the laws of nature are far better guides than the fiats and machinations of medical busybodies. If the latter gentlemen had their way, death, save at the hands of hangmen, policemen and other such legalized assassins, would be abolished altogether, and the present differential in favor of the enlightened would disappear. I can't convince myself that that would work any good to the world. On the contrary, it seems to me that the current coddling of the half-witted should be stopped before it goes too far —if, indeed, it has not gone too far already. To that end nothing operates more cheaply and effectively than the prosperity of quacks. Every time a bottle of cancer oil goes through the mails *Homo americanus* is improved to that extent. And every time a chiropractor spits on his hands and proceeds to treat a gastric ulcer by stretching the backbone the same high end is achieved.

But chiropractic, of course, is not perfect. It has superb potentialities, but only too often they are not converted into concrete cadavers. The hygienists rescue many of its foreordained customers, and, turning them over to agents of the Medical Trust, maintained at the public expense, get them cured. Moreover, chiropractic itself is not certainly fatal: even an Iowan with diabetes may survive its embraces. Yet worse, I have a suspicion that it sometimes actually cures. For all I know (or any orthodox pathologist seems to know) it *may* be true that certain malaises are caused by the pressure of vagrom vertebræ upon the spinal nerves. And it *may* be true that a hearty ex-boilermaker, by a vigorous yanking and kneading, may be able to relieve that pressure. What is needed is a scientific inquiry into the matter, under rigid test conditions, by a committee of men learned in the architecture and plumbing of the body, and of a high and incorruptible sagacity. Let a thousand patients be selected, let a gang of selected chiropractors examine their backbones and determine what is the matter with them, and then let these diagnoses be checked up by the exact methods of scientific medicine. Then let the same chiropractors essay to cure the patients whose maladies have been determined. My guess is that the chiropractors' errors in diagnosis will run to at least 95% and that their failures in treatment will push 99%. But I am willing to be convinced.

Where is such a committee to be found? I undertake to nominate it at ten minutes' notice. The land swams with men competent in anatomy and pathology, and yet not engaged as doctors. There are thousands of hospitals, with endless clinical material. I offer to supply the committee with cigars and music during the test. I offer, further, to supply both the committee and the chiropractors with sound wet goods. I offer, finally, to give a bawdy banquet to the whole Medical Trust at the conclusion of the proceedings.[2]

THE HILLS OF ZION

(FROM *Prejudices: Fifth Series*. In its first form this was a dispatch to the Baltimore *Evening Sun*, in July 1925. I wrote it on a roaring hot Sunday afternoon in a Chattanooga hotel room, naked above the waist and with only a pair of BVDs below.)

It was hot weather when they tried the infidel Scopes at Dayton, Tenn., but I went down there very willingly, for I was eager to see something of evangelical Christianity as a going concern. In the big cities of the Republic, despite the endless efforts of consecrated men, it is laid up with a wasting disease. The very Sunday-school superintendents, taking jazz from the stealthy radio, shake their fire-proof legs; their

[2] This offer was made in 1927. There were no takers. After World War II the jobholders at Washington, many of them patrons of chiropractic themselves, decided that any veteran who longed to study the science was eligible to receive assistance under the G.I. Bill of Rights. Thus a multitude of fly-by-night chiropractic schools sprang up, and their students were ranked, officially, precisely on all fours with those who studied at Harvard.

pupils, moving into adolescence, no longer respond to the proliferating hormones by enlisting for missionary service in Africa, but resort to necking instead. Even in Dayton, I found, though the mob was up to do execution upon Scopes, there was a strong smell of antinomianism. The nine churches of the village were all half empty on Sunday, and weeds choked their yards. Only two or three of the resident pastors managed to sustain themselves by their ghostly science; the rest had to take orders for mail-order pantaloons or work in the adjacent strawberry fields; one, I heard, was a barber. On the courthouse green a score of sweating theologians debated the darker passages of Holy Writ day and night, but I soon found that they were all volunteers, and that the local faithful, while interested in their exegesis as an intellectual exercise, did not permit it to impede the indigenous debaucheries. Exactly twelve minutes after I reached the village I was taken in tow by a Christian man and introduced to the favorite tipple of the Cumberland Range: half corn liquor and half Coca-Cola. It seemed a dreadful dose to me, but I found that the Dayton illuminati got it down with gusto, rubbing their tummies and rolling their eyes. I include among them the chief local proponents of the Mosaic cosmogony. They were all hot for Genesis, but their faces were far too florid to belong to teetotalers, and when a pretty girl came tripping down the main street, which was very often, they reached for the places where their neckties should have been with all the amorous enterprise of movie actors. It seemed somehow strange.

An amiable newspaper woman of Chattanooga, familiar with those uplands, presently enlightened me. Dayton, she explained, was simply a great capital like any other. That is to say, it was to Rhea county what Atlanta was to Georgia or Paris to France. That is to say, it was predominantly epicurean and sinful. A country girl from some remote valley of the county, coming

into town for her semi-annual bottle of Lydia Pink-
ham's Vegetable Compound, shivered on approaching
Robinson's drug-store quite as a country girl from up-
State New York might shiver on approaching the
Metropolitan Opera House. In every village lout she
saw a potential white-slaver. The hard sidewalks hurt
her feet. Temptations of the flesh bristled to all sides
of her, luring her to Hell. This newspaper woman told
me of a session with just such a visitor, holden a few
days before. The latter waited outside one of the town
hot-dog and Coca-Cola shops while her husband nego-
tiated with a hardware merchant across the street. The
newspaper woman, idling along and observing that the
stranger was badly used by the heat, invited her to step
into the shop for a glass of Coca-Cola. The invitation
brought forth only a gurgle of terror. Coca-Cola, it
quickly appeared, was prohibited by the country lady's
pastor, as a levantine and Hell-sent narcotic. He also
prohibited coffee and tea—and pies! He had his doubts
about white bread and boughten meat. The newspaper
woman, interested, inquired about ice-cream. It was,
she found, not specifically prohibited, but going into a
Coca-Cola shop to get it would be clearly sinful. So she
offered to get a saucer of it, and bring it out to the sidewalk. The visitor vacillated—and came near being lost.
But God saved her in the nick of time. When the newspaper woman emerged from the place she was in full
flight up the street. Later on her husband, mounted on
a mule, overtook her four miles out the mountain pike.

This newspaper woman, whose kindness covered city
infidels as well as Alpine Christians, offered to take me
back in the hills to a place where the old-time religion
was genuinely on tap. The Scopes jury, she explained,
was composed mainly of its customers, with a few Dayton sophisticates added to leaven the mass. It would
thus be instructive to climb the heights and observe the
former at their ceremonies. The trip, fortunately, might
be made by automobile. There was a road running out

of Dayton to Morgantown, in the mountains to the westward, and thence beyond. But foreigners, it appeared, would have to approach the sacred grove cautiously, for the upland worshipers were very shy, and at the first sight of a strange face they would adjourn their orgy and slink into the forest. They were not to be feared, for God had long since forbidden them to practise assassination, or even assault, but if they were alarmed a rough trip would go for naught. So, after dreadful bumpings up a long and narrow road, we parked our car in a little woodpath a mile or two beyond the tiny village of Morgantown, and made the rest of the approach on foot, deployed like skirmishers. Far off in a dark, romantic glade a flickering light was visible, and out of the silence came the rumble of exhortation. We could distinguish the figure of the preacher only as a moving mote in the light: it was like looking down the tube of a dark-field microscope. Slowly and cautiously we crossed what seemed to be a pasture, and then we stealthily edged further and further. The light now grew larger and we could begin to make out what was going on. We went ahead on all fours, like snakes in the grass.

From the great limb of a mighty oak hung a couple of crude torches of the sort that car inspectors thrust under Pullman cars when a train pulls in at night. In the guttering glare was the preacher, and for a while we could see no one else. He was an immensely tall and thin mountaineer in blue jeans, his collarless shirt open at the neck and his hair a tousled mop. As he preached he paced up and down under the smoking flambeaux, and at each turn he thrust his arms into the air and yelled "Glory to God!" We crept nearer in the shadow of the cornfield, and began to hear more of his discourse. He was preaching on the Day of Judgment. The high kings of the earth, he roared, would all fall down and die; only the sanctified would stand up to receive the Lord God of Hosts. One of these kings he mentioned by name, the king of what he called Greece-y.[1] The king of Greece-y, he said, was doomed to Hell. We crawled forward a few more yards and began to see the audience. It was seated on benches ranged round the preacher in a circle. Behind him sat a row of elders, men and women. In front were the younger folk. We crept on cautiously, and individuals rose out of the ghostly gloom. A young mother sat suckling her baby, rocking as the preacher paced up and down. Two scared little girls hugged each other, their pigtails down their backs. An immensely huge mountain woman, in a gingham dress, cut in one piece, rolled on her heels at every "Glory to God!" To one side, and but half visible, was what appeared to be a bed. We found afterward that half a dozen babies were asleep upon it.

The preacher stopped at last, and there arose out of the darkness a woman with her hair pulled back into a little tight knot. She began so quietly that we couldn't hear what she said, but soon her voice rose resonantly and we could follow her. She was denouncing the reading of books. Some wandering book agent, it appeared, had come to her cabin and tried to sell her a specimen of his wares. She refused to touch it. Why, indeed, read a book? If what was in it was true, then everything in it was already in the Bible. If it was false, then reading it would imperil the soul. This syllogism from the Caliph Omar complete, she sat down. There followed a hymn, led by a somewhat fat brother wearing silver-rimmed country spectacles. It droned on for half a dozen stanzas, and then the first speaker resumed the floor. He argued that the gift of tongues was real and that education was a snare. Once his children could read the Bible, he said, they had enough. Beyond lay only infidelity and damnation. Sin stalked the cities. Dayton itself was a Sodom. Even Morgantown had begun to forget God. He sat down, and a female aurochs in

[1] Grecia? *Cf.* Daniel viii, 21.

157

gingham got up. She began quietly, but was soon leaping and roaring, and it was hard to follow her. Under cover of the turmoil we sneaked a bit closer.

A couple of other discourses followed, and there were two or three hymns. Suddenly a change of mood began to make itself felt. The last hymn ran longer than the others, and dropped gradually into a monotonous, unintelligible chant. The leader beat time with his book. The faithful broke out with exultations. When the singing ended there was a brief palaver that we could not hear, and two of the men moved a bench into the circle of light directly under the flambeaux. Then a half-grown girl emerged from the darkness and threw herself upon it. We noticed with astonishment that she had bobbed hair. "This sister," said the leader, "has asked for prayers." We moved a bit closer. We could now see faces plainly, and hear every word. At a signal all the faithful crowded up to the bench and began to pray—not in unison, but each for himself. At another they all fell on their knees, their arms over the penitent. The leader kneeled facing us, his head alternately thrown back dramatically or buried in his hands. Words spouted from his lips like bullets from a machine-gun—appeals to God to pull the penitent back out of Hell, defiances of the demons of the air, a vast impassioned jargon of apocalyptic texts. Suddenly he rose to his feet, threw back his head and began to speak in the tongues[2]—blub-blub-blub, gurgle-gurgle-gurgle. His voice rose to a higher register. The climax was a shrill, inarticulate squawk, like that of a man throttled. He fell headlong across the pyramid of supplicants.

From the squirming and jabbering mass a young woman gradually detached herself—a woman not uncomely, with a pathetic homemade cap on her head. Her head jerked back, the veins of her neck swelled, and her fists went to her throat as if she were fighting for breath. She bent backward until she was like half a

[2] Mark xvi, 17.

hoop. Then she suddenly snapped forward. We caught a flash of the whites of her eyes. Presently her whole body began to be convulsed—great throes that began at the shoulders and ended at the hips. She would leap to her feet, thrust her arms in air, and then hurl herself upon the heap. Her praying flattened out into a mere delirious caterwauling. I describe the thing discreetly, and as a strict behaviorist. The lady's subjective sensations I leave to infidel pathologists, privy to the works of Ellis, Freud and Moll. Whatever they were, they were obviously not painful, for they were accompanied by vast heavings and gurglings of a joyful and even ecstatic nature. And they seemed to be contagious, too, for soon a second penitent, also female, joined the first, and then came a third, and a fourth, and a fifth. The last one had an extraordinary violent attack. She began with mild enough jerks of the head, but in a moment she was bounding all over the place, like a chicken with its head cut off. Every time her head came up a stream of hosannas would issue out of it. Once she collided with a dark, undersized brother, hitherto silent and stolid. Contact with her set him off as if he had been kicked by a mule. He leaped into the air, threw back his head, and began to gargle as if with a mouthful of BB shot. Then he loosed one tremendous, stentorian sentence in the tongues, and collapsed.

By this time the performers were quite oblivious to the profane universe and so it was safe to go still closer. We left our hiding and came up to the little circle of light. We slipped into the vacant seats on one of the rickety benches. The heap of mourners was directly before us. They bounced into us as they cavorted. The smell that they radiated, sweating there in that obscene heap, half suffocated us. Not all of them, of course, did the thing in the grand manner. Some merely moaned and rolled their eyes. The female ox in gingham flung her great bulk on the ground and jabbered an unintelligible prayer. One of the men, in the intervals between fits, put on his spectacles and read his Bible. Beside me on the bench sat the young mother and her baby. She suckled it through the whole orgy, obviously fascinated by what was going on, but never venturing to take any hand in it. On the bed just outside the light the half a dozen other babies slept peacefully. In the shadows, suddenly appearing and as suddenly going away, were vague figures, whether of believers or of scoffers I do not know. They seemed to come and go in couples. Now and then a couple at the ringside would step out and vanish into the black night. After a while some came back, the males looking somewhat sheepish. There was whispering outside the circle of vision. A couple of Model T Fords lurched up the road, cutting holes in the darkness with their lights. Once someone out of sight loosed a bray of laughter.

All this went on for an hour or so. The original penitent, by this time, was buried three deep beneath the heap. One caught a glimpse, now and then, of her yellow bobbed hair, but then she would vanish again. How she breathed down there I don't know; it was hard enough six feet away, with a strong five-cent cigar to help. When the praying brothers would rise up for a bout with the tongues their faces were streaming with perspiration. The fat harridan in gingham sweated like a longshoreman. Her hair got loose and fell down over her face. She fanned herself with her skirt. A powerful old gal she was, plainly equal in her day to a bout with obstetrics and a week's washing on the same morning, but this was worse than a week's washing. Finally, she fell into a heap, breathing in great, convulsive gasps.

Finally, we got tired of the show and returned to Dayton. It was nearly eleven o'clock—an immensely late hour for those latitudes—but the whole town was still gathered in the courthouse yard, listening to the disputes of theologians. The Scopes trial had brought them in from all directions. There was a friar wearing a sandwich sign announcing that he was the Bible

champion of the world. There was a Seventh Day
Adventist arguing that Clarence Darrow was the beast
with seven heads and ten horns described in Revelation XIII, and that the end of the world was at hand.
There was an evangelist made up like Andy Gump,
with the news that atheists in Cincinnati were preparing to descend upon Dayton, hang the eminent Judge
Raulston, and burn the town. There was an ancient
who maintained that no Catholic could be a Christian.
There was the eloquent Dr. T. T. Martin, of Blue
Mountain, Miss., come to town with a truck-load of
torches and hymn-books to put Darwin in his place.
There was a singing brother bellowing apocalyptic
hymns. There was William Jennings Bryan, followed
everywhere by a gaping crowd. Dayton was having a
roaring time. It was better than the circus. But the
note of devotion was simply not there; the Daytonians,
after listening a while, would slip away to Robinson's
drug-store to regale themselves with Coca-Cola, or to
the lobby of the Aqua Hotel, where the learned Raulston sat in state, judicially picking his teeth. The real
religion was not present. It began at the bridge over
the town creek, where the road makes off for the hills.

IN MEMORIAM: W. J. B.

(FROM *Prejudices: Fifth Series.* In its first form this was printed in the
Baltimore *Evening Sun*, July 27, 1925, the day after Bryan's death at
Dayton, Tenn. I reworked it for the *American Mercury*, Oct., 1925.
My adventures as a newspaper correspondent at the Scopes trial are
told in my *Heathen Days*.)

Has it been duly marked by historians that
William Jennings Bryan's last secular act on this globe
of sin was to catch flies? A curious detail, and not

without its sardonic overtones. He was the most sedulous fly-catcher in American history, and in many ways
the most successful. His quarry, of course, was not
Musca domestica but *Homo neandertalensis*. For forty
years he tracked it with coo and bellow, up and down
the rustic backways of the Republic. Wherever the flambeaux of Chautauqua smoked and guttered, and the
bilge of idealism ran in the veins, and Baptist pastors
dammed the brooks with the sanctified, and men gathered who were weary and heavy laden, and their wives
who were full of Peruna and as fecund as the shad
(*Alosa sapidissima*), there the indefatigable Jennings
set up his traps and spread his bait. He knew every
country town in the South and West, and he could
crowd the most remote of them to suffocation by simply winding his horn. The city proletariat, transiently
flustered by him in 1896, quickly penetrated his buncombe and would have no more of him; the cockney
gallery jeered him at every Democratic national convention for twenty-five years. But out where the grass
grows high, and the horned cattle dream away the lazy
afternoons, and men still fear the powers and principal-
ities of the air—out there between the corn-rows he
held his old puissance to the end. There was no need
of beaters to drive in his game. The news that he was
coming was enough. For miles the flivver dust would
choke the roads. And when he rose at the end of the
day to discharge his Message there would be such
breathless attention, such a rapt and enchanted ecstasy,
such a sweet rustle of amens as the world had not
known since Johann fell to Herod's ax.

There was something peculiarly fitting in the fact
that his last days were spent in a one-horse Tennessee
village, beating off the flies and gnats, and that death
found him there. The man felt at home in such simple
and Christian scenes. He liked people who sweated
freely, and were not debauched by the refinements of
the toilet. Making his progress up and down the Main

street of little Dayton, surrounded by gaping primates from the upland valleys of the Cumberland Range, his coat laid aside, his bare arms and hairy chest shining damply, his bald head sprinkled with dust—so accoutred and on display, he was obviously happy. He liked getting up early in the morning, to the tune of cocks crowing on the dunghill. He liked the heavy, greasy victuals of the farmhouse kitchen. He liked country lawyers, country pastors, all country people. He liked country sounds and country smells.

I believe that this liking was sincere—perhaps the only sincere thing in the man. His nose showed no uneasiness when a hillman in faded overalls and hickory shirt accosted him on the street, and besought him for light upon some mystery of Holy Writ. The simian gabble of the cross-roads was not gabble to him, but wisdom of an occult and superior sort. In the presence of city folks he was palpably uneasy. Their clothes, I suspect, annoyed him, and he was suspicious of their too delicate manners. He knew all the while that they were laughing at him—if not at his baroque theology, then at least at his alpaca pantaloons. But the yokels never laughed at him. To them he was not the huntsman but the prophet, and toward the end, as he gradually forsook mundane politics for more ghostly concerns, they began to elevate him in their hierarchy. When he died he was the peer of Abraham. His old enemy, Wilson, aspiring to the same white and shining robe, came down with a thump. But Bryan made the grade. His place in Tennessee hagiography is secure. If the village barber saved any of his hair, then it is curing gall-stones down there today.

But what label will he bear in more urbane regions? One, I fear, of a far less flattering kind. Bryan lived too long, and descended too deeply into the mud, to be taken seriously hereafter by fully literate men, even of the kind who write schoolbooks. There was a scattering of sweet words in his funeral notices, but it was no more than a response to conventional sentimentality. The best verdict the most romantic editorial writer could dredge up, save in the humorless South, was to the general effect that his imbecilities were excused by his earnestness—that under his clowning, as under that of the juggler of Notre Dame, there was the zeal of a steadfast soul. But this was apology, not praise; precisely the same thing might be said of Mary Baker G. Eddy. The truth is that even Bryan's sincerity will probably yield to what is called, in other fields, definitive criticism. Was he sincere when he opposed imperialism in the Philippines, or when he fed it with deserving Democrats in Santo Domingo? Was he sincere when he tried to shove the Prohibitionists under the table, or when he seized their banner and began to lead them with loud whoops? Was he sincere when he bellowed against war, or when he dreamed of himself as a tin-soldier in uniform, with a grave reserved at Arlington among the generals? Was he sincere when he fawned over Champ Clark, or when he betrayed Clark? Was he sincere when he pleaded for tolerance in New York, or when he bawled for the faggot and the stake in Tennessee?

This talk of sincerity, I confess, fatigues me. If the fellow was sincere, then so was P. T. Barnum. The word is disgraced and degraded by such uses. He was, in fact, a charlatan, a mountebank, a zany without sense or dignity. His career brought him into contact with the first men of his time; he preferred the company of rustic ignoramuses. It was hard to believe, watching him at Dayton, that he had traveled, that he had been received in civilized societies, that he had been a high officer of state. He seemed only a poor clod like those around him, deluded by a childish theology, full of an almost pathological hatred of all learning, all human dignity, all beauty, all fine and noble things. He was a peasant come home to the barnyard. Imagine a gentleman, and you have imagined everything that he was not. What animated him from end to end of his grotesque career was simply ambition—the ambition of a common man to get his hand upon the collar of his superiors, or, failing that, to get his thumb into their eyes. He was born with a roaring voice, and it had the trick of inflaming half-wits. His whole career was devoted to raising those half-wits against their betters, that he himself might shine.

His last battle will be grossly misunderstood if it is thought of as a mere exercise in fanaticism—that is, if Bryan the Fundamentalist Pope is mistaken for one of the bucolic Fundamentalists. There was much more in it than that, as everyone knows who saw him on the field. What moved him, at bottom, was simply hatred of the city men who had laughed at him so long, and brought him at last to so tatterdemalion an estate. He lusted for revenge upon them. He yearned to lead the anthropoid rabble against them, to punish them for their execution upon him by attacking the very vitals of their civilization. He went far beyond the bounds of any merely religious frenzy, however inordinate. When he began denouncing the notion that man is a mammal even some of the hinds at Dayton were agape. And when, brought upon Clarence Darrow's cruel hook, he writhed and tossed in a very fury of malignancy, bawling against the veriest elements of sense and decency like a man frantic—when he came to that tragic climax of his striving there were snickers among the hinds as well as hosannas.

Upon that hook, in truth, Bryan committed suicide, as a legend as well as in the body. He staggered from the rustic court ready to die, and he staggered from it ready to be forgotten, save as a character in a third-rate farce, witless and in poor taste. It was plain to everyone who knew him, when he came to Dayton, that his great days were behind him—that, for all the fury of his hatred, he was now definitely an old man, and headed at last for silence. There was a vague, unpleasant manginess about his appearance; he somehow seemed dirty, though a close glance showed him as carefully shaven as an actor, and clad in immaculate linen. All the hair was gone from the dome of his head, and it had begun to fall out, too, behind his ears, in the obscene manner of Samuel Gompers. The resonance had departed from his voice; what was once a bugle blast had become reedy and quavering. Who knows that, like Demosthenes, he had a lisp? In the old days, under the magic of his eloquence, no one noticed it. But when he spoke at Dayton it was always audible.

When I first encountered him, on the sidewalk in front of the office of the rustic lawyers who were his associates in the Scopes case, the trial was yet to begin, and so he was still expansive and amiable. I had printed in the *Nation,* a week or so before, an article arguing that the Tennessee anti-evolution law, whatever its wisdom, was at least constitutional—that the yahoos of the State had a clear right to have their progeny taught whatever they chose, and kept secure from whatever knowledge violated their superstitions. The old boy professed to be delighted with the argument, and gave the gaping bystanders to understand that I was a publicist of parts. Not to be outdone, I admired the preposterous country shirt that he wore—sleeveless and with the neck cut very low. We parted in the manner of two ambassadors.

But that was the last touch of amiability that I was destined to see in Bryan. The next day the battle joined and his face became hard. By the end of the week he was simply a walking fever. Hour by hour he grew more bitter. What the Christian Scientists call malicious animal magnetism seemed to radiate from him like heat from a stove. From my place in the courtroom, standing upon a table, I looked directly down upon him, sweating horribly and pumping his palm-leaf fan. His eyes fascinated me; I watched them all day long. They were blazing points of hatred. They glittered like occult and sinister gems. Now and then they wandered to me, and I got my share, for my reports of the trial had come back to Dayton, and he had read them. It was like coming under fire.

Thus he fought his last fight, thirsting savagely for blood. All sense departed from him. He bit right and left, like a dog with rabies. He descended to demagogy so dreadful that his very associates at the trial table blushed. His one yearning was to keep his yokels heated up—to lead his forlorn mob of imbeciles against the foe. That foe, alas, refused to be alarmed. It insisted upon seeing the whole battle as a comedy. Even Darrow, who knew better, occasionally yielded to the prevailing spirit. One day he lured poor Bryan into the folly I have mentioned: his astounding argument against the notion that man is a mammal. I am glad I heard it, for otherwise I'd never believe it. There stood the man who had been thrice a candidate for the Presidency of the Republic—there he stood in the glare of the world, uttering stuff that a boy of eight would laugh at. The artful Darrow led him on: he repeated it, ranted for it, bellowed it in his cracked voice. So he was prepared for the final slaughter. He came into life a hero, a Galahad, in bright and shining armor. He was passing out a poor mountebank.

★

THE AUTHOR AT WORK
(FROM *Prejudices: Sixth Series*, 1926)

★

If authors could work in large, well-ventilated factories, like cigarmakers or garment-workers, with plenty of their mates about and a flow of lively professional gossip to entertain them, their labor would be immensely lighter. But it is essential to their craft that they perform its tedious and vexatious operations *a cappella,* and so the horrors of loneliness are added to stenosis and their other professional infirmities. An author at work is continuously and inescapably in the presence of himself. There is nothing to divert and soothe him. Every time a vagrant regret or sorrow assails him, it has him instantly by the ear, and every time a wandering ache runs down his leg it shakes him like the bite of a tiger. I have yet to meet an author who was not a hypochondriac. Saving only medical men, who are always ill and in fear of death, the literati are perhaps the most lavish consumers of pills and philtres in this world, and the most assiduous customers of surgeons. I can scarcely think of one, known to me personally, who is not constantly dosing himself with medicines, or regularly resorting to the knife.

It must be obvious that other men, even among the intelligentsia, are not beset so cruelly. A judge on the bench, entertaining a ringing in the ears, can do his work quite as well as if he heard only the voluptuous rhetoric of the lawyers. A clergyman, carrying on his mummery, is not appreciably crippled by a sour stomach: what he says has been said before, and only scoundrels question it. And a surgeon, plying his exhilarating art and mystery, suffers no professional damage from the wild thought that the attending nurse is more sightly than his wife. But I defy anyone to write a competent sonnet with a ringing in his ears, or to compose sound criticism with a sour stomach, or to do a plausible love scene with a head full of private amorous fancies. These things are sheer impossibilities. The poor literatus encounters them and their like every time he enters his work-room and spits on his hands. The moment the door bangs he begins a depressing, losing struggle with his body and his mind.

Why then, do rational men and women engage in so barbarous and exhausting a vocation—for there are relatively intelligent and enlightened authors, remember, just as there are relatively honest politicians, and even bishops. What keeps them from deserting it for trades that are less onerous, and, in the eyes of their fellow creatures, more respectable? One reason, I believe, is that an author, like any other so-called artist, is a man in whom the normal vanity of all men is so vastly exaggerated that he finds it a sheer impossibility to hold it in. His overpowering impulse is to gyrate before his fellow men, flapping his wings and emitting defiant yells. This being forbidden by the police of all civilized countries, he takes it out by putting his yells on paper. Such is the thing called self-expression.

In the confidences of the literati, of course, it is always depicted as something much more mellow and virtuous. Either they argue that they are moved by a yearning to spread the enlightenment and save the world, or they allege that what steams them and makes them leap is a passion for beauty. Both theories are quickly disposed of by an appeal to the facts. The stuff written by nine authors out of ten, it must be plain at a glance, has as little to do with spreading the enlightenment as the state papers of the late Chester A. Arthur. And there is no more beauty in it, and no more sign of a feeling of beauty, than you will find in the décor of a night-club. The impulse to create beauty, indeed, is rather rare in literary men, and almost completely absent from the younger ones. If it shows itself at all, it comes as a sort of afterthought. Far ahead of it comes the yearning to make money. And after the yearning to make money comes the yearning to make a noise. The impulse to create beauty lingers far behind. Authors, as a class, are extraordinarily insensitive to it, and the fact reveals itself in their customary (and often incredibly extensive) ignorance of the other arts. I'd have a hard job naming six American novelists who could be depended upon to recognize a fugue without prompting, or six poets who could give a rational account of the difference between a Gothic cathedral and a Standard Oil filling-station.

The thing goes even further. Most novelists, in my experience, know nothing of poetry, and very few poets have any feeling for the beauties of prose. As for the dramatists, three-fourths of them are unaware that such things as prose and poetry exist at all. It pains me to set down such inconvenient and blushful facts. If they ought to be concealed, then blame my babbling upon scientific passion. That passion, today, has me by the ear.

VALENTINO

(FROM *Prejudices: Sixth Series*. Valentino died August 23, 1926. This piece first appeared in the Baltimore *Evening Sun*, August 30, 1926.)

By one of the chances that relieve the dullness of life and make it instructive, I had the honor of dining with this celebrated gentleman in New York, a week or so before his fatal illness. I had never met him before, nor seen him on the screen; the meeting was at his instance, and, when it was proposed, vaguely puzzled me. But soon its purpose became clear enough. Valentino was in trouble and wanted advice. More, he wanted advice from an elder and disinterested man, wholly removed from the movies and all their works. Something that I had written, falling under his eye, had given him the notion that I was a judicious fellow. So he requested one of his colleagues, a lady of the films, to ask me to dinner at her hotel.

The night being infernally warm, we stripped off our coats, and came to terms at once. I recall that he wore suspenders of extraordinary width and thickness. On so slim a young man they seemed somehow absurd, especially on a hot Summer night. We perspired horribly for an hour, mopping our faces with our handkerchiefs, the table napkins, the corners of the tablecloth, and a couple of towels brought in by the humane waiter. Then there came a thunderstorm, and we began to breathe. The hostess, a woman as tactful as she is charming, disappeared mysteriously and left us to commune.

The trouble that was agitating Valentino turned out to be very simple. The ribald New York papers were full of it, and that was what was agitating him. Some time before, out in Chicago, a wandering reporter had discovered, in the men's wash-room of a gaudy hotel, a slot-machine selling talcum-powder. That, of course, was not unusual, but the color of the talcum-powder was. It was pink. The news made the town giggle for a day, and inspired an editorial writer on the Chicago *Tribune* to compose a hot weather editorial. In it he protested humorously against the effeminization of the American man, and laid it lightheartedly to the influence of Valentino and his sheik movies. Well, it so happened that Valentino, passing through Chicago that day on his way east from the Coast, ran full tilt into the editorial, and into a gang of reporters who wanted to know what he had to say about it. What he had to say was full of fire. Throwing off his 100% Americanism and reverting to the *mores* of his fatherland, he challenged the editorial writer to a duel, and, when no answer came, to a fist fight. His masculine honor, it appeared, had been outraged. To the hint that he was less than he, even to the extent of one half of one per cent, there could be no answer save a bath of blood.

Unluckily, all this took place in the United States, where the word honor, save when it is applied to the structural integrity of women, has only a comic significance. When one hears of the honor of politicians, of bankers, of lawyers, of the United States itself, everyone naturally laughs. So New York laughed at Valentino. More, it ascribed his high dudgeon to mere publicity-seeking: he seemed a vulgar movie ham seeking space. The poor fellow, thus doubly beset, rose to dudgeons higher still. His Italian mind was simply unequal to the situation. So he sought counsel from the neutral, aloof and seasoned. Unluckily, I could only name the disease, and confess frankly that there was no remedy— none, that is, known to any therapeutics within my ken. He should have passed over the gibe of the Chicago journalist, I suggested, with a lofty snort—perhaps, better still, with a counter gibe. He should have kept away from the reporters in New York. But now, alas, the mischief was done. He was both insulted and ridiculous, but there was nothing to do about it. I advised him to let the dreadful farce roll along to exhaustion. He protested that it was infamous. Infamous? Nothing, I argued, is infamous that is not true. A man still has his inner integrity. Can he still look into the shaving-glass of a morning? Then he is still on his two legs in this world, and ready even for the Devil. We sweated a great deal, discussing these lofty matters. We seemed to get nowhere.

Suddenly it dawned upon me—I was too dull or it was too hot for me to see it sooner—that what we were talking about was really not what we were talking about at all. I began to observe Valentino more closely. A curiously naïve and boyish young fellow, certainly not much beyond thirty, and with a disarming air of inexperience. To my eye, at least, not handsome, but nevertheless rather attractive. There was some obvious fineness in him; even his clothes were not precisely those of his horrible trade. He began talking of his home, his people, his early youth. His words were simple and yet somehow very eloquent. I could still see the mime before me, but now and then, briefly and darkly, there was a flash of something else. That something else, I concluded, was what is commonly called, for want of a better name, a gentleman. In brief, Valentino's agony was the agony of a man of relatively civilized feelings thrown into a situation of intolerable vulgarity, destructive alike to his peace and to his dignity —nay, into a whole series of such situations.

It was not that trifling Chicago episode that was riding him; it was the whole grotesque futility of his life. Had he achieved, out of nothing, a vast and dizzy success? Then that success was hollow as well as vast—a colossal and preposterous nothing. Was he acclaimed by yelling multitudes? Then every time the multitudes yelled he felt himself blushing inside. The old story of Diego Valdez once more, but with a new poignancy in it. Valdez, at all events, was High Admiral of Spain. But Valentino, with his touch of fineness in him—he had his commonness, too, but there was that touch of fineness—Valentino was only the hero of the rabble. Imbeciles surrounded him in a dense herd. He was pursued by women—but what women! (Consider the sordid comedy of his two marriages—the brummagem, star-spangled passion that invaded his very deathbed!) The thing, at the start, must have only bewildered him. But in those last days, unless I am a worse psychologist than even the professors of psychology, it was revolting him. Worse, it was making him afraid.

I incline to think that the inscrutable gods, in taking him off so soon and at a moment of fiery revolt, were very kind to him. Living, he would have tried inevitably to change his fame—if such it is to be called—into something closer to his heart's desire. That is to say, he would have gone the way of many another actor—the way of increasing pretension, of solemn artiness, of hollow hocus-pocus, deceptive only to himself. I believe he would have failed, for there was little sign of the genuine artist in him. He was essentially a highly respectable young man, which is the sort that never metamorphoses into an artist. But suppose he had succeeded? Then his tragedy, I believe, would have only become the more acrid and intolerable. For he would have discovered, after vast heavings and yearnings, that what he had come to was indistinguishable from what he had left. Was the fame of Beethoven any more caressing and splendid than the fame of Valentino? To you and me, of course, the question seems to answer itself. But what of Beethoven? He was heard upon the subject, *viva voce*, while he lived, and his answer survives, in all the freshness of its profane eloquence, in his music. Beethoven, too, knew what it meant to be applauded. Walking with Goethe, he heard something that was not unlike the murmur that reached Valentino through his hospital window. Beethoven walked away briskly. Valentino turned his face to the wall.

Here was a young man who was living daily the dream of millions of other young men. Here was one who was catnip to women. Here was one who had wealth and fame. And here was one who was very unhappy.

A GLANCE AHEAD
(FROM *Notes on Democracy*, 1926)

★

For all I know, democracy may be a self-limiting disease, as civilization itself seems to be. There are thumping paradoxes in its philosophy, and some of them have a suicidal smack. It offers John Doe a means to rise above his place beside Richard Roe, and then, by making Roe his equal, it takes away the chief usufructs of the rising. I here attempt no pretty logical gymnastics: the history of democratic states is a history of disingenuous efforts to get rid of the second half of that dilemma. There is not only the natural yearning of Doe to use and enjoy the superiority that he has won; there is also the natural tendency of Roe, as an inferior man, to acknowledge it. Democracy, in fact, is always inventing class distinctions, despite its theoretical abhorrence of them. The baron has departed, but in his place stand the grand goblin, the supreme worthy archon, the sovereign grand commander. Democratic man is quite unable to think of himself as a free individual; he must belong to a group, or shake with fear and loneliness—and the group, of course, must have its leaders. It would be hard to find a country in which such brummagem serene highnesses are revered with more passionate devotion than they get in the United States. The distinction that goes with mere office runs far ahead of the distinction that goes with actual achievement. A Harding is regarded as superior to a Halsted, no doubt because his doings are better understood.

But there is a form of human striving that is understood by democratic man even better than Harding's, and that is the striving for money. Thus the plutocracy, in a democratic state, tends inevitably, despite its theoretical infamy, to take the place of the missing aristocracy, and even to be mistaken for it. It is, of course, something quite different. It lacks all the essential characters of a true aristocracy: a clean tradition, culture, public spirit, honesty, honor, courage—above all, courage. It stands under no bond of obligation to the state; it has no public duty; it is transient and lacks a goal. Its most puissant dignitaries of today came out of the mob only yesterday—and from the mob they bring all its peculiar ignobilities. As practically encountered, the plutocracy stands quite as far from the *honnête homme* as it stands from the holy saints. Its main character is its incurable timorousness; it is for ever grasping at the straws held out by demagogues. Half a dozen gabby Jewish youths, meeting in a back room to plan a revolution—in other words, half a dozen kittens preparing to upset the Matterhorn—are enough to scare it half to death. Its dreams are of banshees, hobgoblins, bugaboos. The honest, untroubled snores of a Percy or a Hohenstaufen are quite beyond it.

The plutocracy is comprehensible to the mob because its aspirations are essentially those of inferior men: it is not by accident that Christianity, a mob religion, paves heaven with gold and precious stones, *i.e.*, with money. There are, of course, reactions against this ignoble ideal among men of more civilized tastes, even in democratic states, and sometimes they arouse the mob to a transient distrust of certain of the plutocratic pretensions. But that distrust seldom arises above mere envy, and the polemic which engenders it is seldom sound in logic or impeccable in motive. What it lacks is aristocratic disinterestedness, born of aristocratic security. There is no body of opinion behind it that is, in the strictest sense, a free opinion. Its chief exponents, by some divine irony, are pedagogues of one sort or another—which is to say, men chiefly marked by their haunting fear of losing their jobs. Living under such terrors, with the plutocracy policing them harshly on one side and the mob congenitally suspicious of them on the other, it is no wonder that their revolt usually peters out in metaphysics, and that they tend to abandon it as their families grow up, and the costs of heresy become prohibitive. The pedagogue, in the long run, shows the virtues of the Congressman, the newspaper editorial writer or the butler, not those of the aristocrat. When, by any chance, he persists in contumacy beyond thirty, it is only too commonly a sign, not that he is heroic, but simply that he is pathological. So with most of his brethren of the Utopian Fife and Drum Corps, whether they issue out of his own seminary or out of the wilderness. They are fanatics; not statesmen. Thus politics, under democracy, resolves itself into impossible alternatives. Whatever the label on the parties, or the war cries issuing from the demagogues who lead them, the practical choice is between the plutocracy on the one side and a rabble of preposterous impossibilists on the other. It is a pity that this is so. For what democracy needs most of all is a party that will separate the good that is in it theoretically from the evils that beset it practically, and then try to erect that good into a workable system. What it needs beyond everything is a party of liberty. It produces, true enough, occasional libertarians, just as despotism produces occasional regicides, but it treats them in the same drumhead way. It will never have a party of them until it invents and installs a genuine aristocracy, to breed them and secure them.

★

THE LIBIDO FOR THE UGLY

(FROM *Prejudices: Sixth Series*, 1927)

On a Winter day some years ago, coming out of Pittsburgh on one of the expresses of the Pennsylvania Railroad, I rolled eastward for an hour through the coal and steel towns of Westmoreland county. It was familiar ground; boy and man, I had been through it often before. But somehow I had never quite sensed its appalling desolation. Here was the very heart of industrial America, the center of its most lucrative and characteristic activity, the boast and pride of the richest and grandest nation ever seen on earth—and here was a scene so dreadfully hideous, so intolerably bleak and forlorn that it reduced the whole aspiration of man to a macabre and depressing joke. Here was wealth beyond computation, almost beyond imagination—and here were human habitations so abominable that they would have disgraced a race of alley cats.

I am not speaking of mere filth. One expects steel towns to be dirty. What I allude to is the unbroken and agonizing ugliness, the sheer revolting monstrousness, of every house in sight. From East Liberty to Greensburg, a distance of twenty-five miles, there was not one in sight from the train that did not insult and lacerate the eye. Some were so bad, and they were among the most pretentious—churches, stores, warehouses, and the like—that they were downright startling; one blinked before them as one blinks before a man with his face shot away. A few linger in memory, horrible even there: a crazy little church just west of Jeannette, set like a dormer-window on the side of a bare, leprous hill; the headquarters of the Veterans of Foreign Wars at another forlorn town, a steel stadium like a huge rat-trap somewhere further down the line. But most of all I recall the general effect—of hideousness without a break. There was not a single decent house within eye-range from the Pittsburgh suburbs to the Greensburg yards. There was not one that was not misshapen, and there was not one that was not shabby.

The country itself is not uncomely, despite the grime of the endless mills. It is, in form, a narrow river valley, with deep gullies running up into the hills. It is thickly settled, but not noticeably overcrowded. There is still plenty of room for building, even in the larger towns, and there are very few solid blocks. Nearly every house, big and little, has space on all four sides. Obviously, if there were architects of any professional sense or dignity in the region, they would have perfected a chalet to hug the hillsides—a chalet with a high-pitched roof, to throw off the heavy Winter snows, but still essentially a low and clinging building, wider than it was tall. But what have they done? They have taken as their model a brick set on end. This they have converted into a thing of dingy clapboards, with a narrow, low-pitched roof. And the whole they have set upon thin, preposterous brick piers. By the hundreds and thousands these abominable houses cover the bare hillsides, like gravestones in some gigantic and decaying cemetery. On their deep sides they are three, four and even five stories high; on their low sides they bury themselves swinishly in the mud. Not a fifth of them are perpendicular. They lean this way and that, hanging on to their bases precariously. And one and all they are streaked in grime, with dead and eczematous patches of paint peeping through the streaks.

Now and then there is a house of brick. But what brick! When it is new it is the color of a fried egg. When it has taken on the patina of the mills it is the color of an egg long past all hope or caring. Was it necessary to adopt that shocking color? No more than it was necessary to set all of the houses on end. Red brick, even in a steel town, ages with some dignity. Let it become downright black, and it is still sightly, especially if its trimmings are of white stone, with soot in the depths and the high spots washed by the rain. But in Westmoreland they prefer that uremic yellow, and so they have the most loathsome towns and villages ever seen by mortal eye.

I award this championship only after laborious research and incessant prayer. I have seen, I believe, all of the most unlovely towns of the world; they are all to be found in the United States. I have seen the mill towns of decomposing New England and the desert towns of Utah, Arizona and Texas. I am familiar with the back streets of Newark, Brooklyn and Chicago, and have made scientific explorations to Camden, N.J. and Newport News, Va. Safe in a Pullman, I have whirled through the gloomy, God-forsaken villages of Iowa and Kansas, and the malarious tide-water hamlets of Georgia. I have been to Bridgeport, Conn., and to Los Angeles. But nowhere on this earth, at home or abroad, have I seen anything to compare to the villages that huddle along the line of the Pennsylvania from the Pittsburgh yards to Greensburg. They are incomparable in color, and they are incomparable in design. It is as if some titanic and aberrant genius, uncompromisingly inimical to man, had devoted all the ingenuity of Hell to the making of them. They show grotesqueries of ugliness that, in retrospect, become almost diabolical. One cannot imagine mere human beings concocting such dreadful things, and one can scarcely imagine human beings bearing life in them.

Are they so frightful because the valley is full of foreigners—dull, insensate brutes, with no love of beauty in them? Then why didn't these foreigners set up similar abominations in the countries that they came from? You will, in fact, find nothing of the sort in Europe—save perhaps in the more putrid parts of England. There is scarcely an ugly village on the whole Continent. The peasants, however poor, somehow manage to make themselves graceful and charming habitations, even in Spain. But in the American village and small town the pull is always toward ugliness, and in that Westmoreland valley it has been yielded to with an eagerness bordering upon passion. It is incredible that mere ignorance should have achieved such masterpieces of horror.

On certain levels of the American race, indeed, there seems to be a positive libido for the ugly, as on other and less Christian levels there is a libido for the beautiful. It is impossible to put down the wallpaper that defaces the average American home of the lower middle class to mere inadvertence, or to the obscene humor of the manufacturers. Such ghastly designs, it must be obvious, give a genuine delight to a certain type of mind. They meet, in some unfathomable way, its obscure and unintelligible demands. They caress it as "The Palms" caresses it, or the art of the movie, or jazz. The taste for them is as enigmatical and yet as common as the taste for dogmatic theology and the poetry of Edgar A. Guest.

Thus I suspect (though confessedly without knowing) that the vast majority of the honest folk of Westmoreland county, and especially the 100% Americans among them, actually admire the houses they live in, and are proud of them. For the same money they could get vastly better ones, but they prefer what they have got. Certainly there was no pressure upon the Veterans of Foreign Wars to choose the dreadful edifice that bears their banner, for there are plenty of vacant buildings along the track-side, and some of them are appreciably better. They might, indeed, have built a better one of their own. But they chose that clapboarded horror with their eyes open, and having chosen it, they let it mellow into its present shocking depravity. They like it as it is: beside it, the Parthenon would no doubt offend them. In precisely the same way the authors of the rat-trap stadium that I have mentioned made a deliberate choice. After painfully designing and erecting it, they made it perfect in their own sight by putting a completely impossible pent-house, painted a staring yellow, on top of it. The effect is that of a fat woman with a black eye. It is that of a Presbyterian grinning. But they like it.

Here is something that the psychologists have so far neglected: the love of ugliness for its own sake, the lust to make the world intolerable. Its habitat is the United States. Out of the melting pot emerges a race which hates beauty as it hates truth. The etiology of this madness deserves a great deal more study than it has got. There must be causes behind it; it arises and flourishes in obedience to biological laws, and not as a mere act of God. What, precisely, are the terms of those laws? And why do they run stronger in America than elsewhere? Let some honest *Privat Dozent* in pathological sociology apply himself to the problem.

TRAVAIL

(FROM the Baltimore *Evening Sun*, October 8, 1928)

It always makes me melancholy to see the boys going to school. During the half hour before 9 o'clock they stagger through the square in front of my house in Baltimore with the despondent air of New Yorkers coming up from the ferries to work. It happens to be uphill, but I believe they'd lag as much if they were going down. Shakespeare, in fact, hints as much in the Seven Ages. In the afternoon, coming home, they leap and spring like gazelles. They are tired, but they are happy, and happiness in the young always takes the form of sharp and repeated contractions of the striped muscles, especially in the legs, arms and larynx.

The notion that schoolboys are generally content with their lot seems to me to be a sad delusion. They are, in the main, able to bear it, but they like it no more than a soldier enjoys life in a foxhole. The need to endure it makes actors of them; they learn how to lie—perhaps the most valuable thing, to a citizen of Christendom, that they learn in school. No boy genuinely loves and admires his teacher; the farthest he can go, assuming him to have all of his wits, is to tolerate her as he tolerates castor oil. She may be the loveliest flower in the whole pedagogical garden, but the most he can ever see in her is a jailer who might conceivably be worse.

School days, I believe, are the unhappiest in the whole span of human existence. They are full of dull, unintelligible tasks, new and unpleasant ordinances, brutal violations of common sense and common decency. It doesn't take a reasonably bright boy long to discover that most of what is rammed into him is nonsense, and that no one really cares very much whether he learns it or not. His parents, unless they are infantile in mind, tend to be bored by his lessons and labors, and are unable to conceal the fact from his sharp eyes. His first teachers he views simply as disagreeable policemen. His later ones he usually sets down quite accurately as asses.

It is, indeed, one of the capital tragedies of youth—and youth is the time of real tragedy—that the young are thrown mainly with adults they do not quite respect. The average boy of my time, if he had had his free choice, would have put in his days with Amos Rusie or Jim Corbett; a bit later he would have chosen Roosevelt. But a boy sees such heroes only from afar. His actual companions, forced upon him by the inexorable decrees of a soulless and irrational state, are schoolma'ams, male and female, which is to say, persons of trivial and unromantic achievement, and no more capable of inspiring emulation in a healthy boy than so many midwives or dog-catchers.

It is no wonder that schoolboys so often turn for stimulus from their teachers to their fellows. The fact, I believe, is largely to blame for the juvenile lawlessness that prevails in America, for it is the relatively daring and lawless boys who stand out from the mass, and so attract their weaker brethren. But whatever the consequences, the thing itself is quite natural, for a boy with superabundant energy flogging him yearns for experiment and adventure. What he gets out of his teachers is mainly the opposite. On the female side they have the instincts of duennas, and on the male side they seldom rise above the level of scoutmasters and Y.M.C.A. secretaries. It would be hard enough for a grown man, with alcohol and cynicism aiding him, to endure such society. To a growing boy it is torture.

I believe that things were better in the days before maudlin harridans, searching the world for atrocities to put down, alarmed the school boards into abolishing corporal punishment. The notion that it was degrading to boys is silly. In the main, their public opinion indorsed it as both just and humane. I went to a school where rattanning was resorted to when needed. Its effects, I am convinced, were excellent. It preserved the self-respect of the teachers, and so tended to make the boys respect them. Given command, they actually exercised it. I never heard of a boy complaining, after the smarting in his gluteus maximus had passed off, that he had been used cruelly or unjustly. He sometimes bawled during the operation, but he was content afterward. The teachers in that school were not only respected by the boys, but more or less liked. The males among them seemed to be men, not milksops.

But even so, attendance upon their séances was a dull business far more often than it was exhilarating, and every boy in their classes began thinking of the closing bell the instant the opening bell clanged. Keeping up with the pace they set was cruel to the stupid boys, and holding back to it was even more cruel to the intelligent ones. The things that they regarded as important were not, as a rule, interesting to the boys, and the things that the boys liked they only too often appeared to regard as low. I incline to believe, looking backward, that the boys were right far oftener than they were wrong.

Today the old pedagogy has gone out, and a new and complicated science has taken its place. Unluckily, it is largely the confection of imbeciles, and so the unhappiness of the young continues. In the whole realm of human learning there is no faculty more fantastically incompetent than that of pedagogy. If you doubt it, go read the pedagogical journals. Better still, send for an armful of the theses that *Kandidaten* write and publish when they go up for their Ph.D.'s. Nothing worse is to be found in the literature of astrology, scientific salesmanship, or Christian Science. But the poor schoolma'ams, in order to get on in their trade, must make shift to study it, and even to master it. No wonder their dreams are of lawful domestic love, even with the curse of cooking thrown in.

★

I suggest hanging all the professors of pedagogy, arming the ma'am with a rattan, and turning her loose. Back to Bach! The new pedagogy has got so complicated that it often forgets the pupil altogether, just as the new medicine often forgets the patient. It is driving the poor ma'ams crazy, and converting the children into laboratory animals. I believe that the old sing-song system, with an occasional fanning of the posterior, was better. At all events, it was simpler. One could grasp it without graphs.

A GOOD MAN GONE WRONG

(FROM the *American Mercury*, February 1929. Henry Judd Gray, a corset salesman, and Ruth Brown Snyder killed her husband, Albert, an art editor, on March 20, 1927. They confessed and were executed at Sing Sing, January 12, 1928. A.C.)

Mr. Gray went to the electric chair in Sing Sing on January 11, 1928, for his share in the butchery of Mrs. Ruth Snyder's husband. The present book was composed in his last days, and appears with the imprimatur of his devoted sister. From end to end of it he protests pathetically that he was, at heart, a good man. I believe him. The fact, indeed, is spread all over his singularly naïve and touching record. He emerges from it as the almost perfect model of the Y.M.C.A. alumnus, the conscientious husband and father, the Christian business man, the virtuous and God-fearing Americano. It was his very virtue, festering within him, that brought him to his appalling doom. Another and more wicked man, caught in the net of La Snyder, would have wriggled out and gone on his way, scarcely pausing to thank God for the fun and the escape. But once poor Judd had yielded to her brummagem seductions, he was done for and he knew it. Touched by sin, he shriveled like a worm on a hot stove. From the first exchange of wayward glances to the final agony in the chair the way was straight and inevitable.

All this sounds like paradox, but I offer it seriously, and as a psychologist of high gifts. What finished the man was not his banal adultery with his suburban sweetie, but his swift and overwhelming conviction that it was mortal sin. The adultery itself was simply in bad taste: it was, perhaps, something to be ashamed of, as stealing a poor taxi-driver's false teeth would be something to be ashamed of, but it was no more. Elks and Shriners do worse every day, and suffer only transient qualms. But to Gray, with his Presbyterian upbringing and his idealistic view of the corset business, the slip was a catastrophe, a calamity. He left his tawdry partner in a daze, marveling that there could be so much wickedness in the world, and no belch of fire from Hell to stop it. Thereafter his demoralization proceeded from step to step as inexorably and as beautifully as a case of Bright's disease. The woman horrified him, but his very horror became a kind of fascination. He resorted to her as a Christian dipsomaniac resorts to the jug, protestingly, tremblingly and helplessly. In his blinking eyes she became an amalgam of all the Loreleis, with the Rum Demon peeping over her shoulder. Whatever she ordered him to do he did at once, like a man stupefied by some diabolical drug. When, in the end, she ordered him to butcher her oaf of a husband, he proceeded to the business almost automatically, wondering to the last instant why he obeyed and yet no more able to resist than he was able, on the day of retribution, to resist his 2,000 volts.

In his narrative he makes much of this helplessness, and speculates somewhat heavily upon its cause. That cause, as I hint, is clear enough: he was a sincere Presbyterian, a good man. What is the chief mark of such a good man? That he cannot differentiate rationally between sin and sin—that a gnat gags him as badly as a camel. So with poor Gray. His initial peccadillo shocked him so vastly that he could think of himself thereafter only as a sinner unspeakable and incorrigible. In his eyes the step from adultery to murder was as natural and inevitable as the step from the cocktail-shaker to the gutter in the eyes of a Methodist bishop. He was rather astonished, indeed, that he didn't beat his wife and embezzle his employers' funds. Once the conviction of sin had seized him he was ready to go the whole hog. He went, as a matter of record, somewhat beyond it. His crime was of the peculiarly brútal and atrocious kind that only good men commit. An Elk or a Shriner, persuaded to murder Snyder, would have done it with a certain decency. Moreover, he would have demanded a plausible provocation. But Gray, being a good man, performed the job with sickening ferocity, and without asking for any provocation at all. It was sufficient for him that he was full of sin, that God had it in for him, that he was hopelessly damned. His crime, in fact, was a sort of public ratification of his damnation. It was his way of confessing. If he had any logical motive, it was his yearning to get into Hell as soon as possible. In his book, to be sure, he speaks of Hell under the name of Heaven. But that is mere blarney, set down for the comfort of his family. He was too good a Presbyterian to have any illusions on the point: he was, in fact, an amateur theologian of very respectable attainments. He went to the chair fully expecting to be in Hell in twenty seconds.

It seems to me that his story is a human document of immense interest and value, and that it deserves a great deal more serious study than it will probably get. Its moral is plain. Sin is a dangerous toy in the hands of the virtuous. It should be left to the congenitally sinful, who know when to play with it and when to let it alone. Run a boy through a Presbyterian Sunday-school and you must police him carefully all the rest of his life, for once he slips he is ready for anything.

THE COMEDIAN
(FROM the Baltimore *Evening Sun*, November 18, 1929)

The acting that one sees upon the stage does not show how human beings actually comport themselves in crises, but simply how actors think they ought to. It is thus, like poetry and religion, a device for gladdening the heart with what is palpably not true. But it is lower than either of those arts, for it is forced to make its gaudy not-true absurd by putting it alongside the true. There stands Richard Cœur de Lion—and the plainly enough, also stands a poor ham. Relatively few reflective persons seem to get any pleasure out of acting. They often, to be sure, delight in comedians—but a comedian is not an actor: he is a sort of *reductio ad absurdum* of an actor. His work bears the same relation to acting properly so called as that of a hangman, a midwife or a divorce lawyer bears to poetry, or that of a bishop to religion.

MR. JUSTICE HOLMES

(FROM the *American Mercury*, May 1930. A review of *The Dissenting Opinions of Mr. Justice Holmes*, arranged by Alfred Lief, with a foreword by George W. Kirchwey; New York, 1930. With additions from the *American Mercury*, May 1932.)

Mr. Justice Holmes's dissenting opinions have got so much fawning praise from Liberals that it is somewhat surprising to discover that Mr. Lief is able to muster but fifty-five of them, and even more surprising to hear from Dr. Kirchwey that in only one case did the learned justice stand quite alone, and that the cases "in which he has given expression to the judgment of the court, or in which he has concurred in its judgment, far outnumber, in the ratio of eight or ten to one, those in which he felt it necessary to record his dissent."

There is even more surprising stuff in the opinions themselves. In three Espionage Act cases, including the Debs case, one finds a clear statement of the doctrine that, in war time, the rights guaranteed by the First Amendment cease to have any substance, and may be set aside summarily by any jury that has been sufficiently inflamed by a district attorney itching for higher office. In *Fox vs. the State of Washington* we learn that any conduct "which shall tend to encourage or advocate disrespect for the law" may be made a crime, and that the protest of a man who believes that he has been jailed unjustly, and threatens to boycott his persecutors, may be treated as such a crime. In *Moyer vs. Peabody* it appears that the Governor of a State, "without sufficient reason but in good faith," may call out the militia, declare martial law, and jail anyone he happens to suspect or dislike, without laying himself open "to an action after he is out of office on the ground that he had no reasonable ground for his belief." And in *Weaver vs. Palmer Bros. Co.* there is the plain inference that in order to punish a theoretical man, A, who is suspected of wrong-doing, a State Legislature may lay heavy and intolerable burdens upon a real man, B, who has admittedly done no wrong at all.

I find it hard to reconcile such notions with any plausible concept of Liberalism. They may be good law, but it is impossible to see how they can conceivably promote liberty. My suspicion is that the hopeful Liberals of the 20s, frantically eager to find at least one judge who was not violently and implacably against them, seized upon certain of Mr. Justice Holmes's opinions without examining the rest, and read into them an attitude that was actually as foreign to his ways of thinking as it was to those of Mr. Chief Justice Hughes. Finding him, now and then, defending eloquently a new and uplifting law which his colleagues proposed to strike off the books, they concluded that he was a sworn advocate of the rights of man. But all the while, if I do not misread his plain words, he was actually no more than an advocate of the rights of lawmakers. There, indeed, is the clue to his whole jurisprudence. He believed that the law-making bodies should be free to experiment almost *ad libitum,* that the courts should not call a halt upon them until they clearly passed the uttermost bounds of reason, that everything should be sacrificed to their autonomy, including, apparently, even the Bill of Rights. If this is Liberalism, then all I can say is that Liberalism is not what it was when I was young.

In those remote days, sucking wisdom from the primeval springs, I was taught that the very aim of the Constitution was to keep law-makers from running amok, and that it was the highest duty of the Supreme Court, following *Marbury vs. Madison,* to safeguard it against their forays. It was not sufficient, so my instructors maintained, for Congress or a State Legislature to give assurance that its intentions were noble; noble or not, it had to keep squarely within the limits of the Bill of Rights, and the moment it went beyond them its most virtuous acts were null and void. But Mr. Justice Holmes apparently thought otherwise. He held, it would seem, that violating the Bill of Rights is a rare and difficult business, possible only by summoning up deliberate malice, and that it is the chief business of the Supreme Court to keep the Constitution loose and elastic, so that blasting holes through it may not be too onerous. Bear this doctrine in mind, and you will have an adequate explanation, on the one hand, of those forward-looking opinions which console the Liberals—for example, in *Lochner vs. New York* (the bakery case), in the child labor case, and in the Virginia case involving the compulsory sterilization of imbeciles—and on the other hand, of the reactionary opinions which they so politely overlook—for example, in the Debs case, in *Bartels vs. Iowa* (a war-time case, involving the prohibition of foreign-language teaching), in the Mann Act case (in which Dr. Holmes concurred with the majority of the court, and thereby helped pave the way for the wholesale blackmail which Mr. Justice McKenna, who dissented, warned against), and finally in the long line of Volstead Act cases.

Like any other man, of course, a judge sometimes permits himself the luxury of inconsistency. Mr. Justice Holmes, it seems to me, did so in the wiretapping case and again in the Abrams case, in which his dissenting opinion was clearly at variance with the prevailing opinion in the Debs case, written by him. But I think it is quite fair to say that his fundamental attitude was precisely as I have stated it. Over and over again, in these opinions, he advocated giving the legislature full head-room, and over and over again he protested against using the Fourteenth Amendment to upset novel and oppressive laws, aimed frankly at helpless minorities. If what he said in some of those opinions were accepted literally there would be scarcely any brake at all upon lawmaking, and the Bill of Rights would have no more significance than the Code of Manu.

The weak spot in his reasoning, if I may presume to suggest such a thing, was his tacit assumption that the voice of the legislature was the voice of the people. There is, in fact, no reason for confusing the people and the legislature: the two, in these later years, are quite distinct. The legislature, like the executive, has ceased, save indirectly, to be even the creature of the people: it is the creature, in the main, of pressure groups, and most of them, it must be manifest, are of dubious wisdom and even more dubious honesty. Laws are no longer made by a rational process of public discussion; they are made by a process of blackmail and intimidation, and they are executed in the same manner. The typical lawmaker of today is a man wholly devoid of principle—a mere counter in a grotesque and knavish game. If the right pressure could be applied to him he would be cheerfully in favor of polygamy, astrology or cannibalism.

It is the aim of the Bill of Rights, if it has any remaining aim at all, to curb such prehensile gentry. Its function is to set a limitation upon their power to harry and oppress us to their own private profit. The Fathers, in framing it, did not have powerful minorities in mind; what they sought to hobble was simply the majority. But that is a detail. The important thing is that the Bill of Rights sets forth, in the plainest of plain language, the limits beyond which even legislatures may not go. The Supreme Court, in *Marbury vs. Madison,* decided that it was bound to execute that intent, and for a hundred years that doctrine remained the corner-stone of American constitutional law. But in late years the court has taken the opposite line, and public opinion seems to support it. Certainly Dr. Holmes did not go as far in that direction as some of his brother judges, but equally certainly he went far enough. To call him a Liberal is to make the word meaningless.

Let us, for a moment, stop thinking of him as one, and let us also stop thinking of him as a *littérateur,* a reformer, a sociologist, a prophet, an evangelist, a metaphysician; instead, let us think of him as something that he undoubtedy was in his Pleistocene youth and probably remained ever after, to wit, a soldier. Let us think of him, further, as a soldier extraordinarily ruminative and articulate—in fact, so ruminative and articulate as to be, in the military caste, almost miraculous. And let us think of him still further as a soldier whose natural distaste and contempt for civilians, and corollary yearning to heave them all into Hell, was cooled and eased by a stream of blood that once flowed through the Autocrat of the Breakfast Table—in brief, as a soldier beset by occasional doubts, hesitations, flashes of humor, bursts of affability, moments of sneaking pity. Observe that I insert the wary word, "occasional"; it surely belongs there. On at least three days out of four, during his long years on the bench, the learned justice remained the soldier—precise, pedantic, unimaginative, even harsh. But on the fourth day a strange amiability overcame him, and a strange impulse to play with heresy, and it was on that fourth day that he acquired his singular repute as a sage.

There is no evidence in Dr. Holmes's decisions that he ever gave any really profound thought to the great battle of ideas which raged in his time. He was interested in those ideas more or less, and now and then his high office forced him to take a hand in the battle, but he never did so with anything properly describable as passionate conviction. The whole uproar, one gathers, seemed fundamentally foolish to him. Did he have any genuine belief in democracy? Apparently the answer must be no. It amused him as a spectacle, and there were times when he was in the mood to let that spectacle run on, and even to help it on, but there were other times when he was moved to haul it up with a sharp command. That, no doubt, is why his decisions show so wide a spread and so beautiful an inconsistency, baffling to those who would get him into a bottle. He could, on occasion, state the case for the widest freedom, whether of the individual citizen or of the representative lawmaker, with a magnificent clarity, but he could also on occasion give his vote to the most brutal sort of repression. It seems to me that the latter occasions were rather more numerous than the former. And it seems to me again, after a very attentive reading of his decisions, that what moved him when he was disposed to be complacent was far less a positive love of liberty than an amiable and half contemptuous feeling that those who longed for it ought to get a horse-doctor's dose of it, and thereby suffer a really first-rate belly-ache.

This easy-going cynicism of his is what gave his decisions their peculiar salacity, and made them interesting as literature. It separated them sharply from the writings of his fellow judges, most of whom were frankly dull dogs. He had a considerable talent for epigram, and like any other man who possesses it was not shy about exercising it. I do not go so far as to allege that it colored and conditioned his judgment, that the apt phrase actually seduced him, but certainly it must be plain that once his mood had brought him to this or that judgment the announcement of it was sometimes more than a little affected by purely literary impulses. Now and then, alas, the result was far more literature than law. I point, for example, to one of his most celebrated epigrams: "Three generations of morons are enough." It is a memorable saying, and its essential soundness need not be questioned, but is it really judicial, or even legal, in form and content; does it offer that plain guidance which the higher courts are supposed to provide? What of the *two* generations:

are they too little? I should not want to be a *nisi prius* judge if all the pronunciamentoes of the Supreme Court were so charmingly succinct and memorable— and so vague.

The average American judge, as everyone knows, is a mere rabbinical automaton, with no more give and take in his mind than you will find in the mind of a terrier watching a rathole. He converts the law into a series of rubber-stamps, and brings them down upon the scalped skulls of the just and unjust alike. The alternative to him, as commonly conceived, is quite as bad— an uplifter in a black robe, eagerly gulping every new brand of Peruna that comes out, and converting his pulpit into a sort of soap-box. Mr. Justice Holmes was neither, and he was better than either. He was under no illusions about the law. He knew very well that its aim was not to bring in the millennium, but simply to keep the peace. But he believed that keeping the peace was an art that could be practised in various ways, and that if one of them was by using a club then another was by employing a feather. Thus the Liberals, who long for tickling with a great and tragic longing, were occasionally lifted to the heights of ecstasy by the learned judge's operations, and in fact soared so high that they were out of earshot of next day's thwack of the club. I suspect that Dr. Holmes himself, when he heard of their enthusiasm, was quite as much amused as flattered. Such misunderstandings are naturally grateful to a skeptic, and they are doubly grateful to a skeptic of the military order, with his professional doubt of all persons who think that they think. I can imagine this skepticism—or, if you choose, cynicism—giving great aid and comfort to him on January 1, 1932, when he entered the chamber of the Supreme Court for the last time, and read his last opinion.

The case was that of one James Dunne, an humble bootician of Eureka, Calif., and the retiring justice delivered the majority opinion. Dunne had been tried in

California on an indictment embracing three counts. The first charged him with keeping liquor for sale, the second with possessing it unlawfully, and the third with selling it. The jury acquitted him on the second and third counts, but found him guilty on the first. His counsel thereupon appealed. The evidence as to all three offenses, it was shown, was precisely the same. If the prisoner was innocent of two of them, then how could he be guilty of the third? Mr. Justice Holmes, speaking for himself and all his fellow justices save one, swept away this question in the following words:

> Consistency in the verdict is not necessary. Each count in an indictment is regarded as if it was a separate offense. If separate indictments had been presented against the defendant for possession and for maintenance of a nuisance, and had been separately tried, the same evidence being offered in support of each, an acquittal on one could not be pleaded as *res judicata* of the other. Where the offenses are separately charged in the counts of a single indictment the same rule must hold.

I am not learned in the law, but the special gifts of a lawyer are surely not necessary to see that this judgment disposed completely of the prohibition of double jeopardy in Article I of the Bill of Rights. What it said, in plain English, is that a man may be tried over and over again for what is essentially the same offense, and that if one, two, three or *n* juries acquit him he may yet be kept in the dock, and so on *ad infinitum* until a jury is found that will convict him. And what such a series of juries may do may be done by one single jury—by the simple device of splitting his one offense into two, three, four or *n* offenses, and then trying him for all of them. In order to go free he must win verdicts of not guilty on every count. But in order to jail him all the prosecuting attorney needs is a verdict of guilty on one.

I commend this decision to Liberals who still cherish the delusion that Dr. Holmes belonged to their lodge. Let them paste it in their Sunday go-to-meeting hats. And I commend to them also the astounding but charming fact that the one judge who dissented was Mr. Justice Pierce Butler, for many years the chief demon in their menagerie. This is what he said:

> Excluding the possession negatived by the finding under the second count, there is nothing of substance left in the first count, for its specifications were limited to the keeping for sale of the identical drinks alleged in the second count to have been unlawfully possessed. . . . The evidence having been found insufficient to establish such possession, it cannot be held adequate to warrant conviction under the first count. The finding of not guilty is a final determination that possession, the gravamen of both counts, was not proved.

THE CALAMITY OF APPOMATTOX
(FROM the *American Mercury*, September 1930)

No American historian, so far as I know, has ever tried to work out the probable consequences if Grant instead of Lee had been on the hot spot at Appomattox. How long would the victorious Confederacy have endured? Could it have surmounted the difficulties inherent in the doctrine of States' Rights, so often inconvenient and even paralyzing to it during the war? Could it have remedied its plain economic deficiencies, and become a self-sustaining nation? How would it have protected itself against such war heroes as Beauregard and Longstreet, Joe Wheeler and Nathan B.

Forrest? And what would have been its relations to the United States, socially, economically, spiritually and politically?

I am inclined, on all these counts, to be optimistic. The chief evils in the Federal victory lay in the fact, from which we still suffer abominably, that it was a victory of what we now call Babbitts over what used to be called gentlemen. I am not arguing here, of course, that the whole Confederate army was composed of gentlemen; on the contrary, it was chiefly made up, like the Federal army, of innocent and unwashed peasants, and not a few of them got into its corps of officers. But the impulse behind it, as everyone knows, was essentially aristocratic, and that aristocratic impulse would have fashioned the Confederacy if the fortunes of war had run the other way. Whatever the defects of the new commonwealth below the Potomac, it would have at least been a commonwealth founded upon a concept of human inequality, and with a superior minority at the helm. It might not have produced any more Washingtons, Madisons, Jeffersons, Calhouns and Randolphs of Roanoke, but it would certainly not have yielded itself to the Heflins, Caraways, Bilbos and Tillmans.

The rise of such bounders was a natural and inevitable consequence of the military disaster. That disaster left the Southern gentry deflated and almost helpless. Thousands of the best young men among them had been killed, and thousands of those who survived came North. They commonly did well in the North, and were good citizens. My own native town of Baltimore was greatly enriched by their immigration, both culturally and materially; if it is less corrupt today than most other large American cities, then the credit belongs largely to Virginians, many of whom arrived with no baggage save good manners and empty bellies. Back home they were sorely missed. First the carpetbaggers ravaged the land, and then it fell into the hands of the native white trash, already so poor that war and Reconstruction could not make them any poorer. When things began to improve they seized whatever was seizable, and their heirs and assigns, now poor no longer, hold it to this day. A raw plutocracy owns and operates the New South, with no challenge save from a proletariat, white and black, that is still three-fourths peasant, and hence too stupid to be dangerous. The aristocracy is almost extinct, at least as a force in government. It may survive in backwaters and on puerile levels, but of the men who run the South today, and represent it at Washington, not 5%, by any Southern standard, are gentlemen.

If the war had gone with the Confederates no such vermin would be in the saddle, nor would there by any sign below the Potomac of their chief contributions to American *Kultur*—Ku Kluxry, political ecclesiasticism, nigger-baiting, and the more homicidal variety of wowserism. Such things might have arisen in America, but they would not have arisen in the South. The old aristocracy, however degenerate it might have become, would have at least retained sufficient decency to see to that. New Orleans, today, would still be a highly charming and civilized (if perhaps somewhat zymotic) city, with a touch of Paris and another of Port Said. Charleston, which even now sprouts lady authors, would also sprout political philosophers. The University of Virginia would be what Jefferson intended it to be, and no shouting Methodist would haunt its campus. Richmond would be, not the dull suburb of nothing that it is now, but a beautiful and consoling second-rate capital, comparable to Budapest, Brussels, Stockholm or The Hague. And all of us, with the Middle West pumping its revolting silo juices into the East and West alike, would be making frequent leaps over the Potomac, to drink the sound red wine there and breathe the free air.

My guess is that the two Republics would be getting on pretty amicably. Perhaps they'd have come to terms as early as 1898, and fought the Spanish-American War together. In 1917 the confiding North might have gone out to save the world for democracy, but the South, vaccinated against both Wall Street and the Liberal whim-wham, would have kept aloof—and maybe rolled up a couple of billions of profit from the holy crusade. It would probably be far richer today, independent, than it is with the clutch of the Yankee mortgage-shark still on its collar. It would be getting and using his money just the same, but his toll would be less. As things stand, he not only exploits the South economically; he also pollutes and debases it spiritually. It suffers damnably from low wages, but it suffers even more from the Chamber of Commerce metaphysic.

No doubt the Confederates, victorious, would have abolished slavery by the middle 80s. They were headed that way before the war, and the more sagacious of them were all in favor of it. But they were in favor of it on sound economic grounds, and not on the brummagem moral grounds which persuaded the North. The difference here is immense. In human history a moral victory is always a disaster, for it debauches and degrades both the victor and the vanquished. The triumph of sin in 1865 would have stimulated and helped to civilize both sides.

Today the way out looks painful and hazardous. Civilization in the United States survives only in the big cities, and many of them—notably Boston and Philadelphia—seem to be sliding down to the cow country level. No doubt this standardization will go on until a few of the more resolute towns, headed by New York, take to open revolt, and try to break out of the Union. Already, indeed, it is talked of. But it will be hard to accomplish, for the tradition that the Union is indissoluble is now firmly established. If it had been broken in 1865 life would be far pleasanter today for every American of any noticeable decency. There are, to be sure, advantages in Union for everyone, but it must be manifest that they are greatest for the worst kinds of people. All the benefit that a New Yorker gets out of Kansas is no more than what he might get out of Saskatchewan, the Argentine pampas, or Siberia. But New York to a Kansan is not only a place where he may get drunk, look at dirty shows and buy bogus antiques; it is also a place where he may enforce his dunghill ideas upon his betters.

THE NEW ARCHITECTURE
(FROM the *American Mercury*, February 1931)

The New Architecture seems to be making little progress in the United States. The traces of it that are visible in the current hotels, apartment-houses and office buildings are slight, and there are so few signs of it in domestic architecture and ecclesiastical architecture that when they appear they look merely freakish. A new suburb built according to the plans of, say, Le Corbusier would provoke a great deal more mirth than admiration, and the realtor who projected it would probably be badly stuck. The advocates of the new style are full of earnestness, and some of them carry on in the shrill, pedagogical manner of believers in the Single Tax or the New Humanism, but save on the level of factory design they do not seem to be making many converts. In other directions precious few persons seem to have been persuaded that their harsh and melodramatic designs are either logical or beautiful, or that the conventions they denounce are necessarily meaningless and ugly.

Those conventions, in point of fact, are often informed by an indubitable beauty, as even the most frantic Modernist must admit when he contemplates the Lincoln Memorial at Washington or St. Thomas's Church in New York; and there is not the slightest reason for holding that they make war upon anything essential to the modern spirit. We live in a Machine Age, but there are still plenty of us who have but little to do with machines, and find in that little no answer to our aspirations. Why should a man who hates automobiles build a house designed upon the principles which went into the Ford Model T? He may prefer, and quite honestly, the principles which went into the English dwelling-house of the Eighteenth Century, and so borrow them with a clear conscience.

I can sympathize with that man, for in many ways he is I and I am he. If I were building a house tomorrow it would certainly not follow the lines of a dynamo or a steam shovel; it would be, with a few obvious changes, a replica of the houses that were built in the days when human existence, according to my notion, was pleasanter and more spacious than ever before or since. The Eighteenth Century, of course, had its defects, but they were vastly overshadowed by its merits. It got rid of religion. It lifted music to first place among the arts. It introduced urbanity into manners, and made even war relatively gracious and decent. It took eating and drinking out of the stable and put them into the parlor. It found the sciences childish curiosities, and bent them to the service of man, and elevated them above metaphysics for all time. Lastly and best, it invented the first really comfortable human habitations ever seen on earth, and filled them with charming fittings. When it dawned even kings lived like hogs, but as it closed even colonial planters on the banks of the Potomac were housed in a fashion fit for gentlemen.

The Eighteenth Century dwelling-house has countless rivals today, but it is as far superior to any of them as the music of Mozart is superior to Broadway jazz. It is not only, with its red brick and white trim, a pattern of simple beauty; it is also durable, relatively inexpensive, and pleasant to live in. No other sort of house better meets the exigencies of housekeeping, and none other absorbs modern conveniences more naturally and gracefully. Why should a man of today abandon it for a house of harsh masses, hideous outlines, and bald metallic surfaces? And why should he abandon its noble and charming furniture for the ghastly imitations of the electric chair that the Modernists make of gaspipe? I can find no reason in either faith or morals. The Eighteenth Century house fits a civilized man almost perfectly. He is completely at ease in it. In every detail it accords with his ideas. To say that the florid chicken-coops of Le Corbusier and company are closer to his nature is as absurd as to say that the tar-paper shacks behind the railroad tracks are closer to his nature.

Nor is there any sense in the common contention that Gothic has gone out, and is now falsetto. The truth is that St. Thomas's Church not only represents accurately the Christian mysticism of Ralph Adams Cram, who designed it, but also the uneasy consciences of the rich Babbitts who paid for it. It is a plain and highly intelligible signal to the world that, at least on Sundays, those Babbitts search their hearts and give thought to Hell. It is, in its sordid surroundings, distinctly otherworldly, just as Bishop Fulbert's cathedral was otherworldly when it began to rise above the medieval squalor of Chartres. The otherworldliness is of the very essence of ecclesiastical architecture. The moment it is lost we have the dreadful "plants" that barbaric Baptists and Methodists erect in the Pellagra and Goitre Belts. Of all forms of visible otherworldliness, it seems to me, the Gothic is at once the most logical and the most beautiful. It reaches up magnificently—and a good half of it is palpably useless. When men really begin to build churches like the Bush Terminal there will be no religion any more, but only Rotary. And when they begin to live in houses as coldly structural as step-ladders they will cease to be men, and become mere rats in cages.

THE NOMINATION OF F.D.R.
(FROM the Baltimore *Evening Sun*, July 1 and 2, 1932)

Chicago, July 1

The plan of the Roosevelt managers to rush the convention and put over their candidate with a bang failed this morning, and after a turbulent all-night session and two roll-calls the anti-Roosevelt men fought off a motion to adjourn until this afternoon and the delegates proceeded to a third test of strength.

A few minutes before the first roll-call began, at 4 o'clock this morning, Arthur F. Mullen, of Nebraska, Farley's chief of staff, told me that Roosevelt would receive 675 votes on the first ballot and 763 on the second, and that the third would bring him the two-thirds needed for his nomination. But the first ballot actually brought him only 666¼ and the second only 677¾, and the third had not gone halfway down the roll of States before it was plainly evident that a hard fight was ahead of him, with his chances much slimmer than they seemed to be the time the voting began. In brief, the Roosevelt runaway was stopped.

The first two ballots were taken amid the utmost confusion and to the tune of loud and raucous challenges from unhappy minorities of various delegations. On the first ballot Minnesota demanded to be polled, with the result that its 24 votes under the unit rule went to Roosevelt. New York, which was also polled, split unequally, with 28½ votes going to Roosevelt and 65½ to Al Smith. This was a somewhat unpleasant surprise for the Roosevelt men and they got little consolation out of the second ballot, for on it Roosevelt made a gain of but a single vote. Their total gain of 11½ came mainly from Missouri, where the 12 Roosevelt votes of the first ballot increased to 18, with a corresponding loss to former Senator James A. Reed.

By this time it was clear that the Roosevelt assault had been hurled back, and the allies, who had been apparently trying all night to manufacture as many delays as possible, suddenly demanded action on their own account. This demand was sufficient to block an effort that the Roosevelt men made at 8.05 to adjourn until 4 p.m. It was opposed violently by New York, speaking through the clarion voice of Dudley Field Malone, and a standing vote showed such a formidable party against the adjournment that the proposal was withdrawn.

The second ballot probably took more time than any ever heard of before, even in a Democratic national convention. The roll-call was begun at 5.17 a.m. and it was not until 8.05 that the result was announced. Thus the running time was nearly three hours. Two large States, Ohio and Pennsylvania, demanded to be polled, and there was a battle in the District of Columbia delegation that consumed a full hour. Two of the District delegates were Ritchie men, and they fought hard to throw off the unit rule and have their choice recorded, but Chairman Walsh decided that the rule bound them, and their votes were thus credited to Roosevelt. The same fate befell six Ritchie votes in the Michigan delegation on the third ballot.

Governor Ritchie polled 21 votes on the first ballot— Maryland's 16, 4 from Indiana and 1 from Pennsylvania. On the second ballot he gained 2½ in Pennsylvania, making his total 23½. Meanwhile Al Smith, who started off with 201¾, dropped to 194¼, and slight losses were also shown by Traylor, White, Byrd and Baker, and six of former Senator Reed's Missourians departed

for the Roosevelt camp. Altogether the allies polled
487¾. On the first ballot, a few minutes before the roll-
call began, Howard Bruce of Maryland estimated that
they would poll 484 and that their irreducible mini-
mum of shock troops, good for fifty ballots if necessary,
was 425—40 more than would be needed to prevent
Roosevelt from ever polling a two-thirds majority.

The all-night session was a horrible affair and by the
time the light of dawn began to dim the spotlights, a
great many delegates had gone back to their hotels or
escaped to the neighboring speakeasies. When the bal-
loting began shortly after 5 a.m. scores of them were
missing and the fact explained the worst delays in the
voting and especially some of the quarrels over the
rights and dignities of alternates. When New York was
called Jimmy Walker could not be found, but by the
time the dreadful business of polling the immense State
delegation, with its ninety regular members and eight
members-at-large, neared an end, he somehow turned
up and was presently saying something for the microphone and getting a round of applause for it.

The third ballot showed plainly that Roosevelt was
not going to run the convention amuck, but the same
evidence proved that the allies had likewise failed to
knock him out. He was holding all his principal delegations, and in addition he was making some small
gains in the territory of the enemy. His total vote was
682 79/100, which showed an increase of five and a frac-
tion over the second ballot and of sixteen over the first.
This was surely not disaster. Nevertheless, it was still
sufficient to fill the allies with hope and courage, for
they had been in fear that the first Roosevelt rush
would shake and break their lines, and that had certainly not happened.

The way the tide of battle was going was revealed
dramatically by the attitude of the leaders on the two
sides. All during the infernal night session the Roosevelt men had been trying to wear out and beat down

the opposition, and to push on to a showdown. They opposed every motion to adjourn, and refused every other sort of truce. They wanted to get through with the speeches as soon as possible, but they were confident enough to be still willing to match speech with speech, and they did so until daylight. But after the first ballot they began to play for time, and after the second all of their early bellicosity had gone out of them.

The allies, meanwhile, were gaining in assurance. They knew that Al Smith was ready to talk of delivering his vote to one or another of them after the third ballot, and they were eager to reach it. But the Roosevelt men, by that stage, saw clearly that a hard fight was ahead, and so took their turn at playing for time. The combat of rhetoricians and rooters during the long, hot and weary hours of the night was depressingly typical of a Democratic national convention. The show was almost completely idiotic, with now and then a more or less rational speech to relieve it. Senator Tydings made one such speech, putting Governor Ritchie in nomination, and another was made by Richard F. Cleveland, son of Grover Cleveland, seconding him. A third came from William G. McAdoo in the interest of Garner. But the average was as low as one might look for at a ward club in a mean street and few of the delegates and fewer of the visitors seemed to pay any attention to what was said.

All sorts of grotesque female politicians, most of them with brassy voices and hard faces, popped up to talk to the radio audience back home. The evening session, in fact, had been postponed to nine o'clock to get a radio hookup and every fourth-rate local leader in the hall, male or female, tried for a crack at the microphone. More than once weary delegates objected that the Niagara of bilge was killing them and along toward four in the morning Josephus Daniels went to the platform and protested against it formally. But all of the nine candidates had to be put in nomination, and when they had been put in nomination all of them had to be seconded, not once, but two, four, six or a dozen times. Worse, their customers had to parade obscenely every time one of them was launched and some of the parades ran to nearly an hour.

Here one gang helped another. The Texans, who had a band, lent it to every other outfit that had a candidate, and it brayed and boomed for Ritchie, Byrd, Reed and Al Smith quite as cruelly as it performed for Garner. This politeness, of course, had to be repaid by its beneficiaries, and with interest. The Byrd band, clad in uniforms fit for Arctic exploration, did not let up for hours on end. And while it played one tune, the band of the Texans played another, and the official band in the gallery a third, and the elephantine pipe-organ a fourth. At one stage in the uproar a male chorus also appeared, but what it sang I can't tell you, nor which candidate it whooped and gargled for.

It was hard on the spectators in the galleries, but it was even harder on the delegates, for they had to march in a good many of the parades and they were hoofed and hustled when they kept their seats. Most of them, as is usual at a national convention, are beyond middle life, and a good many of them show obvious marks of oxidation. Two have died since the convention began, a matter of only five days. Scores had to clear out of the hall during the night and seek relief in the corridors.

Toward three o'clock, a thunderstorm came up, and the extreme heat of the early evening began to lessen. By that time, a full half of the spectators had gone home, so the cops were able to open the great doors of the hall without running any risk of being rushed off their feet, and by dawn the place had become relatively comfortable. But then the sun began to shine down through the gallery windows, and presently the floor was a furnace again, and the delegates got out their foul handkerchiefs and resumed their weary mopping and panting.

Under such circumstances, there is always plenty of ill-humor. There is more of it than usual when Democrats meet, for they are divided into implacable factions, and each hates all the others. Many of the more wearisome maneuvers of the three roll-calls were apparently suggested by mere malignancy. The Pennsylvanians, I was told, demanded to be polled simply to bring back to the hall some of their own delegates who had deserted the battlefield and gone home to bed. The row in the District of Columbia delegation was apparently two-thirds personal and only one-third political. And the Smith men carried on their relentless campaign of motions, protests and parliamentary inquiries mainly to annoy the Roosevelt men.

Toward the end the thing became a mere endurance match. It was plain after the second ballot that neither side was going to break, but the allies by now were hungry to punish the Roosevelt outfit, and they did so by opposing adjournment and by raising all sorts of nonsensical difficulties, some of which could be resolved only after long conferences on the platform and a copious consultation of precedent books and parliamentary lawyers.

Old Tom Walsh, the chairman, held out pretty well until eight o'clock, but then he began to cave in, and during the last hour the temporary chairman of the convention, the wet bridegroom, Senator Alben W. Barkley, of Kentucky, operated the bungstarter and struggled with the riddles that were thrown at him from the floor.

★

Chicago, July 2

The great combat is ending this afternoon in the classical Democratic manner. That is to say, the victors are full of uneasiness and the vanquished are full of bile. It would be hard to find a delegate who believes seriously that Roosevelt can carry New York in November, or Massachusetts, or New Jersey, or even Illinois. All of the crucial wet States of the Northeast held out against him to the last ditch, and their representatives are damning him up hill and down dale today. Meanwhile the Southern and Middle Western delegates are going home with a tattered Bible on one shoulder and a new and shiny beer seidel on the other, and what they will have to listen to from their pastors and the ladies of the W.C.T.U. is making their hearts miss every other beat.

The row ended quietly enough last night, but without the slightest sign of genuine enthusiasm. The galleries kept on howling for Al Smith to the finish, but Al himself sulked in his hotel, and placards in the lobbies this morning announced that most of his true friends would leave for Manhattan at noon. When, at 10.32 last night, Chairman Walsh announced the final vote, there was only the ghost of a cheer, and in less than a minute even the Roosevelt stalwarts were back in their seats and eager only for adjournment and a decent night's rest. The convention was worn out, but that was only part of the story. It was also torn by rancors that could not be put down. The Smith men all knew very well that the result was a good deal less a triumph for Roosevelt, who actually seemed to have few genuine friends in the house, than a defeat and rebuke for Smith. As for the Roosevelt men, they found themselves on their repeal honeymoon wondering dismally if the bride were really as lovely as she had seemed last Wednesday. Both sides had won and both had lost, but what each thought of was only the loss.

In all probability the Marylanders, though they lost their fight for Governor Ritchie, came out of the struggle with fewer wounds than any other delegation that played a part of any actual importance in the ceremonies. They had been beaten, but they had not made any enemies. They were on the bandwagon, but the Smith *bloc* had no cause to complain of them. They owed this comfortable result to the fine skill of Governor Ritchie himself. He was his own manager here, just as he had been his own manager in the preliminary campaign, and his coolness resisted a dozen temptations to run amuck and get into trouble. He took the whole thing calmly and good-naturedly, and showed not the slightest sign, at any stage, of the appalling buck fever which so often demoralizes candidates. He kept on good terms with the Smith outfit without getting any of its sulphurous smell upon him, and he submitted to the inevitable in the end in a dignified manner, and without any obscene embracing of Roosevelt. If Roosevelt is elected in November there is a swell place in the Cabinet waiting for him—that is, assuming that he wants it. And if Roosevelt is butchered by the implacable Smith men, then he will have another chance in 1936, and a far better one than he had this week, with the corpse of Al incommoding him.

As you all know by now, the final break to Roosevelt was brought on by the Garner men from California. Garner's friends from Texas were prepared to stick to him until Hell froze over, but in California he was only a false face for McAdoo and Hearst, and McAdoo was far more bent upon punishing Smith for the events of 1924 than he was for nominating Texas Jack, just as Hearst was more eager to block his pet abomination, Newton D. Baker, than to name any other candidate. Hearst was quite willing on Thursday to turn to Ritchie, who was satisfactory to him on all the major issues, including especially the League of Nations. In fact, negotiations with him were in full blast Thursday afternoon, with Arthur Brisbane as the intermediary. But McAdoo had other ideas, chiefly relating to his own fortunes, and he pulled Hearst along. For one thing, McAdoo had a palpable itch for the Vice-Presidency. But above all he yearned to give Smith a beating, and he saw after the third ballot that Roosevelt would be the handiest stick for the job.

The actual nomination of Roosevelt after the turmoils of the all-night session went off very quietly. The delegates appeared in the hall all washed up, with clean collars, pressed suits and palpable auras of witch hazel and bay rum. The scavengers of the stadium had swept up the place, the weather had turned cool and there was the general letting down that always follows a hard battle. No one had had quite enough sleep, but everyone had had at least some. Chairman Walsh, who had been wilting visibly in the horrible early hours of the morning, was himself again by night, and carried on his operations with the bungstarter in his usual fair, firm and competent manner. He is a good presiding officer and he had got through the perils of the night session without disaster. Now he was prepared for the final scene and every spectator in the packed galleries knew where it would lead the plot and who would be its hero.

California comes early on the roll, so there was no long suspense. McAdoo went up to the platform to deliver the State delegation in person. He must be close to seventy by now, if not beyond it, but he is still slim, erect and graceful, and as he made his little speech and let his eye rove toward the New York delegation he looked every inch the barnstorming Iago of the old school. Eight years ago at New York he led the hosts of the Invisible Empire against the Pope, the rum demon and all the other Beelzebubs of the Hookworm Belt, and came so close to getting the nomination that the memory of its loss must still shiver him. The man who blocked him was Al Smith, and now he was paying Al back.

If revenge is really sweet he was sucking a colossal sugar teat, but all the same there was a beery flavor about it that must have somewhat disquieted him. For he is Georgia cracker by birth and has always followed his native pastors docilely, and it must have taken a lot of temptation to make him accept the ribald and saloon-ish platform. Here, indeed, revenge was working both ways, and if Al were a man of more humor he would have been smiling, too.

The other rebellious States fell into line without much ceremony, always excepting, of course, those which held out for Al to the end. Illinois was delivered by Mayor Cermak of Chicago, a Czech brought up on roast goose and Pilsner, and showing the virtues of that diet in his tremendous shoulders and sturdy legs. He spoke also for Indiana, which had been split badly on the first three ballots. When Maryland's turn came Governor Ritchie spoke for it from the floor, releasing its delegates and casting their votes for the winner, and a bit later on former Governor Byrd did the business for Virginia. In the same way Missouri was delivered by former Senator James A. Reed, who somewhat later came up to the platform and made a little speech, de-nouncing Samuel Insull and Lord Hoover in blister-ing terms and calling upon the Smith men to "fall in line like good soldiers and face the common enemy." Senator Reed spoke of the time as "this afternoon," though it was actually nearly ten o'clock at night. But no one noticed, for the all-night session had blown up all reckoning of time and space.

The whole proceedings, in fact, showed a curiously fantastic quality. Here was a great party convention, after almost a week of cruel labor, nominating the weakest candidate before it. How many of the delegates were honestly for him I don't know, but certainly it could not have been more than a third. There was ab-solutely nothing in his record to make them eager for him. He was not only a man of relatively small expe-rience and achievement in national affairs; he was also one whose competence was plainly in doubt, and whose good faith was far from clear. His only really valuable asset was his name, and even that was asso-ciated with the triumphs and glories of the common enemy. To add to the unpleasantness there was grave uneasiness about his physical capacity for the job they were trusting to him.

Yet here they were giving it to him, and among the parties to the business were a dozen who were patently his superior and of very much larger experience. For example, Tom Walsh, the chairman, one of the most diligent and useful Senators ever seen in Washington and a man whose integrity is unquestioned by anyone. For example, Carter Glass of Virginia, an irascible and almost fanatical fellow, but still a very able man and an immensely valuable public servant. For example, Reed of Missouri, the very picture and model of a Roman senator, whose departure from the Senate cost it most of its dramatic effectiveness and a good half of its power. Even McAdoo is certainly worth a dozen Franklin D. Roosevelts. As for Al Smith, though he is now going down hill fast, he was once worth a hundred. But the man who got the great prize was Roosevelt, and most of the others are now too old to hope for it hereafter.

The failure of the opposition was the failure of Al Smith. From the moment he arrived on the ground it was apparent that he had no plan, and was animated only by his fierce hatred of Roosevelt, the cuckoo who had seized his nest. That hatred may have had logic in it, but it was impotent to organize the allies and they were knocked off in detail by the extraordinarily astute Messrs. Farley and Mullen. The first two ballots gave them some hope, but it was lost on the third, for the tide by then was plainly going Roosevelt's way. Perhaps the Al of eight or ten years ago, or even of four years ago, might have achieved the miracle that the crisis called for, but it was far beyond the technique of the golf-playing Al of today. He has ceased to be the wonder and glory of the East Side and becomes simply a minor figure of Park Avenue.

But in the midst of the débâcle he could at least steal

some consolation from the fact that his foes were facing a very difficult and perhaps almost impossible campaign before the people. His sardonic legacy to his party is the platform, and especially the Prohibition plank. It will harass Roosevelt abominably until the vote is counted, and after that it may take first place among his permanent regrets. If his managers had had their way, there would have been a straddle comparable to the one made by the Republicans. But the allies rushed them so savagely that they were taken off their feet. That rush required little leadership. It was spontaneous and irresistible. The big cities poured out their shock troops for it.

The delegates went back to their hotels last night to the tune of "Onward, Christian Soldiers." It was the first time that the tune had been heard in the convention, and probably the first time it had been heard in the hall. But playing it was only a kind of whistling in the dark. For five days the bands had been laboring far different hymns, and their echoes still sounded along the rafters.

A GOOD MAN IN A BAD TRADE

(FROM the *American Mercury*, January 1933. A review of *Grover Cleveland: a Study in Courage*, by Allan Nevins; New York, 1932.)

We have had more brilliant Presidents than Cleveland, and one or two who were considerably more profound, but we have never had one, at least since Washington, whose fundamental character was solider and more admirable. There was never any string tied to old Grover. He got on in politics, not by knuckling to politicians, but by scorning and defying them, and when he found himself opposed in what he conceived to be

sound and honest courses, not only by politicians, but by
the sovereign people, he treated them to a massive dose
of the same medicine. No more self-sufficient man is
recorded in modern history. There were times, of
course, when he had his doubts like the rest of us, but
once he had made up his mind he stood immovable. No
conceivable seduction could weaken him. There was
something almost inhuman about his fortitude, and to
millions of his contemporaries it seemed more satanic
than godlike. No President since Lincoln, not even the
melancholy Hoover, has been more bitterly hated, or
by more people. But Cleveland, though he certainly
did not enjoy it—he was, indeed, singularly lacking in
the shallower and more comforting sort of egoism—
yet did not let it daunt him. He came into office his own
man, and he went out without yielding anything of
that character for an instant.

In his time it was common to ascribe a good part of
this vast steadfastness to his mere bulk. He had a huge
girth, shoulders like the Parthenon, a round, compact
head, and the slow movements of any large animal. He
was not very tall, but he looked, somehow, like an enormous natural object—say, the Jungfrau or Cape Horn.
This aspect of the stupendous, almost of the terrific,
was tempting to the primeval psychologists of that innocent day, and they succumbed to it easily. But in the
years that have come and gone since then we have
learned a great deal about fat men. It was proved, for
example, by W. H. Taft that they could be knocked
about and made to dance with great facility, and it was
proved by Hoover that their texture may be, not that
of Alps, but that of chocolate éclairs. Cleveland, though
he was also fat, was the complete antithesis of these gentlemen. There was far more to him than beam and ton-
nage. When enemies had at him they quickly found
that his weight was the least of their difficulties; what
really sent them sprawling was the fact that his whole
huge carcass seemed to be made of iron. There was no

give in him, no bounce, no softness. He sailed through American history like a steel ship loaded with monoliths of granite.

He came of an excellent family, but his youth had been a hard one, and his cultural advantages were not of the best. He learned a great deal about human nature by sitting with pleasant fellows in the Buffalo saloons, but he seems to have made but little contact with the finer and more elusive parts of the spiritual heritage of man, and in consequence his imagination was not awakened, and he remained all his days a somewhat stodgy and pedantic fellow. There is no sign in his writings of the wide and fruitful reading of Roosevelt I, and they show none of the sleek, shiny graces of Wilson. His English, apparently based upon Eighteenth Century models, was a horrible example to the young. It did not even roar; it simply heaved, panted and grunted. He made, in his day, some phrases, and a few of them are still remembered, but they are all études in ponderosity—*innocuous desuetude, communism of pelf,* and so on. The men he admired were all solid men like himself. He lived through the Gilded Age, the Mauve Decade and the Purple Nineties without being aware of them. His heroes were largely lawyers of the bow-wow type, and it is significant that he seems to have had little acquaintance with Mark Twain, though Mark edited a paper in Buffalo during his terms as mayor there. His favorite American author was Richard Watson Gilder.

The one man who seems to have had any genuine influence upon him was Richard Olney, first his Attorney-General and then his Secretary of State. He had such great respect for Olney's professional skill as a lawyer that he was not infrequently blind to the man's defects as a statesman. It was Olney who induced him to send troops to Chicago to put down the Pullman strike, and Olney who chiefly inspired the celebrated Venezuela message. Cleveland, at the start, seems to have been reluctant to intervene in Chicago, but Olney convinced him that it was both legal and necessary. In the Venezuelan matter something of the same sort appears to have occurred. It was characteristic of Cleveland that, once he had made up his mind, he stuck to his course without the slightest regard for consequences. Doubts never beset him. He banged along like a locomotive. If man or devil got upon the track, then so much the worse for man or devil. "God," he once wrote to Gilder, "has never failed to make known to me the path of duty."

Any man thus obsessed by a concept of duty is bound to seek support for it somewhere outside himself. He must rest it on something which seems to him to be higher than mere private inclination or advantage. Cleveland, never having heard of Kant's categorical imperatives and being almost as innocent of political theory, naturally turned to the Calvinism of his childhood. His father had been a Presbyterian clergyman, and he remained a communicant of the family faith to the end. But the Calvinism that he subscribed to was a variety purged of all the original horrors. He translated predestination, with its sharp cocksureness and its hordes of damned, into a sort of benign fatalism, not unmixed with a stealthy self-reliance. God, he believed, ordained the order of the world, and His decrees must ever remain inscrutable, but there was nevertheless a good deal to be said for hard work, a reasonable optimism, and a sturdy fidelity to what seemed to be the right. Duty, in its essence, might be transcendental, but its mandates were issued in plain English, and no honest man could escape them. There is no record that Cleveland ever tried to escape them. He was not averse to popularity, but he put it far below the approval of conscience. In him all the imaginary virtues of the Puritans became real.

It is not likely that we shall see his like again, at least in the present age. The Presidency is now closed to the kind of character that he had so abundantly. It is going, in these days, to more politic and pliant men. They get it by yielding prudently, by changing their minds at the right instant, by keeping silent when speech is dangerous. Frankness and courage are luxuries confined to the more comic varieties of runners-up at national conventions. Thus it is pleasant to remember Cleveland, and to speak of him from time to time. He was the last of the Romans. If pedagogy were anything save the puerile racket that it is he would loom large in the schoolbooks. As it is, he is subordinated to Lincoln, Roosevelt I and Wilson. This is one of the things that are the matter with the United States.

COOLIDGE

(FROM the *American Mercury*, April 1933. First printed, in part, in the Baltimore *Evening Sun*, January 30, 1933. Coolidge died January 5, 1933.)

The editorial writers who had the job of concocting mortuary tributes to the late Calvin Coolidge, LL.D., made heavy weather of it, and no wonder. Ordinarily, an American public man dies by inches, and there is thus plenty of time to think up beautiful nonsense about him. More often than not, indeed, he threatens to die three or four times before he actually does so, and each threat gives the elegists a chance to mellow and adorn their effusions. But Dr. Coolidge slipped out of life almost as quietly and as unexpectedly as he had originally slipped into public notice, and in consequence the brethren were caught napping and had to do their poetical embalming under desperate pressure. The common legend is that such pressure inflames and inspires a true journalist, and maketh him to sweat masterpieces, but it is not so in fact. Like any other literary man, he functions best when he is at leisure, and can turn from his tablets now and then to run down a quotation, to eat a plate of ham and eggs, or to look out of the window.

The general burden of the Coolidge memoirs was that the right hon. gentleman was a typical American, and some hinted that he was the most typical since Lincoln. As the English say, I find myself quite unable to associate myself with that thesis. He was, in truth, almost as unlike the average of his countrymen as if he had been born green. The Americano is an expansive fellow, a back-slapper, full of amiability; Coolidge was reserved and even muriatic. The Americano has a stupendous capacity for believing, and especially for believing in what is palpably not true; Coolidge was, in his fundamental metaphysics, an agnostic. The Americano dreams vast dreams, and is hag-ridden by a demon; Coolidge was not mount but rider, and his steed was a mechanical horse. The Americano, in his normal incarnation, challenges fate at every step and his whole life is a struggle; Coolidge took things as they came.

Some of the more romantic of the funeral bards tried to convert the farmhouse at Plymouth into a log-cabin, but the attempt was as vain as their effort to make a Lincoln of good Cal. His early days, in fact, were anything but pinched. His father was a man of substance, and he was well fed and well schooled. He went to a good college, had the clothes to cut a figure there, and made useful friends. There is no record that he was brilliant, but he took his degree with a respectable mark, proceeded to the law, and entered a prosperous law firm on the day of his admission to the bar. Almost at once he got into politics, and by the time he was twenty-seven he was already on the public payroll. There he remained without a break for exactly thirty years, always moving up. Not once in all those years did he lose an election. When he retired in the end, it was at his own motion, and with three or four hundred thousand dollars of tax money in his tight jeans.

In brief, a darling of the gods. No other American has ever been so fortunate, or even half so fortunate. His career first amazed observers, and then dazzled them. Well do I remember the hot Saturday in Chicago when he was nominated for the Vice-Presidency on the ticket with Harding. Half a dozen other statesmen had to commit political suicide in order to make way for him, but all of them stepped up docilely and bumped themselves off. The business completed, I left the press-stand and went to the crypt below to hunt a drink. There I found a group of colleagues listening to a Boston brother who knew Coolidge well, and had followed him from the start of his career.

To my astonishment I found that this gentleman was offering to lay a bet that Harding, if elected, would be assassinated before he had served half his term. There were murmurs, and someone protested uneasily that such talk was injudicious, for A. Mitchell Palmer was still Attorney-General and his spies were all about. But the speaker stuck to his wager.

"I am simply telling you," he roared, "what I *know*. I know Cal Coolidge inside and out. He is the luckiest goddam ———— ———— in the whole world."

It seemed plausible then, and it is certain now. No other President ever slipped into the White House so easily, and none other ever had a softer time of it while there. When, at Rapid City, S.D., on August 2, 1927, he loosed the occult words, "I do not choose to run in 1928," was it prescience or only luck? For one, I am inclined to put it down to luck. Surely there was no prescience in his utterances and maneuvers otherwise. He showed not the slightest sign that he smelt black clouds ahead; on the contrary, he talked and lived only sunshine. There was a volcano boiling under him, but he did not know it, and was not singed. When it burst forth at last, it was Hoover who got its blast, and was fried, boiled, roasted and fricasseed. How Dr. Coolidge must have chuckled in his retirement, for he was not without humor of a sad, necrotic kind. He knew Hoover well, and could fathom the full depths of the joke.

In what manner he would have performed himself if the holy angels had shoved the Depression forward a couple of years—this we can only guess, and one man's hazard is as good as another's. My own is that he would have responded to bad times precisely as he responded to good ones—that is, by pulling down the blinds, stretching his legs upon his desk, and snoozing away the lazy afternoons. Here, indeed, was his one peculiar *Fach,* his one really notable talent. He slept more than any other President, whether by day or by night. Nero fiddled, but Coolidge only snored. When the crash came at last and Hoover began to smoke and bubble, good Cal was safe in Northampton, and still in the hay.

There is sound reason for believing that this great gift of his for self-induced narcolepsy was at the bottom of such modest popularity as he enjoyed. I mean, of course, popularity among the relatively enlightened. On lower levels he was revered simply because he was so plainly just folks—because what little he said was precisely what was heard in every garage and barbershop. He gave the plain people the kind of esthetic pleasure known as recognition, and in horse-doctor's doses. But what got him customers higher up the scale of humanity was something else, and something quite different. It was the fact that he not only said little, and that little of harmless platitudes all compact, but did even less. The kind of government that he offered the country was government stripped to the buff. It was government that governed hardly at all. Thus the ideal of Jefferson was realized at last, and the Jeffersonians were delighted.

Well, there is surely something to say for that abstinence, and maybe a lot. I can find no relation of cause and effect between the Coolidge somnolence and the Coolidge prosperity, but it is nevertheless reasonable to argue that if the former had been less marked the latter might have blown up sooner. We suffer most, not when the White House is a peaceful dormitory, but when it is a jitney Mars Hill, with a tin-pot Paul bawling from the roof. Counting out Harding as a cipher only, Dr. Coolidge was preceded by one World Saver and followed by two more. What enlightened American, having to choose between any of them and another Coolidge, would hesitate for an instant? There were no thrills while he reigned, but neither were there any headaches. He had no ideas, and he was not a nuisance.

THE WALLACE PARANOIA

(The Progressive Party convention at Philadelphia at the end of July 1948 was Mencken's last reporting assignment. This piece appeared in the Baltimore *Evening Sun*, July 26, 1948. A.C.)

After another long and dismal day of pathological rhetoric relieved only by the neat and amusing operations of the party-line steamroller, the delegates to the founding convention of the third and maybe last Progressive party began shuffling off for home tonight.

On the whole, the show has been good as such things go in the Republic. It has provided no sharp and gory conflict of candidates like that which marked the Republican Convention. It has offered no brutal slaughter of a minority like that which pepped up the Democratic Convention, but it has at least brought together a large gang of picturesque characters, and it has given everyone a clear view of its candidates and its platform. The former certainly do not emerge from it with anything properly describable as an access of dignity. Wallace started off by making a thumping ass of himself in his preliminary press conference and did nothing to redeem himself by his bumbling and boresome delivery of his speech of acceptance (otherwise not a bad one) last night. As for Taylor, he has made it plain to all that there is nothing to him whatever save a third-rate mountebank from the great open spaces, a good deal closer to Pappy O'Daniel than to Savonarola. Soak a radio clown for ten days and ten nights in the rectified juices of all the cow-state Messiahs ever heard of and you have him to the life. Save on the remotest fringes of the intellectually underprivileged it is highly unlikely that he will add anything to the strength of the new party.

Wallace's imbecile handling of the Guru matter revealed a stupidity that is hard to fathom. He might have got rid of it once and for all by simply answering yes or no for no one really cares what foolishness he fell for ten or twelve years ago. He is swallowing much worse doses of hokum at this minute, and no complaint is heard. But he tried disingenuously to brush off the natural and proper questions of the journalists assembled and when they began to pin him down and press him he retreated into plain nonsense. Worse, he had begun this sorry exhibition by a long and witless tirade against the press. He went into the conference with every assumption in his favor. He came out of it tattered and torn.

The convention naturally attracted swarms of crackpots of all sorts and for three days and three nights they did their stuff before the sweating platform committee ostensibly headed by the cynical Rexford Tugwell. But the platform was actually drawn up by the Communists and fellow-travelers on the committee, and when it got to the floor this afternoon they protected it waspishly and effectively against every raid from more rational quarters. When an honest but humorless Yankee from Vermont tried to get in a plank disclaiming any intention to support the Russian assassins in every eventuality, no matter how outrageous their doings, it was first given a hard parliamentary squeeze by the Moscow fuglemen on the platform, and then bawled to death on the floor.

No one who has followed the proceedings can have any doubt that the Communists have come out on top. Wallace, a little while back, was declaring piously that he didn't want their support, but certainly made no effort to brush it off during the convention. In any case, his effort to climb from under, like Eleanor Roosevelt's, came far too late, and no person of any common sense took it seriously. As for Taylor, he has been cultivating the Kremlin, openly and without apology, all week, and the comrades in attendance seem to have no doubt of his fealty. When he got up in Shibe Park to make his so-called speech of acceptance—an effort worthy of a corn doctor at a county fair—he actually held it up long enough to throw them a bucket of bones.

The delegates, taking them one with another, have seemed to me to be of generally low intelligence, but it is easy to overestimate the idiocy of the participants in such mass paranoias. People of genuine sense seldom come to them, and when they do come, they are not much heard from. I believe that the percentage of downright half-wits has been definitely lower than in, say, the Democratic Convention of 1924, and not much higher than in the Democratic Convention of this year. This is not saying, of course, that there were not plenty of psychopaths present. They rolled in from North, East, South and West, and among them were all of the types listed by Emerson in his description of the Chandos street convention of reformers, in Boston more than a century ago. Such types persist, and they do not improve as year chases year. They were born with believing minds, and when they are cut off by death from believing in a F.D.R., they turn inevitably to such Rosicrucians as poor Henry. The more extreme varieties, I have no doubt, would not have been surprised if a flock of angels had swarmed down from Heaven to help whoop him up, accompanied by the red dragon with seven heads and ten horns described in Revelation xii, 3. Alongside these feebleminded folk were gangs of dubious labor leaders, slick Communists, obfuscators, sore veterans, Bible-belt evangelists, mischievous college students, and such-like old residents of the Cave of Adullum.

But it would be unfair to forget the many quite honest, and even reasonably intelligent folk, male and female, who served as raisins in the cake. Some of them I recalled seeing years ago at other gatherings of those born to hope. They were veterans of many and many now-forgotten campaigns to solve the insoluble and remedy the irremediable. They followed Bryan in their day, then T.R. and the elder LaFollette and all the other roaring magicians of recent history. They are survivors of Populism, the Emmanuel movement, the no-more-scrub-bulls agitation, the ham-and-eggs crusade of Upton Sinclair, the old-age pension frenzy of Dr. Francis Townsend, the share-the-wealth gospel of Huey Long, and so on without end. They are grocery-store economists, moony professors in one-building "universities," editors of papers with no visible circulation, preachers of lost evangels, customers of a hundred schemes to cure all the sorrows of the world.

Whether they will muster enough votes on Election Day to make a splash remains to be seen. In the United States new parties usually do pretty well at the start and then fade away. Judging by the speeches they listen to here in Philadelphia their principal current devil is the embattled gents furnisher, Harry S. Truman. I heard very little excoriation of Dewey, but they screamed against Harry at every chance.

MENCKEN'S LAST STAND

(Mencken ended his newspaper career where he had begun it: plaguing the Baltimore city fathers. The piece explains itself. But this local challenge to race relations was only one of many that harassed American cities everywhere and would lead, so early as May of 1954, to an historic change in the Supreme Court's working doctrine on segregation. This, so far as I can discover, was the last piece that Mencken wrote and published. It appeared in the Baltimore *Evening Sun* on November 9, 1948. Two weeks later, to the day, he had a cerebral thrombosis. He was despaired of for a time and rallied at one point to say only, "Bring on the angels." But he was tougher than he felt and by Christmas his paralysis had vanished and he went home again, where, ever since, he has been devotedly nursed by his brother August. However, he did not recover from a semantic aphasia, which left him able to focus images and words but not, alas, into any communicable sense. He has not been able to write or read since. A.C.)

When, on July 11 last, a gang of so-called progressives, white and black, went to Druid Hill Park to stage an inter-racial tennis combat, and were collared and jugged by the cops, it became instantly impossible for anyone to discuss the matter in a newspaper, save, of course, to report impartially the proceedings in court.

The impediment lay in the rules of the Supreme Bench, and the aim of the rules is to prevent the trial of criminal cases by public outcry and fulmination. I am, and have always been, in favor of the aim. I was in favor of it, in fact, long before any of the judges now extant arose to the bench from the underworld of the bar, and I argued for it at great length in the columns of the *Sunpapers*. But four months is a long while for journalists to keep silent on an important public matter, and if I bust out now it is simply and solely because I believe that the purpose of the rule has been sufficiently achieved. The accused have had their day in court, and no public clamor, whether pro or con, has corrupted the judicial process. Seven, it appears, have been adjudged guilty of conspiring to assemble unlawfully and fifteen others have been turned loose.

To be sure, the condemned have petitioned the Supreme Bench, sitting *en banc,* for new trials, but it is not my understanding that the rule was designed to protect the reviewing lucubrations of the Supreme Bench. I simply can't imagine its members being swayed by newspaper chit-chat; as well think of them being swayed by the whispers of politicians. Moreover, I have no desire to sway them, but am prepared to accept their decision, whatever it is, with loud hosannahs, convinced in conscience that it is sound in both law and logic. As for the verdict of Judge Moser below, I accept it on the same terms precisely. But there remains an underlying question, and it deserves to be considered seriously and without any reference whatever to the cases lately at bar. It is this: Has the Park Board any right in law to forbid white and black citizens, if they are so inclined, to join in harmless games together on public playgrounds? Again: Is such a prohibition, even supposing that it is lawful, supported by anything to be found in common sense and common decency? I do not undertake to answer the first question, for I am too ignorant of law, but my answer to the second is a loud and unequivocal No. A free citizen in a free state, it seems to me, has an inalienable right to play with whomsoever he will, so long as he does not disturb the general peace. If any other citizen, offended by the spectacle, makes a pother, then that other citizen, and not the man exercising his inalienable right, should be put down by the police.

Certainly it is astounding to find so much of the spirit of the Georgia Cracker surviving in the Maryland Free State, and under official auspices. The public parks are supported by the taxpayer, including the colored taxpayer, for the health and pleasure of the whole people. Why should cops be sent into them to separate those people against their will into separate herds? Why should the law set up distinctions and discriminations which the persons directly affected themselves reject? If the park tennis courts were free to all comers no white person would be compelled to take on a colored opponent if he didn't care to. There would be no such vexatious and disingenuous pressure as is embodied, for example, in the Hon. Mr. Truman's Fair Employment Practices Act. No one would be invaded in his privacy. Any white player could say yes or no to a colored challenger, and any colored player could say yes or no to a white. But when both say yes, why on earth should anyone else object?

It is high time that all such relics of Ku Kluxry be wiped out in Maryland. The position of the colored people, since the political revolution of 1895, has been gradually improving in the State, and it has already reached a point surpassed by few other states. But there is still plenty of room for further advances, and it is irritating indeed to see one of them blocked by silly Dogberrys. The Park Board rule is irrational and nefarious. It should be got rid of forthwith.

Of equal, and maybe even worse, irrationality is the rule regarding golf-playing on the public links, whereby colored players can play on certain links only on certain days, and white players only on certain other days. It would be hard to imagine anything more ridiculous. Why should a man of one race, playing *in forma pauperis* at the taxpayers' expense, be permitted to exclude men of another race? Why should beggars be turned into such peculiarly obnoxious choosers? I speak of playing *in forma pauperis* and that is precisely what I mean. Golf is an expensive game, and should be played only by persons who can afford it. It is as absurd for a poor man to deck himself in its togs and engage in its witless gyrations as it would be for him to array himself as a general in the army. If he can't afford it he should avoid it, as self-respecting people always avoid what they can't afford. The doctrine that the taxpayer should foot the bills which make a bogus prince of pelf of him is New Dealism at its worst. I am really astonished that the public golf links attract any appreciable colored patronage. The colored people, despite the continued efforts of white frauds to make fools of them, generally keep their heads and retain their sense of humor. If there are any appreciable number of them who can actually afford golf, then they should buy some convenient cow-pasture and set up grounds of their own. And the whites who posture at the taxpayers' expense should do the same.

In answer to all the foregoing I expect confidently to hear the argument that the late mixed tennis matches were not on the level, but were arranged by Communists to make trouble. So far as I am aware this may be true but it seems to me to be irrelevant. What gave the Communists their chance was the existence of the Park Board's rule. If it had carried on its business with more sense they would have been baffled. The way to dispose of their chicaneries is not to fight them when they are right.

SENTENTIÆ [1912–48]

(These maxims, epigrams and apothegms cover a long range in time. The earliest were first printed in the *Smart Set* in 1912; the latest come from note-books never printed at all. In 1916 I published a collection under the title of *A Little Book in C Major*. Four years later it was taken, in part, into a revised edition of *A Book of Burlesques*, and there survived until that book went out of print in the late 30's.)

The Mind of Man

When a man laughs at his troubles he loses a good many friends. They never forgive the loss of their prerogative.

The chief value of money lies in the fact that one lives in a world in which it is overestimated.

Never let your inferiors do you a favor. It will be extremely costly.

Whenever you hear a man speak of his love for his country it is a sign that he expects to be paid for it.

Conscience is the inner voice which warns us that someone may be looking.

An idealist is one who, on noticing that a rose smells better than a cabbage, concludes that it will also make better soup.

The difference between a moral man and a man of honor is that the latter regrets a discreditable act, even when it has worked and he has not been caught.

Self-Respect—The secure feeling that no one, as yet, is suspicious.

Masculum et Feminam Creavit Eos.

At the end of one millennium and nine centuries of Christianity, it remains an unshakable assumption of

the law in all Christian countries and of the moral judgment of Christians everywhere that if a man and a
woman, entering a room together, close the door behind them, the man will come out sadder and the
woman wiser.

When women kiss it always reminds one of prize-
fighters shaking hands.

Alimony—The ransom that the happy pay to the
devil.

A man always remembers his first love with special
tenderness. But after that he begins to bunch them.

Women have simple tastes. They can get pleasure out
of the conversation of children in arms and men in love.

How little it takes to make life unbearable. . . . A
pebble in the shoe, a cockroach in the spaghetti, a
woman's laugh.

Women always excel men in that sort of wisdom
which comes from experience. To be a woman is in itself a terrible experience.

Adultery is the application of democracy to love.

The Citizen and the State

Syllogisms à la Mode—If you are against labor rack-
eteers, then you are against the working man. If you
are against demagogues, then you are against democracy. If you are against Christianity, then you are
against God. If you are against trying a can of Old Dr.
Quack's Cancer Salve, then you are in favor of letting
Uncle Julius die.

Democracy is the theory that the common people
know what they want, and deserve to get it good and
hard.

The believing mind reaches its perihelion in the so-
called Liberals. They believe in each and every quack
who sets up his booth on the fair-grounds, including the
Communists. The Communists have some talents too,
but they always fall short of believing in the Liberals.

Judge—A law student who marks his own examination-papers.

Arcana Cœlestia

Archbishop—A Christian ecclesiastic of a rank superior to that attained by Christ.

Puritanism—The haunting fear that someone, somewhere, may be happy.

This and That

To believe that Russia has got rid of the evils of capitalism takes a special kind of mind. It is the same kind that believes that a Holy Roller has got rid of sin.

Psychotherapy—The theory that the patient will probably get well anyhow, and is certainly a damned ijjit.

EXEUNT OMNES
(FROM the *Smart Set*, December 1919)

Go to any public library and look under "Death: Human" in the card index, and you will be surprised to find how few books there are on the subject. Worse, nearly all the few are by psychical researchers who regard death as a mere removal from one world to another or by mystics who appear to believe that it is little more than a sort of illusion. Once, seeking to find out what death was physiologically—that is, to find out just what happened when a man died—I put in a solid week without result. There seemed to be nothing whatever on the subject, even in the medical libraries. Finally, after much weariness, I found what I was looking for in Dr. George W.

Crile's "Man: An Adaptive Mechanism." [1] Crile said
that death was acidosis—that it was caused by the failure of the organism to maintain the alkalinity necessary
to its normal functioning—and in the absence of any
proofs or even argument to the contrary I accepted his
notion forthwith and have cherished it ever since. I
thus think of death as a sort of deleterious fermenta-
tion, like that which goes on in a bottle of Château
Margaux when it becomes corked. Life is a struggle,
not against sin, not against the Money Power, not
against malicious animal magnetism, but against hydrogen ions. The healthy man is one in whom those ions,
as they are dissociated by cellular activity, are immediately fixed by alkaline bases. The sick man is one in
whom the process has begun to lag, with the hydrogen
ions getting ahead. The dying man is one in whom it
is all over save the charges of fraud.

But here I get into chemical physics, and not only
run afoul of revelation but also reveal, perhaps, a degree
of ignorance verging upon the indecent. The thing I
started out to do was simply to call attention to the
only full-length and first-rate treatise on death that I
have ever encountered or heard of, to wit, "Aspects
of Death and Correlated Aspects of Life," by Dr. F.
Parkes Weber,[2] a fat, hefty and extremely interesting
tome, the fruit of truly stupendous erudition. What Dr.
Weber has attempted is to bring together in one volume all that has been said or thought about death since
the time of the first human records, not only by poets,
priests and philosophers, but also by painters, engravers,
soldiers, monarchs and the populace generally. One
traces, in chapter after chapter, the ebb and flow of
human ideas upon the subject, of the human attitude
to the last and greatest mystery of them all—the notion
of it as a mere transition to a higher plane of life, the

[1] New York, 1916. Dr. Crile died in 1943.
[2] New York, 1919.

notion of it as a benign panacea for all human suffering, the notion of it as an incentive to this or that way
of living, the notion of it as an impenetrable enigma,
inevitable and inexplicable. Few of us quite realize how
much the contemplation of death has colored human
thought throughout the ages, despite the paucity of
formal books on the subject. There have been times
when it almost shut out all other concerns; there has
never been a time when it has not bulked enormously
in the racial consciousness. Well, what Dr. Weber does
is to detach and set forth the salient ideas that have
emerged from all that consideration and discussion—
to isolate the chief theories of death, ancient and modern, pagan and Christian, scientific and mystical, sound
and absurd.

The material thus accumulated and digested comes
from sources of great variety. The learned author, in
addition to written records, has canvassed prints, medals, paintings, engraved gems and monumental inscrip-
tions. His authorities range from St. John on what is
to happen at the Day of Judgment to Sir William Osler
on what happens upon the normal human deathbed,
and from Socrates on the relation of death to philosophy to Havelock Ellis on the effects of Christian ideas
of death upon the medieval temperament. The one
field that Dr. Weber overlooked is that of music, a
somewhat serious omission. It is hard to think of a
great composer who never wrote a funeral march, or a
requiem, or at least a sad song to some departed love.
Even old Papa Haydn had moments when he ceased to
be merry, and let his thought turn stealthily upon the
doom ahead. To me, at all events, the slow movement
of the Military Symphony is the saddest of music—an
elegy, I take it, on some young fellow who went out in
the incomprehensible wars of those times and got himself horribly killed in a far place. The trumpet blasts toward the end fling themselves over his hasty grave in a
remote cabbage field; one hears, before and after them,

the honest weeping of his comrades into their wine-pots. Beethoven, a generation later, growled at death surlily, but Haydn faced it like a gentleman. The romantic movement brought a sentimentalization of the tragedy; it became a sort of orgy. Whenever Wagner dealt with death he treated it as if it were some sort of gaudy tournament or potlatch—a thing less dreadful than ecstatic. Consider, for example, the *Char-Freitag* music in "Parsifal"—death music for the most memorable death in the history of the world. Surely no one hearing it for the first time, without previous warning, would guess that it had to do with anything so gruesome as a crucifixion. On the contrary, I have a notion that the average auditor would guess that it was a musical setting for some lamentable fornication between a baritone seven feet in height and a soprano weighing three hundred pounds.

But if Dr. Weber thus neglects music, he at least gives full measure in all other departments. His book, in fact, is encyclopedic; he almost exhausts the subject. One idea, however, I do not find in it: the conception of death as the last and worst of all the practical jokes played upon poor mortals by the gods. That idea apparently never occurred to the Greeks, who thought of almost everything else, but nevertheless it has an ingratiating plausibility. The hardest thing about death is not that men die tragically, but that most of them die ridiculously. If it were possible for all of us to make our exits at great moments, swiftly, cleanly, decorously, and in fine attitudes, then the experience would be something to face heroically and with high and beautiful words. But we commonly go off in no such gorgeous, poetical way. Instead, we died in raucous prose—of arteriosclerosis, of diabetes, of toxemia, of a noisome perforation in the ileocaecal region, of carcinoma of the liver. The abominable acidosis of Dr. Crile sneaks upon us, gradually paralyzing the adrenals, flabbergasting the thyroid, crippling the poor old liver, and throwing its fog upon the brain. Thus the ontogenetic process is recapitulated in reverse order, and we pass into the mental obscurity of infancy, and then into the blank unconsciousness of the prenatal state, and finally into the condition of undifferentiated protoplasm. A man does not die quickly and brilliantly, like a lightning stroke; he passes out by inches, hesitatingly and, one may almost add, gingerly.

It is hard to say just when he is fully dead. Long after his heart has ceased to beat and his lungs have ceased to swell him up with the vanity of his species, there are remote and obscure parts of him that still live on, quite unconcerned about the central catastrophe. Dr. Alexis Carrel used to cut them out and keep them alive for months. No doubt there are many parts of the body, and perhaps even whole organs, which wonder what it is all about when they find that they are on the way to the crematory. Burn a man's mortal remains, and you inevitably burn a good portion of him alive, and no doubt that portion sends alarmed messages to the unconscious brain, like dissected tissue under anesthesia, and the resultant shock brings the deceased before the hierarchy of Heaven in a state of collapse, with his face white, sweat bespangling his forehead and a great thirst upon him. It would not be pulling the nose of reason to argue that many a cremated pastor, thus confronting the ultimate in the aspect of a man taken with the goods, has been put down as suffering from an uneasy conscience when what actually ailed him was simply surgical shock. The cosmic process is not only incurably idiotic; it is also indecently unjust.

Thus the human tendency to make death dramatic and heroic has little excuse in the facts. No doubt you remember the scene in the last act of "Hedda Gabler," in which Dr. Brack comes in with the news of Lövborg's suicide. Hedda immediately thinks of him putting the pistol to his temple and dying instantly and magnificently. The picture fills her with romantic delight. When Brack tells her that the shot was actually through the breast she is disappointed, but soon begins to romanticize even *that*. "The breast," she says, "is also a good place. . . . There is something beautiful in this!" A bit later she recurs to the charming theme, "In the breast—ah!" Then Brack tells her the plain truth —in the original, thus: "*Nej,—det traf ham i underlivet!*" . . . Edmund Gosse, in his first English translation of the play, made the sentence: "No—it struck him in the abdomen." In the last edition William Archer makes it "No—in the bowels!" Abdomen is nearer to *underlivet* than bowels, but belly would probably render the meaning better than either. What Brack wants to convey to Hedda is the news that Lövborg's death was not romantic in the least—that he went to a brothel, shot himself, not through the cerebrum or the heart, but the duodenum or perhaps the jejunum, and is at the moment of report awaiting autopsy at the Christiania Allgemeinekrankenhaus. The shock floors her, but it is a shock that all of us must learn to bear. Men upon whom we lavish our veneration reduce it to an absurdity at the end by dying of cystitis, or by choking on marshmallows or dill pickles. Women whom we place upon pedestals worthy of the holy saints come down at last with mastoid abscesses or die obscenely of female weakness. And we ourselves? Let us not have too much hope. The chances are that, if we go to war, eager to leap superbly at the cannon's mouth, we'll be finished on the way by being run over by an army truck driven by a former bus-boy and loaded with imitation Swiss cheeses made in Oneida, N.Y. And that if we die in our beds, it will be of cholelithiasis.

The aforesaid Crile, in one of his other books, "A Mechanistic View of War and Peace," [3] has a good deal

[3] New York, 1915.

to say about death in war, and in particular, about the disparity between the glorious and inspiring passing imagined by the young soldier and the messy finish that is normally in store for him. He shows two pictures, the one ideal and the other real. The former is the familiar print, "The Spirit of '76," with the three patriots springing grandly to the attack, one of them with a neat and romantic bandage around his head—apparently, to judge by his liveliness, to cover a wound no worse than a bee-sting. The latter picture is a close-up of a French soldier who was struck just below the mouth by a German one-pounder shell—a soldier suddenly converted into the hideous simulacrum of a cruller. What one notices especially is the curious expression upon what remains of his face—an expression of the utmost surprise and indignation. No doubt he marched off to the front firmly convinced that, if he died at all, it would be at the climax of some heroic charge, up to his knees in blood and with his bayonet run clear through a Bavarian at least four feet in diameter. He imagined the clean bullet through the heart, the stately last gesture, the final words: "Thérèse! Sophie! Olympe! Marie! Suzette! Odette! Dénise! Julie! . . . France!" Go to the book and see what he got.

Alas, the finish of a civilian in a luxurious hospital, with trained nurses fluttering over him and his pastor whooping and heaving for him at the foot of his bed, is often quite as unesthetic as any form of exitus witnessed in war. "No. 8," says the apprentice nurse in faded pink, tripping down the corridor with a hooch of rye for the diabetic in No. 2, "has just passed out." "Which is No. 8?" asks the new nurse. "The one whose wife wore that awful hat this afternoon?" . . . But all the authorities, it is pleasant to know, report that the final scene, though it may be full of horror, is commonly devoid of terror. The dying man doesn't struggle much and he isn't much afraid. As his alkalies give out he succumbs to a blest stupidity. His mind fogs. His will power vanishes. He submits decently. He scarcely gives a damn.

EPITAPH
(FROM the *Smart Set*, December 1921)

If, after I depart this vale, you ever remember me and have thought to please my ghost, forgive some sinner and wink your eye at some homely girl.

ABOUT THE AUTHOR

Henry Louis Mencken was born in Baltimore in 1880 and died there in 1956. Educated at Baltimore Polytechnic, he began his long career as a journalist, critic, and philologist on the Baltimore Morning Herald in 1899. In 1906 he joined the staff of the Baltimore Sun papers and thus began an association with the distinguished Sun papers that lasted until a few years before his death. He was co-editor of The Smart Set with George Jean Nathan from 1908 to 1923, and with Nathan he founded in 1924 The American Mercury, of which he was editor until 1933. Among his many books are the three-volume The American Language, six volumes of Prejudices, and three autobiographical books: Happy Days, Heathen Days, and Newspaper Days. He also edited A New Dictionary of Quotations. The Diary of H. L. Mencken, edited by Charles A. Fecher, was published in 1989.